REMEMBERING AND BECOMING

REMEMBERING AND BECOMING

ORAL HISTORY IN AOTEAROA NEW ZEALAND

EDITED BY
ANNA GREEN AND
MEGAN HUTCHING

OTAGO UNIVERSITY PRESS
Te Whare Tā o Ōtākou Whakaihu Waka

Published by Otago University Press
Te Whare Tā o Ōtākou Whakaihu Waka
533 Castle Street, Dunedin, New Zealand
university.press@otago.ac.nz
oup.nz

First published 2024
Copyright © The moral rights of the authors as listed on the contents page have been asserted.

ISBN 978-1-99-004883-8

A catalogue record for this book is available from the National Library of New Zealand. This book is copyright. Except for the purpose of fair review, no part may be stored or transmitted in any form or by any means, electronic or mechanical, including recording or storage in any information retrieval system, without permission in writing from the publishers. No reproduction may be made, whether by photocopying or by any other means, unless a licence has been obtained from the publisher.

Published with the assistance of Creative New Zealand

Editor: Liz Wilson
Index: Lee Slater
Design/layout: Fiona Moffat

Printed in New Zealand by Ligare

CONTENTS

PREFACE 7

1 WHAT IS ORAL HISTORY?
  MEGAN PŌTIKI AND ANNA GREEN 9

2 PROMISES AND POSSIBILITIES: NGĀTI WHĀTUA VOICES
  IN THE TREATY CLAIM PROCESS
  MARGARET KAWHARU 25

3 GETTING INSIDE PEOPLE'S HEADS: WHAT ORAL HISTORY
  CAN TELL US ABOUT CLASS IN NEW ZEALAND IN THE
  LATE TWENTIETH CENTURY
  JANE MOODIE 41

4 RE-REMEMBERING THE DAWN RAIDS: AN ORAL HISTORY
  OF WILL 'ILOLAHIA AND THE POLYNESIAN PANTHERS
  HELENA COOK 57

5 'A PEASANT FARMER': NARRATIVE IDENTITY AND
  A SENSE OF BELONGING
  ANNA GREEN 71

6 'SHE WOULD ALWAYS BE THERE': THE (IM)MATERIAL LIFE
  AND HOME OF MISS MARION STEVEN
  NATALIE LOOYER 83

7 WRITING ANGLO–INDIAN STORIES
  ROBYN ANDREWS 95

8 'I FELT I WAS MASTER OF MY OWN DESTINY'
  MEGAN HUTCHING 113

9   THE KITCHEN: INSIGHTS FROM A 1950s DOMESTIC
    WORKPLACE
    HELEN FRIZZELL AND PIP OLDHAM 123

10 REVISITING CONSENT IN ORAL HISTORIES OF SEX WORK
    CHERYL WARE 139

11 TED, MARGARET AND SUE TOO
    DEAN BROUGHTON 151

12 'I REMEMBER, I WAS THERE': THE EXPERIENCES OF
    CHILDREN IN INSTITUTIONAL CARE
    ELIZABETH WARD 161

13 REMEMBERING THE MAKING OF RURAL HUAPAI
    DURING THE 1910s AND 1920s
    DEBORAH DUNSFORD 173

GLOSSARY 185
NOTES 187
ABOUT THE CONTRIBUTORS 207
SELECT BIBLIOGRAPHY 210
INDEX 219

Preface

Oral historians record memories about the past that reveal new aspects of history and deepen our understanding of well-known historical events. Their research sits at the intersection of the discipline of history and the interdisciplinary fields of memory studies and indigenous studies. The contexts in which oral historians work may be collective, recording the memories shared among a specific community, or with individuals remembering their life history. This information and knowledge, therefore, can be based upon personal experience or stories orally transmitted from earlier generations. Over the past decades oral historians have built a resource of social memory in the archival historical record and contributed new insights into the experiences of those who lived in the past. Oral history, you might say, is the people's history.

This book demonstrates that oral histories can contribute to historical understanding in three different and significant ways.

1. They frequently illuminate aspects of the past that are difficult or impossible to reach through conventional written sources, such as the impact of state policies or events upon those who experienced or were subjected to them, or the interior world of the family.
2. They may challenge or reframe existing historical perspectives. This can include bringing to the forefront neglected historical agents with contrary perspectives leading to more nuanced understandings; demonstrating how social norms played out in practice; or revealing the uneven adoption of cultural change.

3   And finally, oral histories also reveal the continuing connections between past and present in human thought and practice. Remembering the past, thinking about the present and planning the future are inextricably interconnected in both personal and collective human consciousness.

The following chapters include substantial interview extracts to demonstrate how oral history contributes to reflections on iwi, whānau and hapū, communities, class, trauma and distress, work, migration, gender, and family relations.

We would like to thank the contributors, those who shared their oral histories, the anonymous readers for their thoughtful comments on the text, and the staff at Otago University Press.

Anna Green and Megan Hutching

1
What is oral history?

MEGAN PŌTIKI
KĀI TAHU, KĀTI MĀMOE, TE ĀTI AWA

AND **ANNA GREEN**

Megan Pōtiki and Anna Green explore two approaches to oral history and the remembered past in Aotearoa me Te Waipounamu New Zealand. They argue that oral histories expand our historical knowledge of wāhi and hapori, place and community, on personal, kinship and national levels, and also illuminate the connections between the past, present and future in contemporary society. In dialogue with the 'history of historians', shorthand for scholarly histories based upon textual archival sources, oral histories have the potential to deepen and transform our understanding of the history of Aotearoa me Te Waipounamu New Zealand.

MEGAN PŌTIKI

What is oral history? This is an interesting and challenging question for me, and I have chosen to answer it from an insider's viewpoint. I come from and was raised in a village named Ōtākou. Today, Ōtākou sits on the outer eastern part of the Otago Peninsula. In the past Ōtākou had a far larger footprint, stretching across the whole peninsula and into the present-day city of Dunedin. It is worth noting that Ōtākou remains to this day the name of the Otago Harbour.

Our village is a strong Māori community with generations of whānau still living in the vicinity. Our people continue to fish and farm and are engaged with the heart of the village, our marae. All this, despite the fact we were overwhelmed by colonisation in the early 1800s. This wave of modernity eroded our language so it began to die out, which in turn meant we lost important cultural and historical knowledge, significantly weakening our tikanga for the generations that followed.

Colonisers brought other negative influences that systematically undermined our Māori community. These included foreign diseases, which heightened mortality rates, land loss due to forced sales and confiscations, which depleted our food sources, and broken promises within the deeds of the sale of land and the Treaty of Waitangi. We became increasingly marginalised as new unsympathetic education systems were introduced that did not consider our people's religion, traditions and self-governance or place any value on our tikanga and te reo. The final blow came in the first half of the twentieth century with the impact of World War I and World War II. These wars took our men and undermined our ability to maintain intergenerational language transmission. They were fluent speakers of the Māori language, repositories of knowledge and tikanga, who left behind a community of mothers and children who simply needed to survive.

I was raised in a community that was still operating in a traditional Māori way during the 1970s and 1980s. We were just about holding on to the last bastions of tikanga like the tangihanga. We were still burying our dead in a deeply Māori way, we continued to make speeches in English that followed a Māori oratory pattern. We were practising our long-standing food gathering tikanga, including the harvesting of mutton birds, which is something we have done sustainably for generations. In order to keep the whakapapa strong and our land intact, we were still marrying within the hapū, all the while continuing a 150-year fight for a Waitangi Tribunal claim.

It is important to provide this backdrop when considering what oral history means to me. My knowledge about tikanga and te reo comes from a formal learning process I undertook in my twenties. However, if I look back to my childhood, I can say that I learnt first-hand through the experience of living alongside my elders, who in turn had knowledge, wisdom and insight that was passed down to them through generations of history. Even if significant tracts were fractured, eroded or lost in more recent times, the essential remnants of history and whakapapa are still there. As a starting point, through lived experience, I understand that Māori oral history is the simple transmission of experience and knowledge from one generation to another.

I was very fortunate to be close to my grandparents on both sides of my family. My Pākehā Nana was a formidable character and an important person in my life. She and my Pākehā grandfather were extremely supportive of me. When I was born, my grandfather was known to have said that he was thrilled that his grandchild would have a firm footing in this country because I was Māori. My Pākehā grandparents' experiences in life shaped my thinking. They were poor and ate any food that was cheap to put on the table like tripe, tongue and brains. They came from a community where families didn't go to university. In contrast, my Māori family had land in their ancestral village, ate like kings off the fat of the land and succeeded academically as well as in sport – I am from a long line of Māori high achievers who graduated from university or played rugby for Aotearoa New Zealand. With hindsight, I realise it was no wonder that my Pākehā grandparents behaved as if my Pākehā mother had married into Māori royalty.

I am also related to a line of staunch Māori women who were the backbone of our community. My Nana told stories about what it was like growing up in the 'sugar bag years' (the Great Depression of the 1930s) and how she had drawn a line down the back of her leg to feign the wearing of stockings as you simply couldn't buy them. Once, she nonchalantly talked to me about the loss of her mother when she was a pre-teen. Her mother, my great-grandmother, on a visit to New Plymouth, was pulled under a train and killed when her fur coat got caught. I was astounded when she told me that she wasn't allowed to attend the funeral and that she was immediately expected to help her father, a Gallipoli survivor, raise her younger brother and sister. In my late twenties, not long before my Nana passed away, I bought her a diary and a pen and asked her if she could write her life story for me. She made a good attempt at it, and I am so fortunate to have her story. I named my daughter after her because she was a wonderful and remarkable role model for me.

When talking to people about their thoughts on oral history, a friend stated that 'oral history is a legitimate method of passing knowledge from one generation to the next so should be acknowledged as such'. Concluding that just because there was no written language (until their adoption of Western literacy) doesn't mean knowledge wasn't transmitted accurately and efficiently. Within my tribe, we understand that there were key informants who transmitted knowledge in the 1800s. These people were steeped in generations of knowledge as their mātauranga was corroborated with each other. Some were students or the children of people who attended our last whare wānanga traditional school of learning. They transmitted their information in various ways, some told missionaries who wrote their knowledge down, others learnt to write and documented their knowledge in the form of whakapapa, waiata, narratives, maps, mahinga kai lists, dreams and letters. Tribally we have been left with an incredible corpus of knowledge with which we can revitalise tikanga and language idiom, turn of phrase, vocabulary and dialect.

Therefore, oral history is not necessarily something that is transmitted from person to person, but it includes the repositories that have been left for us from tūpuna. Oral transmission is protected by the key informants but also left to us in certain resources that transmit our narratives. These may take the form of photographs, interviews, manuscripts, whakapapa, books, maps, newspapers and so on. We were able to revive certain tikanga at our marae based on photographs discovered in old newspapers. We hadn't worn pare kawakawa for a century at our tangihanga, and these images, published in the 1890s, showed us women and men dripping in greenery, so we decided to bring that tikanga back and re-embed it, restoring it within our processes. Our children will see the wearing of pare kawakawa as normal and relate to it as something we have always done.

We are challenged to transmit and receive oral knowledge in different forms and in different ways. The notion that when a person arrives at their marae there will be many kaumātua (elders) to talk to who can provide incredible mātauranga is not a realistic experience for my own people. This also challenges the concept of what defines a kaumātua? Where I come from, I place a different lens on this and that may be confronting to some philosophical views. I believe that a kaumātua is an individual who is deeply knowledgeable about particular tikanga, practices, history and te reo. This means that a kaumātua might not be someone who is 65 years old but potentially a person in their twenties. As an example, my husband, who died in 2019, was an advocate and stalwart of te reo Māori revitalisation, particularly our tribal dialect. He dedicated a lifetime to researching our tribal manuscripts and bringing our language to life. At his tangi the paepae was full of our young men who had been the product of this revitalisation journey and were fluent speakers of te reo Māori. I am sure that a paepae full of young men was somewhat confronting to people, but in many regards their knowledge and expertise in oratory was that of a kaumātua. They executed each kōrero beautifully, carving our idiom, our dialect, our waiata, our proverbial sayings into their speeches. We were all extremely proud.

Sometimes the loss of language and tikanga gives rise to people and mātauranga that attempt to fill a gap. In the 1980s we were possibly at our lowest ebb as a hapū. We were barely managing to pull the funds together to keep gathering evidence to fight a Waitangi Tribunal claim, and we had no speakers and were culturally teetering on the edge. The exhibition *Te Māori* came to town and forced us to take a look at ourselves. As a result, some individuals went on a language learning journey and pushed themselves to become culturally stronger and wiser. This has also taken our people on a journey of reclaiming authentic knowledge and deciphering dubious and incorrect language and history. As my friend above stated, just because we didn't have a written language to start doesn't mean knowledge wasn't transmitted accurately and efficiently. That is the truth. My iwi was left with copious amounts of resources and information that stem from senior informants and that can be cross-referenced with each other and so we know it is authentic knowledge. Our stalwarts who ferociously pursued history, whakapapa and te reo Māori from the key tūpuna sources came to realise that, in some instances, placenames were renamed with names that had no historical foundation and new narratives were told that had no whakapapa to us.

We have been on a journey as a people, and we have learnt that we must work hard to maintain our authenticity and protect our identity. We must continue to question ourselves and our knowledge as we grow and move in to the twenty-first century. The Ngāi Tahu mapping system, Kā Huru Manu goes someway to rectifying the odd kōrero that is out there. It follows a process whereby a placename must be found in a number of authentic manuscripts and maps in order for us to include it on the map. This allows us to study the name and really understand its meaning and whakapapa. When considering the restoration of our authentic history, traditions and language I look to my children. I talk openly to them about the importance of careful evaluation and encourage them to question something if it doesn't feel right. I challenge them to be that critical eye and not simply take a story or narrative as the truth but to cross-reference information and research the source. Let us raise disrupters and critical thinkers, our future really does depend on that!

I have given you my very personal journey, which I hope illuminates my position that oral history is layered like whakapapa. It is multi-dimensional and can be attained in several different forms. We need to look forward with open eyes and taringa areare, gathering layers of oral tradition and history and truly questioning what is authentic mātauranga.

ANNA GREEN

In contrast to Megan, I am an immigrant to New Zealand, having arrived here in 1980, but my path to becoming an oral historian shares a parallel influence of family and place. I grew up on a farm in the Wye Valley on the Welsh border, which is now classified as an area of outstanding natural beauty. Landmarks and archaeological traces from thousands of years of human habitation and conflict were visible on the hills, meadows and along the winding river. My father, born in 1898, told me stories about our forebears from both sides of Offa's Dyke.[1] And on our farm rounds together he would talk about village life and what farming was like during his childhood before World War I (he rarely spoke to me about his experiences in the trenches). My sense of family history is therefore embedded in this historically distinctive region. In my final year at school, I read *Ask the Fellows Who Cut the Hay* by George Ewart Evans, often described as an oral history even though the conversations were not audio recorded.[2] Given my farming family background I was absorbed by the stories Evans documented with farm labourers remembering their working lives in the late nineteenth century. The foundations for my love of history and oral history were surely laid in this time and place. It therefore really goes without saying that the oral transmission of stories about the past, particularly within families and indigenous communities, long precedes their emergence in published histories.

My early interest in oral history developed further when I studied history at university. Around the middle of the twentieth century technological advances in portable sound recording equipment made it possible for researchers to travel and record oral histories in the field, dramatically enlarging, diversifying, and ultimately democratising the practice of historical research. Over the following decades oral history emerged as a multidisciplinary formal and critical research methodology in universities around the world.[3] Methodologies, as well as analytic and interpretive approaches to oral history, were subsequently debated internationally and developed, adopted and adapted in diverse cultural, linguistic, legal and historical contexts. While there are cultural differences in approaches among oral historians, there is also shared ground. National associations, and later the International Oral History Association in 1996, were established with regular conferences and online journals. These global exchanges about methodology and analysis were very productive and led to a rich body of literature in the field. Oral historians in Aotearoa me Te Waipounamu New Zealand[4] contribute to these discussions and debates, and the National Oral History Association Te Kete Kōrero-a-Waha o Te Motu (NOHANZ), founded in 1986, holds biennial conferences and has published the journal *Oral History in New Zealand* annually since 1988.[5]

NOHANZ was conceived from the beginning as a place where community and academic oral historians could meet and share their research and examples of good practice. It has, therefore, always had a strong community orientation, encouraging and enabling those whose experiences and perspectives were rarely collected for the archives or represented in written form to be recorded. These aims were enhanced by the 1990 sesquicentennial gift from the Australian government of one million dollars to support the collection of the peoples' oral histories. The fund is administered by Manatū Taonga Ministry for Culture and Heritage and supports a range of oral history projects each year, with the interviews preserved in the Oral History and Sound Collection in the Alexander Turnbull Library or iwi and regional libraries.[6]

I would argue that there are five principal streams in contemporary New Zealand oral history, and while each frames its purpose in a particular way they also overlap and share aspects of common methodologies. The work of an oral historian could well fall within more than one of these streams. The first is *Māori oral history*, and Megan has described her personal approach to the question of 'what is oral history?' in the first part of this chapter.[7] A second stream focuses on a specific community or group. These *community oral histories* may revolve around a geographical place or a particular experience, such as shared memories of the Christchurch earthquake, the working lives of butchers or drovers, or life histories of LGBTQI+ people or refugees.[8] The oral historian may or may not be a member of that community, and these projects often draw upon a range of sources as well as oral history. *Commissioned oral histories* form the third oral history stream. These oral history projects are commissioned by both public and private agencies and organisations to ensure that the memories of an event or individual are preserved in the archives for future researchers. Commissioned interviews tend to be more focused on elite individuals or groups who have sufficient resources to fund the project, although this is not always the case.[9] They range, to take just two examples undertaken by Megan Hutching, from oral histories recorded with women judges to a large national project interviewing those who fought in each theatre of war during World War II.[10]

The final two streams represent a partial shift from the oral history approaches above in one specific way. While oral historians have always recognised, of course, that we remember the past in the present, the purpose of oral history research has generally remained primarily fixed on the past. The final two streams of oral history spin researchers' lenses more towards the present-day context. The fourth stream of *activist oral history* is driven by the desire to rectify inequities in the present and overlaps with qualitative social science research into contemporary social issues.[11] Memory activism can be defined as 'the strategic commemoration of a contested past to achieve mnemonic or political change by working outside state channels'.[12] It emerges, as Aleida Assman points out in the preface to a new anthology on the subject, 'from bottom-up movements that react against repressive structures of silence and injustice, recuperating events of the past for the sake of restorative justice and social inclusion'.[13] The activist approach to memory has expanded in international contexts of globalisation, decolonisation, and identity politics, and often seeks to address the exclusion of ethnic minorities. In New Zealand, recent projects that also fall within this stream of oral history include interviews with disabled, homeless, trans and gender-diverse individuals, and others.[14]

The fifth and final stream of oral history is *academic oral history*. While the practice of oral history began with a focus on oral history as a verifiable historical source, contemporary academic approaches have increasingly turned to investigate how we remember in the present and the relationship between social memory and 'the history of historians'. Oral historians working within an academic context may conduct their interviews in more experimental ways and ground their analyses and interpretations within interdisciplinary theories and concepts. An academic analysis of the oral history interview is likely, for example, to assess the methodology, discuss the structure of the oral narrative, and contextualise and interpret the specific content. Some take an analytical approach that is often described as 'reading against the grain', broadly defined as seeking to understand the unstated or unconscious dimensions of the interview. These can include cultural beliefs and myths, social norms, silences, misremembering and contradictions.[15] Academic oral historians have therefore drawn from a wide range of disciplinary insights and approaches and benefitted from the growth of a new international field – that of memory studies.

Oral history is fundamentally about memory and remembering. Researching the physiological and neurological dimensions of memory in the brain is largely conducted in laboratories by neuroscientists and cognitive psychologists interested in the systems and functions of memory recall and retention. Understanding what memory does well, and not so well, in the laboratory context is a useful exercise for oral historians harbouring unrealistic expectations of their interviewees.[16] But the focus of this research often revolves around forgetting and identifying the deficits of memory. The neuroscientist and psychologist Charan Ranganath suggests that 'instead of asking "Why do we forget?" we should really be asking "Why do we remember?"'[17] Over more than 30 years investigating this question Ranganath has explored the development of memory and how it changes during life stages. He argues that at each phase of the lifecycle, memory is doing exactly what it has evolved to do. In this understanding of memory, the 'remembering self' is 'a powerful force that can shape everything from our perceptions of reality to the choices and plans we make …'[18] Ranganath's approach also reflects a wider temporal shift from a single research focus upon recall of the past to recognition of memory's dynamic role in shaping perceptions of the past, present and future.[19]

The everyday social contexts of remembering, however, remain primarily the province of the humanities and social sciences. These collectively comprise, along with oral history, an interdisciplinary research community within the Memory Studies Association, which was launched in 2016.[20] This multidisciplinary research field explores many levels of memory from the collective to the individual, as represented in written, visual and oral forms. A fundamental principle widely shared by memory studies researchers is that remembering is a social practice. Although oral histories are narrated by individuals, the stories about the past are shared in social contexts with particular audiences and also reflect the norms, values and forms of cultural expression drawn from the social environment. These social influences range from family stories, community memories, religious beliefs, and popular culture to national narratives and commemorations.

The cultural and social dimensions of remembering should not, I would argue, imply a predetermined outcome. Our experiences, understood in a context of multiple potential meanings, may lead us to reflect upon whether we wish to adopt, challenge or reject certain beliefs or cultural scripts. This capacity for critical engagement with our cultural and social environment is why I prefer the term 'social memory' to that of 'collective memory'.[21] In addition, while the emotions and the senses, such as smell, sound, sight or touch, are important triggers activating long-term personal memories, these memories gain meaning and significance from the wider culture and sharing them with others.[22]

METHODOLOGY

At the centre of oral history research practice is the recorded audio or audiovisual interview with one person or a small group of people about the past, and there are some excellent sources of information about planning and carrying out an oral history project.[23] It is important to note here that oral histories conducted within kaupapa Māori will be grounded in mātauranga Māori and the practices and protocols of tikanga Māori.[24] The NOHANZ Code of Ethical and Technical Practice sets out the general responsibilities of an interviewer based on the fundamental principle of informed consent. This requires interviewees to be given a comprehensive explanation concerning the purpose of the research and research process and the relevant legislative context relating to, for example, copyright and privacy. Interviewees are then able to make knowledgeable decisions about whether to participate, understand where their recordings will be preserved, and the conditions of public access and publication. These decisions are documented in signed Recording Agreement Forms and archived with the recording.[25]

The interview itself may follow different forms, depending upon the cultural context and purpose of the research. If, for example, the interview is commissioned to acquire specific information for an archive or business/professional organisation, the oral historian may take a more structured approach with prepared questions on specific topics in order to generate the required information. Indeed, the oral historian may go further and engage in a process of ethical contestation with elite interviewees, providing counterpoints to the perspectives being presented.[26] Alternatively, if the interview is being recorded for a life narrative, or a topic about which less is known in advance, a more flexible, open-ended interview format that builds upon the narrative trajectory of the interviewee is likely to be preferred.[27] In either case, as Alessandro Portelli – a leading oral historian of his generation – recently reminded us, the oral history interview consists of a dialogue shaped by 'the researchers' desire to gather knowledge relevant to their project and the narrators' desire to speak about themselves and be heard'. This means, Portelli concludes, that oral history is fundamentally 'co-created' within the interview. Rather than present oral history as if it were a monologue, he argues that it should be presented as what it is, a dialogue.[28] This runs counter to the historian's traditional practice of effacing themselves from the research process but supports the recent critical emphasis on the interactive nature of the oral history interview.[29]

THE HISTORICAL INTEGRITY AND ANALYSIS OF ORAL HISTORY

All historical sources need to be approached with informed caution, whether written, visual, material or oral. How should we approach oral history sources of information about the past? In New Zealand it could be said that there are two broad approaches to oral history. The first is collective in orientation and founded in iwi and hapū oral histories and traditions, including pūrākau and waiata, as discussed by Megan Pōtiki in the first part of this chapter. The integrity of these sources is grounded in whakapapa, place, and the formal processes of transmission across generations.[30] But, in common with all other forms of knowledge about the past, there can be debate concerning content and interpretation both within and between whānau, hapū and iwi.[31] The second stream of oral history in New Zealand centres primarily upon the individual recorded interview, and there are two distinct, but not incompatible, approaches to the value and veracity of this form of the remembered past.

The reliability of information in individual oral histories can be sought by the conventional empirical method of cross-referencing with other history interviews or historical documentation. In my history of work on the New Zealand waterfront in the first half of the twentieth century both these types of corroboration were possible. For example, detailed memories about the nature of the work and workplace relationships were repeated and discussed by many of those I recorded, both workers and employers. There were clear thematic patterns across the interviews.[32] Many of the stories about the difficulties and dangers of unloading and loading cargo were also raised by the union in negotiations with the shipping company employers and recorded in written documentation. But not all oral histories can be corroborated or supported in this way, and some research topics simply make this impossible. Furthermore, this approach, by insisting upon triangulation and factual verification, misses perhaps the most valuable dimension of the individual oral history interview, the individual's subjective understanding.

Italian cultural historian Luisa Passerini published a seminal article in 1979 which demonstrated an alternative interpretative approach that actively sought to understand the subjective dimensions of remembering. In 'Work Ideology and Consensus under Italian Fascism' Passerini drew upon interviews with around 60 Italian men and women from two generations. She suggested that oral histories were a much richer source for historians than had been previously understood.[33] Rather than simply mine oral histories for factual, verifiable information, or literal representations of the past, Passerini argued that oral historians should also turn their attention to what she called the 'subjectivity', or consciousness, of the interviewee. It is essential, she maintained, that historians recognise the 'subjective reality' that framed an interviewee's understanding of the past. Passerini defined subjective reality as the interaction between cultural structures of belief handed down through family and social groups, and the capacity for self-reflection. This complex interaction between inheritance and reflection could provide the oral historian with insights into how people attach meaning to their experiences and their lives.

Furthermore, it was subsequently argued that understanding the subjective reality of ordinary people is essential if we are to fully understand the trajectory of history or 'evolution of societies'.[34] Passerini's approach to oral history combined a focus on the lives and perspectives of the majority, or 'ordinary' people (a term I do not like but struggle to find an alternative), attentiveness to gender, and a powerful, conceptually informed analysis of oral narratives. She provided a new explanation and understanding of the response of working-class Italians to the fascist government during the inter-war period. I was a postgraduate student at the time and this article was the intellectual spark that illuminated the invaluable contribution oral history could make to our understanding of both past and present.

In 1991 Alessandro Portelli again made the point that historians were missing an important dimension of the past by ignoring the subjectivity inherent in all oral history interviews. He also stressed that 'subjectivity is as much the business of history as are the more visible "facts"'. 'What informants believe', he argued, 'is indeed a historical fact (that is, the fact that they believe it), as much as what really happened.'[35] The failure to comprehend the significance of human subjectivity and the meanings individuals attach to their experiences, even when they do not accord with objective facts, is one of the more perplexing dimensions of conventional historical practice. Oral history interviews enable the historian to explore subjectivity in depth and ask the 'why' and 'how' questions that we often cannot ask directly of written sources. For example, we can ask interviewees why they took a course of action, what they hoped to accomplish, and what they think they achieved.

Unpacking the subjective dimensions of the oral history interview is complex and requires, as Portelli put it, 'different and specific interpretative instruments'.[36] There are many different ways to approach the expression of subjective reality or meaning in the remembered past. Here I would like to focus on just two that have deeply influenced my approach to oral histories: orality and narrative.

The first of these, the *orality* of the source, is all too often ignored and rarely directly addressed in published oral histories. In each oral history recording we enter a rich linguistic universe of intonation, unique phrases, irregular cadences, and patterns of speech. The tone, volume, speed of narration, or pauses in the interview are all bearers of meaning. The same sentence spoken with altered intonation, vocal emphasis or velocity may convey a very different meaning or nuance. If we ignore these valuable indicators of meaning, Portelli suggested, we 'flatten the emotional content of speech down to the supposed equanimity and objectivity of the written document'.[37] Unfortunately, the need to represent spoken sources in writing can make conveying the rich aural dimensions of oral history difficult, and oral history excerpts are often edited and polished for the reader, in the process losing vernacular authenticity.

The second dimension of oral history concerns the centrality of the *narrative form* in remembered experiences and life stories.[38] To recount memories and find meaning in their lives and experiences, interviewees draw upon established cultural forms of telling a story. The stories can be short (an anecdote) or long (the life story). The narratives include a temporal dimension, usually the sequential ordering of events or experiences over a short or long period of time, although the structure of the narrative can take a different form.[39] Both Passerini and Portelli were acutely aware of the ways in which their oral history participants drew upon the narrative frameworks of popular stories and Italian folklore. Stories revolving around cultural archetypes, such as the witch, were also evident in the oral histories I recorded in the 1990s with my students in the railway township of Frankton Junction.[40] Subsequently researchers across multiple disciplines have identified many generic story types or genres in oral histories, including the epic or ironic form of story, origin myth, trickster tale, triumph over adversity, cautionary tale, and parable.[41]

There are two additional aspects of narrative that are particularly relevant here. The American psychologist Jerome Bruner argued that at the heart of a story or narrative something unforeseen must happen. Another term for this 'breach in the expected state of things' is the peripeteia, and Bruner concluded that narrative 'in all its forms is a dialectic between what was expected and what came to pass'.[42] This is why oral histories can be uniquely revealing of the tensions and contradictions within past social and cultural contexts. Oral history narratives may also end with a coda, a retrospective evaluation or reflection about what the story means to the narrator. Whether or not the narrator articulates a coda, oral histories will usually follow a narrative form that builds a framework of meaning.

Finally, academic researchers in many different fields contend that our interior life history narratives are crucial in creating human identities. Cultural psychologists, sociologists and anthropologists, among others, claim that stories we tell about our lives play a foundational role in our sense of self and identity. In other words, 'we *are* the stories we tell', although not everyone agrees with this statement.[43] The psychologist Oliver Sachs described this process:

> We have each of us, a life story, an inner narrative – whose continuity, whose sense, is our lives. It might be said that each of us constructs and lives 'a narrative' and that this narrative is our identities ... Biologically, physiologically, we are not different from each other; historically, as narratives, we are each of us unique.[44]

THE RELATIONSHIP BETWEEN HISTORY AND SOCIAL MEMORY

Where does this leave us in terms of the relationship between oral history and the 'history of historians'? This question is currently the focus of a critical debate revolving specifically around teaching history and national historical narratives. For some time, those working in the field of history education and pedagogy have discussed teaching practice in contexts where students appear to have limited historical knowledge and are greatly influenced by one-dimensional narratives or collective memories embedded in popular culture. The history teachers' concerns have been driven by the desire to challenge or provide a counterbalance to these 'mythistories', the exclusionary, simplistic or damaging narratives that can dominate public perceptions of the past. Historians regard the past as infinitely complex, and historical research and critical thinking often challenge popular historical beliefs.[45] Students, however, may be deeply attached to those family and cultural memories that 'tend to reaffirm connections with the past' and support personal identities.[46] This attachment can create a tension between memory and history, between the capacity of memory and remembering to build coherent personal and collective narratives of identity and belonging, and the opposite tendency of empirical history to challenge, complicate and fragment community and national narratives. These tensions are not always easily resolved.[47]

It is important to emphasise that nuanced and sophisticated understandings of both 'the history of historians' and social memory are essential if we are to more fully comprehend all dimensions of past and present.[48] Writing in the New Zealand historical context, the historian Bain Attwood argues that we need to consider abandoning the search for a singular narrative and recognise the diversity of stories about the past. He describes this as 'sharing histories', recognising that no one narrative has a monopoly upon truth.[49] But he makes this recommendation with a significant qualification. 'Contrary to what some might assume,' he says, 'the project of sharing histories does not take up a relativist position. It does not hold that all historical accounts are equal or that anything goes. It simply recognizes that the most significant parts of any historical narrative are always partial and so the knowledge they produce is limited.' This approach, I believe, represents a positive way forward and opens the door to a more constructive engagement between history and memory.

What can memory and oral history contribute to our understanding of the past in New Zealand? The capacity of oral histories to reveal the subjective reality of remembered experience and thereby bring new dimensions to our understanding of the past is evident in each chapter of this book. From the legacy of whakamā or shame for the Pacific Island community following the Dawn Raids to the disparaging remarks of a husband to his hard-working farming wife on Mount Aspiring Station, the chapters reveal the intense emotional and sensory history that is so often missing from conventional historical accounts. The sensory elements of the remembered past are particularly vivid in the construction of a collective biography of Marion Stevens through memories of her house. The depth and significance of emotional memories permeate virtually every chapter.

Oral histories illuminate the social structures of inclusion and exclusion, challenging dominant popular perceptions of the New Zealand past. The attachment to the idea of a relatively egalitarian national past is put under the microscope in the memories and experiences of class by two descendants of the missionary Williams family. Oral history may also challenge social attitudes relating to difficult or intimate topics, such as those explored in the chapter on sex workers and the issue of consent.

The actions and impact of state policies are a major focus. These include the oral histories of those remembering their experiences in state care, and the consequences for one child of the judicial decision to deport a British ship-jumping seaman. State-sponsored commemorations and public memories of war that focus on combat are also problematised through the remembered experience of a prisoner of war.

Aspects of the past that have been neglected come to the fore. The experiences and perceptions of Anglo-Indians in New Zealand provide a good example of this. There are also important areas of rural history about which little has been written. The chapter on the development of Huapai reveals the contrast between sales pitches promising easy profits and the impact of unrelenting and exploitative labour upon a family and a father's mental health.

Finally, past and present are profoundly connected in all of these oral history stories. We see how an individual farmer on the Banks Peninsula shaped his sense of identity in a circular life history narrative drawing upon his family past. In the context of Māori history, past and present are inseparable in the collective cultural imperatives and memories of Ngāti Whātua and Ngāi Tahu whānau that have ultimately challenged and altered the trajectory of our society.

2

Promises and possibilities: Ngāti Whātua voices in the Treaty claim process

MARGARET KAWHARU
TE TAOŪ, NGĀTI WHĀTUA

This chapter concerns itself with 'oral history' associated with the Treaty of Waitangi claim process. The treaty claim process has been sanctioned as a restorative, reconciliation process between the Indigenous Māori people and the New Zealand state, often referred to as the Crown. With mounting pressure from Māori to deal with outstanding historical grievances, Parliament passed the Treaty of Waitangi Act in 1975, which established a commission of inquiry called the Waitangi Tribunal.[1] It has been charged with investigating and making recommendations on claims brought by Māori relating to actions or omissions of the Crown that breach the country's founding document, Te Tiriti o Waitangi, since it was signed by representatives of the British Crown and tribal leaders in 1840. One of the great innovations of the Waitangi Tribunal has been its choice to hold hearings on a marae of the claimant group, with the intention of enabling the claimant group to speak of their grievances, in their own way – for the first time, in a manner sympathetic and respectful of Māori practices, so that the tribunal may 'reach the real heart of the matter'.[2]

Ngāti Whātua o Kaipara is a claimant group situated in a rural area north of New Zealand's largest city, Tāmaki Makaurau.[3] They lodged their treaty claim in 1992, research began in 1995 and the claimant group presented their claim to the Waitangi Tribunal over four separate weeks in 1999 at Haranui marae, overlooking the Kaipara Harbour. A claim committee, consisting of five elders who represented each of the five marae communities in south Kaipara, led the process. The claim

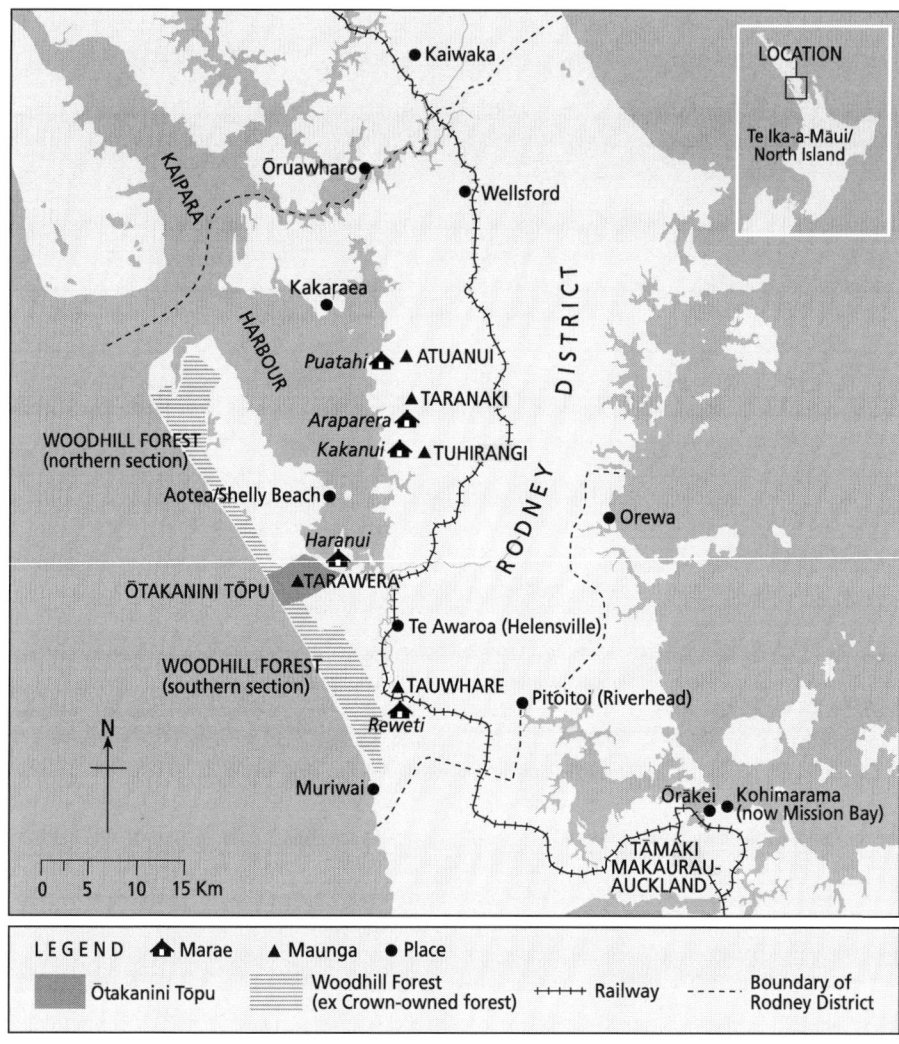

The Kaipara claimant group area and the location of the five marae: Reweti, Haranui, Kakanui, Araparera and Puatahi. Areas of redress: Woodhill Forest land; The railway line, completed in 1876, on land given by Māori as their contribution to mutual prosperity in 1871. Map by Allan Kynaston was part of the tribunal's Kaipara Inquiry District, planned in three stages to hear 30 claims. The tribunal issued an interim report in 2002 recommending that the claimants enter political negotiations with the Crown and, in their Kaipara Report of 2006, confirmed this direction. However, the Crown were very slow and did not begin to negotiate with the Kaipara claimant group until 2008 under Minister Michael Cullen. A settlement was finally achieved in 2011 and enshrined in an act of Parliament in 2013.[4] To give some context, I would like to reference one example of a significant grievance for Kaipara: the gifting of Māori land for the construction of a railway.[5]

During 2008 to 2009, as part of my postgraduate study in social anthropology, I interviewed the claim committee for Ngāti Whātua o Kaipara, with whom I had been working as claim manager since 1995. I wanted to encourage them to reflect on their own life stories and their experiences of prosecuting a Treaty claim. By that time, they were in negotiations with the Crown.[6] Using a combination of earlier oral interviews, formal briefs of evidence to the Waitangi Tribunal, video footage of hui/meetings and copious meeting notes and observations, I wanted to give voice to the fears, aspirations, contradictions and predicaments the claim committee had faced during the claim process that lasted almost two decades. I rely on various forms of oral history associated with the treaty claim process to portray something of the two eldest claim committee members: Reverend Takutaimoana Wikiriwhi (known as Taku or Uncle Doc) and Gloria Timoti (known as Aunty Gloria). Through their words and reflections, we discover that they are very different characters on different life journeys, each with their own hopes and motivations. By listening first-hand to their stories, we can begin to understand some of the challenges and compromises they made as they worked together to let the voices of the past and the present speak.

REVEREND DR TAKUTAIMOANA WIKIRIWHI

Taku was one of the most senior kaumātua in the area, a devoted minister of the Rātana faith and well respected for his untiring service to other people and upholding the mana and authority of Ngāti Whātua everywhere he went. He grew up at Ōruawharo and Reweti but lived for many years at Ōrākei. During the claim he held a kaumātua position at the Mental Health Unit, Manawanui, in Point Chevalier, Auckland. He celebrated his eightieth birthday in 2009 at Reweti marae in the company of all his whānau and the Governor General, Sir Anand Satyanand and his wife, which is indicative of the personal relationships Ngāti Whātua maintained with the British monarch's representative. It was he who lodged the claim with the Waitangi Tribunal in 1992 and when I asked Taku why he got involved, he replied:

> I felt the importance of it. I wasn't concerned whether I knew what it was all about – I felt confidence. I signed for our continuation, for the importance of our continuing existence of ourselves in Kaipara.[7]

In the first tribunal hearing in 1999, Taku, speaking first in Māori then in English, introduced himself by reciting his whakapapa, explained his connections to Reweti marae, as its representative, and addressed everyone:

> Greetings to us all. No matter what happens I feel our togetherness within and that makes me happy. Although I am finding it hard to attend these hui, due to other commitments, my desire is 100 percent here. I look to my elder and younger brothers to speak on our behalf in support of this important issue. Each and every one of us has history and experiences we are able to recall. For me, the bonding as one shows our strength. It does not matter who has been given the responsibility to speak on our behalf, because of our strength and bonding we are all able to speak on behalf of us, about us. It all comes from the heart, so, we show to you, the Crown, our togetherness and strength.

> You, the Crown, show high regard for us, to Ngāti Whātua, to this part of Ngāti Whātua. For me I give this address to you so that you may hear our plea. How do I present this? We will look at one part, seek an area in which we can justify ownership from the past. We lay before you our grievance so that you may hear and feel our suffering. This is not just for me, it is for five marae.

> I understand the circumstances surrounding our marae, surrounding all of us here, surrounding all Ngāti Whātua, but we know that our treasure will be returned. Therefore, on behalf of all of us, I greet you and thank you for taking care of this serious issue, for giving me the opportunity to lay our thoughts before you and for allowing us this time to address our concerns. God gives us the strength and spirit and hears our cries like you are hearing them now, today. Although this issue is deep-rooted the majority of us do not think like that. I speak for myself; when I was young we did not address these issues, but the time has come today for us to do so. We are fortunate in that we have been given this time to address our concerns and have our history and grievances recorded in your books with your records. This will allow our people to seek any information within these records pertaining to Ngāti Whātua.

PROMISES AND POSSIBILITIES

Reverend Dr Takutaimoana Wikiriwhi (Uncle Doc) at the signing of the Deed of Settlement on 9 September 2011 at Aotea (Shelly Beach), Kaipara Harbour. Courtesy of Office of Treaty Settlements

> The greatest joy for us is to see this treasure returned so that we may hold the power and control for tomorrow. Our work goes on regardless and our talks must go on until a solution is found and we are all satisfied. Therefore, I stand here with these words from our people; leave this for you to respond to, for you to give direction. I greet you and thank you. So, to you the Crown, to all of us here, I say again we have come to the end of this day, and I thank you all. To our meeting house and all the memories of our ancestors that lie within, Thank you! Thank you! Thank you one and all.[8]

His address to the tribunal is remarkable for the way it evokes a similar tone to oratory given by Ngāti Whātua tūpuna, ancestors, in the nineteenth century. He acknowledges the status and authority of the Waitangi Tribunal and the Crown, to whom he looks for 'taking care of this serious issue' and 'allowing us this time to address our concerns'. He pays tribute to the value of the written word and the expectation that having 'our history and grievances recorded in your books with your records' can be relied on.

At the Kohimarama Conference in 1860, Wiremu Tipene had stated, 'Christianity will guard the soul, and the law of the Queen will improve our temporal condition: there will I take refuge.'[9] In a comparable vein, Taku refers to the claimant group's unity and strength and he appeals to the tribunal, as one might make a plea before God, 'that you may hear and feel our suffering'. He is confident that the treaty claim processes will return 'our treasure', meaning land, in particular Woodhill Forest land. He is equally confident of Ngāti Whātua's right to 'hold the power and control for tomorrow'.

The substance of Taku's message resides in tikanga Māori, specifically in the principle of utu or reciprocity, a fundamental driver to the whole of Māori life.[10] Ngāti Whātua's response to the Crown in regards to the proposed Kaipara railway in 1871 was, 'You ask us for the land for the railway, and we consent, we believe that out of it you will do good for us all.'[11] Despite the Crown's failure to deliver on the promises from Ngāti Whātua's point of view, Taku leaves his talk 'for you to respond, for you to give direction.' That the relationship is between equals, it is reciprocal, ongoing and mutually beneficial is captured in Taku's reference to 'our talks must go on until a solution is found and we are all satisfied'. His mana would not have let him do otherwise, as he was upholding a continuity of approach from the past to the present and beyond, by uplifting the mana of those whom he was addressing.

Taku's main concern was the continuity of existence in spite of the imposition of Pākehā laws and ways. Privately he felt that 'Pakeha [are] over here to dictate the terms, no matter what you do, they'll do it entirely to their advantage.' Yet when called upon to open and bless a building, he explained his intention as being, 'I open your place to make security of conditions to enable us to work as one and for you to acknowledge that I'm tangata whenua.' He emphasised the need for association, and through association comes understanding, respect and 'the betterment of our people'.[12]

Taku presented matters that were important to him, to re-establish relations and rely on the continuity between the past and the present, rather than to just pursue reparations.[13] But conceptual differences between the parties in approach and methodology meant that they were often talking at cross purposes during the tribunal hearings. Crown counsel focused on historical context including an assessment of the choices Māori made, and referred to 'the complexity of the task of reconstructing history and of judging values and actions of the past'.[14] Claimant counsel criticised Crown counsel for disregarding 'the cultural imperatives which underlay Ngāti Whātua's actions throughout the period covered by the claim'.[15] The tribunal would not accept the idea of any other kind of relationship with mutual obligations over and above the Treaty of Waitangi. Its task was confined to investigating claims against the Crown and determining whether there had been a breach of the principles of the treaty (as defined by the tribunal and the courts) and whether the Crown's action or inaction toward Māori was reasonable or unreasonable in the circumstances of the time.[16] Ultimately, the outcome would be a political one.

GLORIA TIMOTI

Gloria was one of the early protestors against sand mining on the west coast near Woodhill Forest and Reweti marae and one of the original signatories to the statement of claim in 1992. She closely identified with Kakanui and Araparera marae where she grew up. She was educated first at the Kakanui Native School, then went on to Turakina Māori Girls School in Marton and finished at Kaipara College in Helensville. She was a staunch supporter of Māori tino rangatiratanga/self-determination. Gloria lived most of her life in the Kaipara, raised seven children, and worked hard to make ends meet. During much of the claim, she was living on ancestral land at Kakanui (in which she did not have a shareholding, although her sister did), in poor conditions with no power or running water. She was well-known on the claim committee for her quip, 'The Crown is the perpetrator, chief judge, defendant and final arbiter!'

In her brief of evidence, Gloria was one who recounted a story about the Kaipara railway:

> When the railways came through and we gave our land for them we were promised free travel to Auckland. My grandmother went to catch the train to Auckland and a guard asked her for a ticket. She socked him one because she knew she had been promised free travel. She was prosecuted and fined as a result.[17]

Gloria's evidence was based on a recollection of her beloved grandmother. Oral historians acknowledge that oral stories function to connect a crucial aspect of a remembered past with present concerns.[18] They often serve as parables, warnings or predictions for a community, especially in situations where people feel subjugated. Stories can change in the retelling as there are always multiple memories, understandings and imperatives. In referring to the railway in her evidence, Gloria was, in all likelihood, defending her grandmother, for later she said:

> I grieve for my grandmother sometimes because … by the time her grandchildren were in their teens, she couldn't converse with us because we didn't know how to … speak Māori … They alienated her from her own people, from her own.[19]

Treaty claims are principally about alienation from the whenua and from whānau and community with the consequent loss of identity. When Crown counsel argued that the alleged promise of three years of free travel on the Kaipara railway was not supported by the facts,[20] it simply confirmed that sense of alienation again for people like Gloria. It dismissed her story and made her invisible. The tribunal report, however, did acknowledge that Ngāti Whātua had donated most of the land taken up by the Kaipara railway, and the Crown had failed to fulfil the promise to create reserves and provide accommodation for Māori at each terminus, thereby failing to act reasonably and in good faith towards Ngāti Whātua.[21]

Understanding Gloria's life story is to understand some of the lived effects of alienation and marginalisation in postcolonial New Zealand. It was a truly humbling experience to hear Gloria say:

> I don't like me, you know. I don't like the way I am. I don't like the way I am. Because no matter what you do, they still, they still know better than you do and I've got the numbers, I've got the money, I've got the power, I make the laws, you do as I say.[22]

PROMISES AND POSSIBILITIES

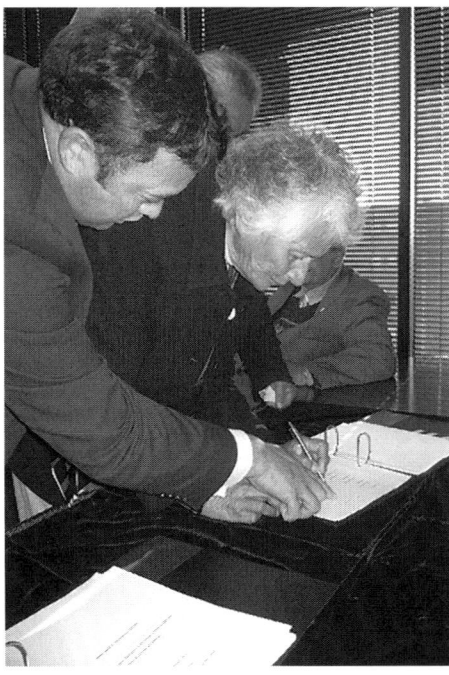

Gloria Timoti signing the Terms of Negotiation on 5 June 2008 in Auckland.

Photo courtesy of Margaret Kawharu

Gloria's disgruntlement wasn't solely directed at historic grievances. When I interviewed her in 2008, she was 78 years old and struggling with Housing New Zealand bureaucrats to get a decent roof over her head for herself and her adult son, Manny. Gloria told me:

> Manny and I had our names down for a Housing Corp. [sic] thing. I'd be happy with just one room, you know a bed sitting room, a unit. But we've been on it since we've been here but last week, they took our names off the thing … I think I attract bad luck! (laughs) I don't know! (laughs) But I can't dwell on it, I get very, yeah, I can take it, I suppose. So long as they stay away from me. What hurt more was they, they spent a lot of time out here you know, planning, and, they could've told me, they knew I had no children … I said, but you knew that from the beginning, when you asked us in the beginning if we had children we said no, and she said, well I'm sorry, we can't do it. They get paid good money to do that eh? I think Housing Corp. [sic] is in disarray … When you go to WINZ, they act like the money that goes out to the beneficiaries is from their own pockets, you know … And I said, look here, if it wasn't for people like me you wouldn't have a job![23]

GIVING VOICE TO THE PAST AND THE PRESENT

Many Māori people often feel invisible, the treaty claim was the first time they felt they were able to voice their grievances against the 'system' and tell their story. For others, who have been veteran campaigners for Māori rights and addressing injustices, the tribunal provides an opportunity to challenge the Crown with a comprehensive inventory of grievances and the impact of them on the whānau community over generations. Early in the preparation of the Ngāti Whātua o Kaipara claim, people were encouraged to be interviewed individually and oral histories, in the form western oral historians are familiar with, played a significant part in the process of gathering information through personal memories of family, events, places, activities, choices and consequences. Oral histories were also gathered collectively at hui to confirm key episodes and key tūpuna in tribal histories to define the claimant group for the tribunal. But it quickly became clear that oral history and 'telling their story' were to be differentiated from oral 'evidence'. While the oral history collected was immensely valuable for a potential tribal archive, much of it was superfluous to substantiating the causes of action in the statement of claim alleging breaches of the principles of Te Tiriti o Waitangi by the Crown.

There were three key areas in the Waitangi Tribunal proceedings where oral evidence was critical to underpin the main causes of action against the Crown. The first was in support of the claimants' basis of authority and representation, where traditional origin narratives and the recitation of whakapapa to confirm the status of the connection of the tangata to the whenua were given by knowledgeable kaumātua/kuia. The second was a more demonstrative form of the claimants' connection to the area in the pōwhiri, welcoming the tribunal to each of the five marae and hosting them on a tour of the claim area by bus and by boat to show them significant sites. The third was oral testimony from claimants more generally, giving indicators of their identity and the socio-economic impact of the grievances and loss on them and their whānau.

Equally as critical was legal counsel's ability to orchestrate the claim against the Crown with the claim committee and the claimant group. Legal counsel interviewed witnesses and drafted most briefs of evidence in collaboration with them before submission to the tribunal. Some of these witnesses did not wish to divulge detailed information, for example, the whereabouts of sacred sites and resources, for fear it might be misappropriated by the local council or developers. Some testimony was not considered helpful to the overall thrust of the claim if it didn't contribute to the main points. Evidence given orally gained usefulness for the tribunal by being in English and written into the record of claim. All in all, 30 claimant witnesses gave evidence before the tribunal. Waiata, songs specially composed to support the claimant witnesses, also formed part of the official record. Some video recordings of these proceedings conducted orally remain in the tribunal's off-site storage.[24]

Less public, however, were the unofficial proceedings. As the venue was Haranui marae, Ngāti Whātua protocol governed proceedings and an oral culture dominated by te reo Māori language presided. For the tribunal to hold the hearings, the hau kāinga opened and closed each day with appropriate karakia. They would tuku their permission to the tribunal to run the hearing and take back their authority at the end of the day, often summarising the day's highlights and checking on the next day's schedule. Debrief sessions were held with whānau and legal counsel after the tribunal had gone home for the day to discuss the overall strategy, assess how well the hearings were going, whether any adjustments needed to be made, and to practise waiata.

These were all, in a sense, forms of oral history in the making. But they went largely unrecorded, untranslated, and did not form part of the 'official' proceedings. Yet they were as much part of memory-making as the prepared written briefs of evidence and recorded oral testimony. More importantly perhaps, these were moments when collectively the claimants were 'remembering the past, thinking about the present and planning the future'. It was one of the few fora in which they could share the collective mamae, realise how that pain had been inflicted on their community, and acknowledge the consequences and the damage. Some of these memories have been captured and more work could be done to collate this material into a tribal archive.

MAKING SENSE OF GRIEVANCE

The historical basis of any Treaty claim is a tracking process of the interaction between Māori and the Crown since 1840. From Ngāti Whātua o Kaipara's perspective, the claim was based on their particular relationship with the Crown, a relationship that their forebears expected to be for mutual prosperity with reciprocal obligations. However, official records attest to alienation, disenfranchisement, marginalisation and protest over long-held grievances, particularly over land. Earlier, I referred to the gifting of Māori land for the construction of a railway and briefly describe the history here.[25]

In 1866, Ngāti Whātua leaders Apihai Te Kawau and Te Tinana promised a stretch of land from Pitoitoi/Riverhead to the Awaroa Creek/Helensville for the much-needed railway as an alternative transport route to the portage roads. At the end of February 1871 the Auckland Provincial Treasurer John Sheehan met with an assembly of 200 Ngāti Whātua to publicly discuss the proposed rail link to Auckland and the voluntary ceding of land required from the different owners along the Pitoitoi-Awaroa route for the purpose. According to the *Daily Southern Cross* newspaper, Sheehan's address 'dwelt upon the many advantages that would result to both races by the opening of the line',[26] and he concluded by informing them that 'it was for them, the native people of Kaipara, to decide the fate of the railway'.[27]

In response, Ngāti Whātua rangatira recalled their long-standing support for the Crown. Te Otene Kikokiko's wife, Maata Tira Koroheke, spoke directly to Sheehan:

> We give the land you ask for and we give it willingly, without cost. You know my lands; take your railway through them. It will do good. Our land will rise in value. We can travel quickly, provisions and clothing will be cheap, and Europeans will come to dwell amongst us. Kaipara will come to be a dwelling place of chiefs, as Auckland now is. When we die, we will leave our children among a people who will treat them kindly, as we, when living, treated the pakeha.[28]

It was agreed that accommodation for Māori would be erected by the government on reserves set aside at each terminus and free travel passes would be granted to the donors of the land for the first three years of the completed railway. Issues raised included payment for refencing and the opportunity for work during the building of the railway. At the close of the hui all the 'native landowners' present, as well as those Europeans interested as mortgagees, signed the deed of concession. Understanding that the Māori landowners were trustees for a much wider tribal group, Sheehan returned in early May 1871 for a rūnanga at Muriwai and gained the consent of 169 signatories to ratify the deed of concession. At the sod-turning ceremony on 31 August 1871 near Pitoitoi the official party included about 20 rangatira. Wiremu Te Reweti told the gathered officials and settlers that: '[w]e have given the land for the railway and we now confirm that gift … You ask us for the land for the railway, and we consent, we believe that out of it you will do good for us all.'[29]

Despite Ngāti Whātua gaining some employment as labourers in the early years of the railway line construction, the longer-term benefits remained something of an illusion. They made suggestions for the siting of new stations and additional daily trips, but these were declined. The Crown took additional land for more stations and sidings without consultation or compensation. By the time Paora Tuhaere petitioned the government in 1877 that Ngāti Whātua had not received the promised three years of free travel, landing reserves or tribal accommodation for Māori at Helensville and Riverhead, the provinces had been disestablished. Although the Native Affairs Committee of 1877 recommended the promises be fulfilled, nothing was done. When Ngāti Whātua lobbied their Member of Parliament, Hone Mohi Tawhai, who took the issues to the House of Representatives in 1882, the government responded that there was nothing in writing that could substantiate the claims. Yet when Tawhai raised the matter of compensation due to the chiefs of Ngāti Whātua, for the lands on which railway stations had been erected, the two deeds of concession signed in 1871 were referred to as the reason that 'no valid claim could be made for compensation in respect to the land so given'.[30] The Crown went on to reinterpret the meaning of the term 'gifting' replacing it with 'taking' the land utilised under the Public Works Act in July 1884.[31]

Appropriating the land in this way, effectively rendered the substantial gift Ngāti Whātua had made in 1871 null and void. Tuhaere felt that 'the Province has deceived and cheated them'.[32] The gifting of their land had made the proposed railway line possible but there was no statutory process by which to recognise a gift within the Public Works.[33] The land was surveyed only when the line was completed. Herein lies the sense of grievance, the lack of acknowledgement of the gifting or the mana of the donors, the failure to properly document the transaction at the time and the failure to deliver on clearly articulated understandings and promises of reciprocity. After various petitions to the government throughout the nineteenth century, it was not until 1985 that the treaty claim process opened a way to address such historical grievances.

Despite the inherent difficulties in the treaty claim process, both Taku and Gloria were dedicated members of the claim committee for over 20 years. They utilised the Waitangi Tribunal to underline Ngāti Whātua's continuity and resilience and encouraged the five marae to collectivise for the purpose. In doing so, oral traditions, oral recollections and oral history contributed to the evidence, which, combined with the written record, much of it from the Crown's own archives, achieved a comprehensive and well-founded claim that eventually led to a settlement. Taku and Gloria witnessed the passing of the settlement legislation in the House of Representatives[34] and Taku responded on behalf of Ngāti Whātua o Kaipara on that memory-making occasion.

There is no doubt that the claim process is well-intentioned and does bring cultural and psychological benefits for Māori communities, as well as a significant financial outcome. The Waitangi Tribunal was founded on an acceptance of Te Tiriti o Waitangi and its work contributes to an ever-expanding body of Treaty jurisprudence by its willingness to incorporate a Māori worldview and value oral tradition and oral testimony.

Oral evidence helps illuminate the past that has not yet been acknowledged. It challenges accepted historical and political perspectives and forces engagement with complex and contested issues. With more nuanced understandings of past events, new insights can be gained into what is required in reconciliation processes from a Māori and Crown perspective.

But the process can also be disempowering. It is a Crown-driven process, mediated by 'professionals' predominantly from western legal and historical disciplines, each with its own methodology.[35] The Crown is fixed on verifiable facts and objective evidence as to how the Crown's actions and omissions have impacted on Māori to create breaches of the treaty because the outcome is directly linked to political decisions around fiscal reparations which must pass parliamentary scrutiny and public acceptability.[36]

Tribunal hearings are considered cathartic. Once the past is remembered and the trauma is revealed and acknowledged, the hope is that recovery and healing can take place, Māori can move on from 'grievance to development mode'.[37] Testimony given orally helps the tribunal 'reach the real heart of the matter', by witnessing the burden of pain, hurt, feelings of injustice and shame people carry in speaking of their personal experiences of being subjected to and impacted by Crown policies. But how to assuage pain is the question.[38] How do we find a way to heal as individuals and as part of the five marae communities as a whole? The remedy is not the responsibility of the tribunal; it is now for the claimant group to negotiate with public servants approved by politicians. I fear there is a risk that in exchange for a settlement, a new collective narrative will emerge, one that serves as a nation-building exercise and tries to hide the past, potentially masking the power imbalances that perpetuate socio-economic disparities and silence the stories of ongoing struggles. However, what the claim process has achieved is the foundation for potential transformation. There is a shared memory of collective effort in asserting Ngāti Whātua o Kaipara's Treaty rights. There is a treaty settlement to show for it. There is a collection of well-documented material amassed from the process pertaining to the history and heritage of Ngāti Whātua o Kaipara that requires organising and protection. Oral history played a crucial part in creating that legacy and anchoring it in the recording of voices no longer with us. As one notable Māori leader told me:

> Unless you own your own memory as a people, you have no functional narrative about who you are, where you're from, and you're not in any position to discuss what you want to be … You've got to be the primary controller over your own knowledge base.[39]

To repay the faith kaumātua like Taku and Gloria put into the claim process for our continuation, there is still work to do.

3

Getting inside people's heads: What oral history can tell us about class in New Zealand in the late twentieth century[1]

JANE MOODIE

In 1998 one branch of my family, the Williamses, celebrated 175 years since the arrival of their missionary ancestors in New Zealand.[2] As an oral historian I was curious to understand in what ways that family's history might influence the lives of descendants at the end of the twentieth century. So began a project involving life narrative interviews with 50 members of the family. I was interested to see how past, present and future were connected in social memory by exploring the relationship between individual memory and family myth, and how these in turn interacted with certain public meanings and ideologies in New Zealand.[3] Among other things, many of the oral testimonies were concerned with class and often with ways in which the belief in egalitarianism cut across the family's class values and attitudes.[4] It is this aspect of the Williams oral testimonies I have chosen in order to demonstrate the potential of oral history to expand our understanding of class in the New Zealand context.

Conceptually class can be understood in several ways: once viewed as a hierarchy of economic (and hence social) inequality based on relationships of domination and exploitation, a more nuanced understanding has since evolved, including that of Pierre Bourdieu who contended that class formation is not exclusively a manifestation of economic relations, nor status guaranteed by wealth alone. British social historian E.P. Thompson pointed to the historical and cultural nature of class when he wrote: 'When we speak of a class, we are thinking of a very loosely defined body of people who share the same congeries of interests, social experiences, traditions and value-system, who have a disposition to behave as a class, to define themselves in their actions and in their consciousness in relation to other groups of people in class ways.'[5]

Recent approaches to the study of class have often drawn on the work of Bourdieu who has identified three main different kinds of capital, each conveying certain advantages.[6] These are:

1 Economic capital (wealth and income).
2 Cultural capital (has three forms: the embodied form, a long-lasting disposition of the mind and body mainly transmitted through family, such as pronunciation; the objectified form, which consists of accumulated cultural goods such as books, pictures, instruments, homes; and the institutionalised form such as educational success).
3 Social capital (a durable network of more or less institutionalised relationships of mutual recognition including family and school, which provide useful contacts).

It is possible to 'draw distinctions between people with different stocks of each of the three capitals', thus providing a 'more complex model of social class'.[7] But Thompson also insisted that 'class itself is not a thing, it is a happening'.[8] And indeed, Patrick Ongley has said that 'people *actively create class through practices of social inclusion and exclusion* based on the possession of different types of capital: cultural, social symbolic as well as economic'.[9] Thus, alongside the possession and longevity of wealth, things like education, skills, occupation, family, friends and other networks, manners, taste and lifestyle can all influence how people are connected to or divided from others. These dimensions of class are evident in the oral testimonies of many of the Williams family.

Throughout most of the twentieth century, many New Zealanders were proud of the idea of being part of an aspiring egalitarian society, but in recent decades in many countries including this, class has often been seen as an outdated category, the focus being more often on identity politics: questions of gender and ethnicity. In New Zealand historiography, as well as this recent neglect of class, the discussion has 'long been lopsided and meagre'.[10] Some studies of colonial society have emphasised the urban working class, others the wealthy South Island 'oligarchy'; some have seen class as irrelevant due to high social mobility and the dominance of regional and personality politics, while others have argued that class was central to colonial society from the outset.[11] More recently, Tom Brooking has described how the colony was founded on the ideal of a landed gentry, with yeoman farmers (working family farms) forming a middle class and labourers filling the lower ranks. Economic and political power lay mainly with the gentry.[12] He has traced the triumph of the yeoman ideal over the gentry ideal from the late nineteenth century to the late twentieth century, giving the rural middle class both economic and political heft. He further suggested that this 'Yeotopia' began to fade after 1990, following the neoliberal reforms, with the economic and political power of the owners of family farms being gradually transferred to the owners of agribusiness and others.

Studies of the wealthy in New Zealand have drawn on a variety of sources including biographies, family papers (histories, financial accounts, diaries, journals, and letters), station records, company records and letterbooks, company histories and probate files, as well as government publications such as the New Zealand Parliamentary Debates, and the census and survey records of Statistics New Zealand. These provide information on property ownership, income, occupation, education, material well-being, inheritance patterns, philanthropy, political orientations and also some insight into family life and values. But do they necessarily speak the language of class? E.P. Thompson wrote, 'Class is defined by men as they live their own history, and, in the end, this is its only definition.'[13] It is in this respect, by listening to people reflecting on their own lives, that oral history has so much to offer in understanding the workings of class in New Zealand society.[14] So let us turn to the Williams family oral histories as an example.

Before doing so, however, it is important to note that oral history involves two people, and the narrative is framed in light of the relationship to the interviewer. This person may be an 'insider', a member of the same organisation or family as the narrator, and therefore assumed by him or her to have a similar social and cultural understanding; or they may be an 'outsider', in which case the narrator will likely not make this assumption and frame their narrative accordingly. In the interviews presented here, I am an 'insider' interviewer, being a member of the same family as those interviewed, and also coming from a farming background. This is important in identifying the assumptions that are being made.

The family's English background was that of the Dissenting urban middle class.[15] They lived comfortably, took part in civic and church affairs, valued education, showed business acumen, and were philanthropic. In New Zealand, as the children of the missionaries Henry and Marianne Williams reached adulthood, they either acquired large tracts of land for pastoral farming or entered the church, while subsequent generations also entered the professions or went into business. The family became very wealthy and influential, and many members remain so. I propose to focus on the narratives of two Williams men, both farmers, born between the two world wars and so belonging to the Silent Generation. Tom Williams, however, was born in 1939, growing up in post-war prosperity, while Eric Williams was born in 1924, experiencing the Great Depression and war during his formative years. The working lives of both spanned the second half of the twentieth century: Tom, in partnership with his brother, ran racehorses and developed deer farming alongside sheep and beef farming, while Eric was influential in Coopworth sheep breeding and a leader in farm forestry in the Waikato. Both speak the language of class but from different perspectives. One of them appeared quite at ease with his family history and privileged upbringing, his narrative revealing how class consciousness can continue to define and unite the large landowning families and allow them to exercise power. The other, however, had spent a lifetime attempting to rebel against class differences, his narrative revealing his awareness of the more nuanced fractures and fissures of society. Both are examples of how oral history can bring fresh understanding to the question of class as it was lived.

Tom Williams was raised at 'Te Parae' in the Wairarapa. It was there that I interviewed him, sitting at the large kitchen table in the old homestead, which was built in the early 1900s. While acknowledging that his family narrative could have an earlier starting point, 1823 perhaps, Tom decided to begin with a story of land and family inheritance. In 1857 Hugh and William Beetham leased 'Brancepath', 10,000 acres in the Wairarapa, but were struggling to stock it and break in the land. When Tom's great-grandfather, Thomas Coldham (T.C.) Williams, married their sister Annie Beetham in 1858, he formed a development partnership with the brothers, funding the freehold and expansion of the station to 'about 70,000' acres by 1888.[16] In 1905, following the Lands for Settlement Act, the partnership was dissolved, with T.C. receiving two thirds of the land and stock, which he then divided between his 13 children.

Much of the original land is still owned by Williams family descendants. The block known as 'Te Parae' was passed to T.C.'s son, Guy, and eventually to the present owner, Tom and his brother. In Tom's opinion 'Te Parae' is now at the economic limit of divisibility, and while it may be a family home base, it can no longer serve as the basis of family wealth. All this was described by Tom in some detail, but in

GETTING INSIDE PEOPLE'S HEADS

the interests of brevity I include here only his description of the disbursements to his father's generation as an example of this narrative of marriage and inheritance.

> Guy Williams, my grandfather, got the 'Te Parae' block and he had four children, three girls and a boy. The oldest was N. who married [a] Borthwick, the second one was B. who married [a] Deans, and the third one was my father Alister, and the fourth child was J. who married [a] Dillon from Marlborough. And my grandfather, Guy, split 'Te Parae' … between three of his four children.

Tom then explained that the eldest daughter received no land because she was considered sufficiently wealthy by marriage, and that this was later a bone of contention. He continued:

> So B. was given about seven or 800 acres … called 'Kautatane' … J., the youngest daughter was given part of 'Te Parae' called 'Wiremu' … The rest of the property, 'Te Parae' was 1500 acres, and that was my father's, Alister, and my brother and I have farmed the land since we both took over round about early 1960s … Mother, my mother, was Nancy Teschemaker and she came from the South Island from Marlborough, not far from 'Leefield', the Dillon family's home. She was a Teschemaker, Nancy Teschemaker was her maiden name, and my father and mother married in 1938 and … I was born in 1939 and my brother in 1942.

> And I guess I'm Thomas Coldham, named after my great-grandfather. And my great-grandfather, Thomas, had a son called Guy who was Guy Coldham, and he had a son called Alister who was Alister Coldham, and he had a son called Thomas, myself, who was Thomas Coldham, and I have a son called Guy, Guy Coldham. So I guess the Coldham bit has sort of stuck and that's in recognition of Marianne, Henry's wife who was, I think, Marianne Coldham.[17]

Having thus established his family background, Tom embarked on the story of his own life. He attended the local rural school before going to Hereworth Preparatory School and Wanganui Collegiate. Unlike his father, who was sent to Cambridge University, Tom was directed to work first in the local abattoir and then on two South Island farms, before travelling overseas for one year. He returned to work on 'Te Parae', taking over completely after his father's death in 1972. Not only did he inherit the farm, but also appeared to have accepted the associated duties of public life. In the following sequence of extracts, he gave a sense of how this baton of public duty was expected to pass from generation to generation.

In about 1972 my father died in December. [He was a county councillor] and in 1973 … I was persuaded to stand, and eventually took over from him. I was in the local government scene for 12 years; I was deputy chairman for three and chairman for six … And the deer industry in 1984 was looking to set up a marketing organisation … It was called the Game Industry Board and I was persuaded to put my name forward … and so I ultimately ended up being appointed as the chairman of that organisation, its inaugural chairman. And I spent 10 years as the chairman of the board. And during that time, I also … was a member of the Thoroughbred Breeders Council.

[My father had] come back from the war and got involved in the horses, recognised that there needed to be an organisation to represent the views of the breeders and so he formed the Breeders Association. He rang up a lot of people like Jack Alexander, Tom Lowry, Jack Grigg, and with his lawyer drafted the constitution of the Breeders Association, and so it's with some pride that all those years later, both my brother and I served on the Breeders Council.

Then the Minister of Racing, the Honourable John Falloon, set up a Ministerial Committee of Inquiry into racing … and race betting systems and any other matters relevant to the racing industry. [I was 'invited' to be on the committee] so I said that I would be prepared to put some time into this … and we came out with a very substantial report. So one of the recommendations was that there be an overall organisation, and … I recommended that it should be called the Racing Industry Board … And so the Racing Industry Board was brought into being by Falloon, to his credit. And ultimately, and to my absolute horror and surprise, he asked me to chair the Racing Industry Board, and after saying no I certainly wouldn't under any circumstances, and then going off to England and coming back, and a few heavyweights saying, 'You'd better do it', I said I would. And so for two years I ran both the Racing Industry Board and the Game Industry Board.[18]

Tom had also been involved in a number of local beneficent initiatives, establishing a theatre trust and a local aviation society, while 'Te Parae' had gradually become the 'centre of the community', holding regular Anglican communion services and hosting events like the annual Wainuioru carol service.[19] In 1991 Tom had arranged for David Yerex to write the story of 'Brancepeth' and 'Te Parae', the Beetham and Williams families' homesteads. I asked him why he had asked Māui Pomare to write the foreword for this book. His reply was that there was a valued association of long standing between the families, the Williams and Pomare boys having been at Wanganui Collegiate and in the first XV rugby teams together for three generations.[20] Later, as we drew the interview to a close, Tom reflected at length on the wider relationship between Māori and Pākehā in recent times, expressing sadness and pondering the responsibilities of certain families in both communities.

> **Tom**: I used to have quite significant discussions with Māui about this, and Pom's views were that his family and my family … had a significant leadership role in trying to wrest this problem from government and get on with the practical solution to it … And I mean he was quite an eminent Māori in my view, and his family [certainly are].

> *Jane: You were speaking earlier of the values of the family. I wondered how you would describe those?*

> **Tom**: I suppose they're more values I hold dear, sort of honesty and integrity. But I mean the fact of the matter is that the [Williams] family have made a very significant contribution to New Zealand and continue to do so … The values that have given us these opportunities [to become involved in public service] are still the values that I think are pretty important, and the ones that I'm sure the younger generation look up to and aspire to … I guarantee that my kids know pretty much about their family, where they come from and the reasons why they are who they are, and I think those are values that we need to continue to instil in … the next generations of the family … Yeah, the things that we are proud of in our ancestry are the sort of things that the next generation need to be proud of.[21]

On the whole Tom's narrative was marked by a sense of composure. Without appearing conceited he was proud of his extended family and its connections, of its multigenerational association with the land, and of the Coldham name, which linked him back to the missionaries and their early arrival in New Zealand. It was a statement of identity and seemed to indicate an easy acceptance of the class origins of the Williams family in New Zealand as a simple matter of fact, past and present.

In contrast, Eric Williams's narrative was one of unease, often ironic in tone, a story of early and continuing resistance to his elitist upbringing. Both narratives are class-coded conversations but Eric's was much more consciously and explicitly so. As such, it revealed the small gradations of social acceptability and the many cleavages and cracks that existed in society, the pressures to meet family and class obligations and some of the changes occurring over time.

Eric was born at Te Aute, Hawkes Bay, where 70 years earlier his great-grandfather, Samuel Williams, had established the college for Māori boys. Unlike Tom he had moved a long way since his boyhood; I spoke with him in the new house he and his wife had retired to in Pirongia, after a lifetime farming in the Waikato. He began with the painful memory that the Williams children were not allowed to attend the local Te Aute school nor play with the local children. For Eric there was one exception to this rule; he was permitted to play with the son of his grandmother's chauffeur, a retired army captain and therefore presumably more socially acceptable.[22] The four Williams children were taught by governesses for some years, and Eric was then sent to a private prep school, Hereworth, and later to Wanganui Collegiate. Although he did quite well both on the playing field and in the classroom, he was not happy in either school. He recalled that he always felt a 'considerable misfit', made fun of by other kids because he was naïve, less worldly than other boys because of his 'secluded' upbringing and perhaps his missionary connections.[23] He left school to join the air force in 1942.

This was how Eric described Te Aute when he was growing up, and immediately after World War II, when he worked on the farm.

Jane: So the relatives were all within walking distance?

> **Eric**: Oh yes, it was a little settlement, the college was at the centre and Aunt Lydia was across the limestone track … A little bit further along from Lydia's house, along a nice wooded path, was 'Roxton', where the two aunts, Ellen and Ada, lived. They had a very nice garden and we used to enjoy visiting them and having bread and butter sandwiches and chocolate biscuits and things with them. And across from them on the main road was the general Pukehou store … And next to that was the blacksmith, where I used to love going and blowing the bellows … Past him … was a garage where they sold petrol, and then there was the local school … And then there was the establishment where my grandfather lived, with the house where we were brought up. And then down below them the three cottages for the gardener, the cowman and the shepherd, the head shepherd, J.L. who was a Scot. I used to enjoy going out with J. on the horses around the farm.
>
> [My father] was, I suppose you'd say, the squire of the Pukehou village at that time, because he was the principal landowner and employer around there. On the farm there were three cottages over by the railway line … and there was a Māori couple in one cottage, M.W., he worked on the farm … He and I used to

do quite a lot together, we worked a lot together like in the harvesting, growing crops and everything else, we worked side by side ... M. was there for most of his life and moved up on to the main road into one of the cottages there.

There was [also] an Irish couple who we used to visit [every now and then], because they were tenants ... They were also very near to the slaughterhouse where we killed cattle and sheep ... I remember when we visited this Irish couple we were 'dearie' and we were intrigued by their accent and so on, but now looking back I felt rather sorry for them too – the sort of conditions – though I suppose as far as they were concerned they were living in clover compared to what they'd left behind in Ireland ... But I didn't think so, no.

We used to have a doctor there, we had a minister there in the village. The doctor was Doctor Jarvis ... Arthur was the local vicar, Arthur Williams. He was just across the gully from my father's house. There was a gully there and we had a track through it and we used to go and visit them. They had a tennis court, quite a nice place. We used to have the odd party, afternoon tea parties and things there. And across the road from them, which was just on the Hastings side of the big house, were three or four houses for people who worked on the station – ploughman, I don't know what they all did, but they all worked there on the farm ...

I think my father was probably a sort of a benefactor, he looked on [Māori] as people who, although they were respected to some extent, they were still a little bit different, a bit of the apartheid system still going in those days and the Māoris who had been deprived of their land were then – they had to work on the land for the Pākehā who'd taken over ... By various means a tremendous number of Māori were deprived of their land. I don't think so much by my immediate family there, they did respect them, but they accepted the lower status of the Māori. I felt that anyway.

Then there was a cookhouse just near the college ... a place where the labourers, so to speak, on the farm – ploughmen and fencers and so on would live, and there was a cook who would cook for all of them, and they'd come into a great big room with long tables and they'd all sit down to their tucker ... I used to go there and have meals with them every now and then. I don't think my parents minded. And we used to play cards. I accepted them I think possibly more so than a lot of people round there, as equals, and I felt sorry for them, I thought they had been given a bad trot. I'm perhaps more of an egalitarian than a lot of people.

Jane: So that was a huge setup, and you guys are there with your governess?

Eric: Yep, yep, and I told my father on one occasion that that was one of the regrets I had.²⁴

Eric painted a picture of a thoroughly hierarchical social structure: the owner's big house, 'the establishment', stood on the hill, connected by a 'nice wooded path' to the homes of other members of the family where, among lovely gardens, you drank tea, ate polite sandwiches and played tennis; below were the houses of the various farm workers, near to the dusty road, the noise of the railway, and the unpleasantness of the slaughterhouse. The unmarried workers ate in the cookhouse, completely separate from the owner's family.²⁵

Later in his narrative Eric made an even stronger declaration of his views. Going to the Pukehou church he recalled that the landowners, mostly relatives, occupied the front pews while their employees sat in the back pews.

Eric: It wasn't long before I was questioning things like 'All things bright and beautiful':

> 'The rich man in his castle,
> The poor man at his gate,
> God made them high and lowly,
> And ordered their estate.'

And I thought, 'Crap!' (I didn't say crap in those days.)

Jane: But you lived in that situation almost.

Eric: I did – and I couldn't see the reasoning or the sense in it.²⁶

World War II proved to be a turning point in Eric's life. His flying instructor was the butcher from Taradale, but nevertheless, 'a god to any of us training pilots', someone Eric could look up to, despite his lowly background.²⁷ In Eric's view, 'everything was stirred up after the war, there was the opportunity to go out on a different channel if [he] wanted to'. He resented the 'strong expectation' placed upon him as the oldest son and grandson to carry on the family farming tradition at Te Aute, to go to church, to always 'do the right thing'.²⁸ This lies at the heart of Eric's story.

Returning home, Eric worked on the station with his brother-in-law, Jim Maclean, who was also a member of the Williams family. He continued to resist the family and class traditions constraining him, a resistance only partially successful.

When his father decided he should follow the family tradition of going to Oxford or Cambridge before settling down at 'Te Aute', Eric managed to persuade him that Cirencester Agricultural College would be more suitable – still an English education but one that did not conform in all respects to expectation. Once in England, Eric left Cirencester after only two terms, finding it irrelevant to New Zealand conditions and to his growing interest in forestry.

Before leaving for England, he had met Heather Scott, a physiotherapist at the local hospital. Part of her attraction was her failure to be 'swayed by the so-called glamour of the Williams family', a fellow rebel. Although Eric clearly liked this, she herself pointed out during the interview that her family had a long-standing connection to the Williamses through the Anglican Church.[29] In reality Heather and Eric shared a somewhat similar background, although the farm on which she had grown up was certainly smaller and less developed than 'Te Aute'. Before coming home, he and Heather were married in London; some of the family attended and Eric noted somewhat apologetically that the Bishop of Lichfield officiated. He seemed aware that having a bishop officiate at his wedding was not altogether consistent with his desire to escape his class origins, but he explained that the bishop had stayed at 'Te Aute' on a visit to New Zealand, and so was known to Eric's family. These class connections repeatedly creep into Eric's narrative.

Back at 'Te Aute', Eric had to finally confront the expectations that weighed upon him and make a decision about his future. 'I think that I was a little bit antipathetic towards my many relatives who were so marvellous … I did my best to divorce myself from them. And when the opportunity came to get away … Heather and I [decided we] would far rather get out of it.'[30] Leaving his brother-in-law in charge at 'Te Aute', they moved to the Waikato where the Scott family lived. Working on the Scott's farm at Pirongia was clearly a shock. It was a situation that exemplified the yeoman farmer, hitherto unfamiliar to Eric. They lived with Heather's family in a house that Eric felt was not much more than 'shearers' accommodation'. The farm was 'very basic, no tractors or machinery, [just] draught horses and sledges … and tossing fertiliser out by hand'. He confessed: 'I felt a little bit out of place there, it was the type of family that I had not experienced before.'[31] So, despite the similarities between the two, the disparity in wealth and material comforts between their two families presented a challenge at first.

As a returned serviceman, Eric was able to apply for a farm by ballot but was never successful in this. Eventually, using a government rehabilitation loan, he bought an undeveloped farm at Te Miro, near Cambridge. Eric now revelled in the primitive state of the farm, which lay up a clay road with a basic four-roomed house and no electricity. He enjoyed recalling that he did all his own shearing with Heather holding the throttle open on the old engine. He had finally broken free. However, he did confess, as an aside, that he had received financial help from his father to buy the stock.[32]

Conflict between his experience of the class attitudes of his family, reinforced by his schooling, and adherence to the wider societal discourse of egalitarianism was never fully resolved in Eric's narrative. Listening to him you hear a man approaching 80 still struggling against class attitudes and practices inculcated since childhood. Even as we sat recording at his table after lunch, he was anxious to point out the changes he had made in his life and, indicating the plastic container of butter, he recalled the dinner table at 'Te Aute'.

> The butter would be rolled into butter pats, and put on a special little plate and a butter knife [with] which you took the butter pat off and put it on your plate and 'Don't take two, dear – that's rude and greedy.' You'll have noticed the 'butter plate' that I brought out for you. I kicked against all those things, and I still do. I mean we still eat with soup spoons because my wife says that's right [but] I'm quite happy to eat with an ordinary dessert spoon.[33]

So here are two men whose family background is that of the North Island landed gentry, although both, through their working lives, may be said to fit the yeoman ideal of family farmer. And yet, both men still speak the language of class, demonstrating the power and persistence of class conditioning in their lives, even though their responses to it are very different. This persistence may suggest a relative impermeability of class hierarchies: usually understood as being difficult to break into, they may also be difficult to break out of. But what to make of the differences in their narratives? The social nature of memory and of class conditioning does not mean it is pre-determined. Eric's rebellion points to the fact that there is a choice in whether or not to buy into inherited beliefs. To ask what may have occasioned the divergence between the two risks venturing into a mire of speculation concerning personality and upbringing. Perhaps the answer lies partly in the 15-year age gap between them. In his formative years Eric experienced the Great Depression and World War II, while Tom, growing up in times of increasing affluence, had not been so starkly confronted with the issues of wealth, poverty and class.

Family is an important locus of class conditioning, so oral histories such as these, which focus on personal life stories and family memories, are a valuable source of information about the social, cultural and symbolic capitals of class in New Zealand society, defined by people as they live their lives. The formation and use of social capital has been clearly indicated here, particularly by Tom's recitation of family marriages over generations. With one exception, the marriages involved descendants of early settlers like the Williamses themselves; the Deans, the Dillons and the Teschemakers, all of whom had become large landowners in the South Island.[34] These marriages were the norm, cementing relationships between such families over generations, but also shoring up landed wealth, creating local class-based communities, and ensuring continued status. Eric's discombobulating first experience on his wife's family farm in the Waikato speaks to the differences between them, despite claims to the contrary.

What is revealing about Tom's testimony was not so much its content but the apparent assumption that I, as a member of the family, needed no explanation of the origins of these families, nor of the 'dynastic' significance of the marriages. These are class-coded conversations that allow people to understand one another in subtle but almost unspoken ways. The use of the indefinite article in the statement, 'she was a Teschemaker', was an important class signifier here. The awkwardness connected with the Borthwick marriage indicated a transgression of the norm; Tom acknowledged the possible unfairness and alluded to an attitude that appeared to place different values on 'old' landed wealth and 'new' business money. Further discussion may have revealed more about the class attitudes that lay behind this decision; without this probing, which I felt would have been inappropriate, it stands as an example of a conversation in which both participants, myself and Tom, appeared to share a mutual understanding of the class traditions and values expressed.

The sequence of inheritance and marriages was then concluded with a recitation of Tom's own line of descent from the family patriarch, with the name Coldham a constant throughout. This allows an acknowledgement of Tom's illustrious ancestor, Henry Williams, as well as his wife, Marianne Coldham, who with a 'pedigree' traceable to the eleventh century was widely regarded in the family as being the most 'upper class' of the two original missionary couples.[35] So the use of the Coldham name connects the New Zealand family, and hence Tom, to his English class roots. This was not alluded to directly, but once again 'insider knowledge' was assumed in this class-coded conversation.

Beyond the family are wider social networks, all helping to develop a sense of class unity and continuity, creating communities of shared values and interests. They also lead to the creation and maintenance of business and political networks.

Tom's narrative makes clear that public duty was an expectation that carried over from generation to generation; if one was asked to serve it was an obligation, born of privilege, to do so. Although Tom was proud of his work, he tried to keep the tone of his narrative matter of fact, not bragging or conceited. And, as with the family genealogy, the networking and names are vital to the account; they often involve people who have been connected over generations through private schooling, marriages, and shared interests, who have the influence and power to get things done. The connections of which Tom speaks are part of the social and cultural capital of the upper class, enabling the power relations that are part of the economic base of class formation.

Oral history encompassing family memory can also provide evidence of the many forms of cultural capitals of class suggested by Bourdieu. These are what Brooking has called the 'more nebulous indicators of social position'.[36] Sometimes these were explicit. Eric's narrative provided good examples: the degree of material comfort expressed in large, older houses with beautiful gardens suggestive of longevity of wealth and position, descriptions of farm layouts that reflect the social hierarchy between owner and workers, also replicated in seating arrangements at church, right down to the minutiae of good manners and acceptable behaviour, and an 'Oxbridge' education.

But there was an awkwardness about Eric's description of 'Te Aute', and therein lies its real value for the oral historian. He adopted an ironic tone, using words and phrases like 'the establishment', 'I suppose you'd say, the squire', and 'the labourers, so to speak', as a way of distancing himself from this hierarchical social structure. Although he appeared to have enjoyed tea and tennis with the family, he established a pattern in which he constantly situated himself with the workers, preferring the company of the blacksmith, the shepherd, the Māori farm worker. To work alongside these people was acceptable, but eating with the ploughman and fencers was breaking the usual class taboo of the two-table family. His comment regarding his parents' attitude to this showed he was well aware of the transgression. He also expressed ambivalence about the family's relationship with the Irish couple; although intrigued by their accents, he cannot quite 'place' them in a social sense, and while appreciative of their apparent welcome, he was nevertheless aware of the condescension implicit in visiting the tenants. Eric appeared uncertain of an appropriate response to the situation. Even though his description of these class signifiers is explicit, this awkwardness and his ironic tone imply his disavowal of the class system.

Sometimes these indicators of cultural capital are more difficult to detect. Tom's hope that 'Te Parae' will remain as a home base if not an economic one for his descendants is, I think, a recognition of the importance of the grand home in this connection. Other examples include the mention of a father's military background as a means to make a small boy more socially acceptable, or the assumption of Anglicanism as a class signifier. And, in the very interstices of oral narrative, we find the odd remark about voice, the telling use of the indefinite article, the awkward, sometimes confusing, moments when speaking of class transgressions. All this gives a much more nuanced understanding of how class operated in New Zealand towards the end of the twentieth century: where the fine fissures in society occurred and how inclusion or exclusion was communicated.

These family narratives also demonstrate how class and race interweave in complex and sometimes contradictory ways. Tom's assumption of easy familiarity (indicated by the use of a nickname) and shared interests with a particular Māori family of higher status was not unusual in the Williams family. Certain Māori are seen as rangatira who share similar values, traditions and a sense of public responsibility in common with Pākehā families like the Williamses, and there is mutual recognition of their parallel positions and influential roles in society. In a number of the Williams narratives, the motif of intergenerational friendship with leading Māori families was also a class signifier, speaking to the longevity of the family in New Zealand; they are not just early settlers, they have deeper roots here, and their long-lasting relationship with Indigenous New Zealanders is evidence of this.[37] In the New Zealand context these claims are also part of the Williams family's social and cultural capital.

In contrast to Tom, when Eric spoke about Māori his discomfiture was pronounced. Although the Māori farm worker at 'Te Aute' was also a tenant on the station, Eric did not speak of visiting his home on that account as he did the Irish worker. He well knew that in the eyes of most Pākehā, Māori were of lower social status, but the conflict for Eric also lay in the attitude of his own family; is it possible to be respectful of Māori while still accepting their lower status and employing them as servants on the land that once was theirs? And are Eric's own family outliers in Pākehā society because of their attitude to Māori? These complex, awkward passages are of enormous value in oral history, and similar passages can be found in a number of the Williams's life narratives particularly when, like Eric, they claimed to espouse egalitarian ideals. Oral history offers a unique means to explore the relationship between class and race in much greater depth than this. (In a similar way the interweaving of class and gender issues is also open to investigation through oral history. Although not so obvious in these two narratives, those of some Williams women would provide excellent examples.

Oral history can also reflect some of the intergenerational changes and adaptations over time. For instance, it was clear that just as an education with a governess was becoming a thing of the past, so an Oxbridge education was no longer requisite in maintaining class superiority. And while Tom acknowledged that for future generations 'Te Parae' can no longer serve as the basis of family wealth, he remained hopeful that other forms of class capital would serve his children well. They know 'why they are who they are', they have been imbued with the right values, they have good social connections through family and school, they have a family history that is significant in New Zealand. For how long can class distinction survive the loss of its wealth base by these means? Time will tell, and in this connection, intergenerational oral history may be useful. Looking at such things as material well-being, occupation, education and political orientation reveals much about class, but oral history is another valuable and neglected source that can tell us something different; it can tell us how people themselves define class as they live their own lives, and how they actively work to create and maintain, or conversely, try to diminish, class differences.

4

Re-remembering the Dawn Raids:
An oral history of Will 'Ilolahia and the Polynesian Panthers

HELENA COOK

Oral history has traditionally been seen as a way of recording stories, of 'exploring the many ways in which individuals construct frameworks of meaning'.[1] Oral history in Aotearoa New Zealand has a history that goes far beyond audio recordings of lived memory, and for Māori and people from the Pacific Islands, oral history has long been a source of passing down knowledge, memories and experiences.[2] This chapter records some of the memories of Will 'Ilolahia, a founding member of the Polynesian Panthers. Inspired by the civil rights struggles of the Black Panthers in the US, the Polynesian Panthers came together in Auckland at a time when Pacific peoples faced racism, oppression and discrimination. The Dawn Raids of the 1970s, where police targeted people they suspected of being visa overstayers (those who remain in New Zealand past the end date of their work visa), are an example of the kind of policies employed by the state that have left a legacy of hurt, shame and disillusionment with government relationships among the Pacific community.

Reflecting on Will's memories as a leading figure involved in fighting institutional racism allows us to tell part of a story that has been traditionally neglected by the writers of New Zealand's history books. Oral history provides the means to hear aspects of the past that are challenging to reach in more traditional written forms; the words and experiences of Pacific people are frequently absent from histories of New Zealand and their stories are often confined to Pacific-specific publications, with a lack of acknowledgement of their long and interwoven history with Aotearoa.

Listening to Pacific voices through oral histories provides the opportunity for stories to be told in a person's own words, allowing for a richer and more nuanced understanding of the lived experiences of the Dawn Raids. This can help reframe the narrative of migrants and overstayers in a Pacific cultural context, challenging assumptions about how people experienced this time in New Zealand's history.

The migration story of Pacific people to Aotearoa New Zealand is one that started before contemporary recorded history. Ancient explorers navigated their way between their home islands in the Pacific to the shores of Aotearoa and back again.[3] This marked the first stage of migration, creating a symbiotic relationship that supposedly benefits both those who come from the Pacific in search of a new life and those who receive Pacific labour, resources, culture and diversity in Aotearoa. The experience of those who came to New Zealand in search of a 'land of milk and honey' has not always been a positive one and this chapter traces a part of New Zealand's history that still haunts many Pacific communities today. By using oral history to reflect on the Dawn Raids, I explore themes of identity, of shame, and the ways traumatic memory influences the past and the present. The kind of future Aotearoa may have as a nation in the Pacific depends both on how we see ourselves now and how we view our past, the kind of acknowledgements and reparations we make for hurts caused, and an honest exploration of the memories that communities carry within them.

THE PACIFIC DIASPORA IN NEW ZEALAND

Migration from the Pacific to New Zealand has traditionally been seen in three main waves. The first was exploration from the Pacific Islands between 1200–1300 AD, when the ancestors of Māori came to settle in Aotearoa. The second wave was during the colonial period, in the 1800s, when Pacific settlers came as sailors, missionaries, teachers and whalers. Finally, a large wave of Pacific migrants, hoping to find a new life for themselves and their families, came to work as labourers from the 1950s right up until the 1980s.[4] Many of them settled permanently in New Zealand, resulting in a new generation of New Zealand-born Pacific people.

Will describes his identity as:

> a Tiwi, which is a New Zealand-born Tongan. So born here in New Zealand, in 1951. Went to school here and I got the opportunity to study in England. I went there at the tender age of 11 but I got homesick.[5]

Once he returned to New Zealand, he settled into life at Mount Albert Grammar in Auckland but found that his experiences overseas had opened his eyes to what life was like for other people of colour.

> I had a little incident, a little experience of racism in England with a friend of mine called George Washington, who was a Trinidadian. We're staying in Paddington, which is sort of like, the Coronation Street kind of houses, and we were always talking in the back yard about the islands, you know about the open window buses and the sound systems, and going down to the sea to jump off the wharf, and by the time you get home your clothes are all dry, cleaned, and you know. In the school I was idealised as the South Sea Islander, sitting underneath the coconut tree playing the ukulele. But my friend George, he was called n*gger, and put down because of his skin. That was my first inkling of what racism was all about. But I didn't really think about it at all until I became George Washington at Mount Albert Grammar and I thought, oh OK![6]

While Will was eventually made a prefect at Mount Albert Grammar, even as a young man he was aware of the divides between white and brown people that he could see in Auckland. The relationships he formed with Māori and Pacific people created a sense of unity among those who found themselves on the receiving end of racism and prejudice.

> All the kids knew me, all the Polynesian kids, because most of them were from Ponsonby, they all knew me because I was in the Niggs [gang] outside. We called ourselves Niggs, because, you know, everyone's calling us n*gger. We didn't wear a patch or anything, it was just a group of us, rural Māori coming up to urban Polynesia, and us born here, and you know we just all combined because we're getting that uh name calling and all that kind of thing. And when I was at Mount Albert Grammar, I could see it quite openly, you know?[7]

ATTITUDES TO PACIFIC PEOPLE IN NEW ZEALAND

Migration from the Pacific Islands to New Zealand came about because people believed in the possibility of a better life.[8] They dreamt of a future when their children would become doctors and lawyers and own houses and big cars. They aspired to send money home and provide for their loved ones. In order to do that, they needed to earn a New Zealand wage and occasionally this was obstructed by the lack of a work visa or residency permit. When faced with the choice between supporting their families or returning home, some migrants decided to risk everything and remain as overstayers (illegal immigrants subject to the penalties for breaking the law) living alongside Pacific people who were in New Zealand legally. In the often tense social and political environment of 1970s New Zealand, 'Pacific people' were often classed together as a unified group despite the vast differences between countries in the region. Many Pākehā New Zealanders saw Pacific people as a community with shared beliefs, culture and behaviours and this led to racial assumptions and behaviours.[9]

Pacific peoples in New Zealand, especially the young ones, were used to being harassed on the streets of Auckland. Conflicts among groups of young men were common; Pākehā boys shouting racist slurs they had heard from their parents or the media, 'Island boys' responding with physical aggression or with direct confrontation.

> What it was like for us walking down the street was, especially in Ponsonby because all these pālangis from North Shore were cutting through Ponsonby to get onto the bridge, and they were hanging out car windows and shouting 'you n*ggers'. And this is how I found out that the Samoans were good at throwing rocks! Some of the Samoan members, like John, they would throw the rocks and hit the cars and then go up to them and open the doors and say, 'What did you say?'[10]

These attitudes towards Pacific people were encouraged by the rhetoric and actions from various New Zealand governments towards the Pacific community. Demand for labour in New Zealand was growing after World War II, often as a result of increased urbanisation. As New Zealand citizens, people from the Cook Islands, Tokelau and Niue were able to migrate to New Zealand freely. In the early 1960s, new agreements signed with Samoa, Tonga and Fiji allowed their citizens to come to New Zealand on short-term work permits.[11] In 1945 there were 2159 Pacific peoples in Aotearoa; by 1971, numbers had reached 43,752.[12] The increase in numbers of Pacific migrants was initially supported by Norman Kirk's Labour government but as the population grew, cracks in relationships became evident. Pacific communities emerged in suburbs like Ponsonby and Ōtara; the majority were poor and working class, with low levels of education and poor health statistics. The New Zealand media increasingly portrayed these communities as criminals, dangerous or drains on public services and the police responded in kind, arresting groups of young Pacific men hanging around the streets.

> The majority of the cops we were dealing with were guys from the South Island, they were pālangis from the country and their only lesson about Polynesians were at Trentham ... if you see a bunch of Polynesians hanging around, they must be up to something. So if they couldn't charge us with anything, they'd charge us with I and D which is Idle and Disorderly. And this is where our lawyer David Lange [helped], he'd got the highest number of dropped convictions because he argued you can't call a Polynesian Idle and Disorderly because he has a home, he has his aunty down the road, his uncle on the next block ... so you can't say that to us. As for the fact that these people don't have money in their pocket, well they don't need money! They can go to the aunty to grab a feed, go to the uncle and have a sleep ... so he got all these convictions thrown out and the cops were pissed off![13]

Will 'Ilolahia and his mates were on the receiving end of abuse from the police, the Pākehā public and the media. During his university studies, Will was inspired by the book *Seize the Time: The story of the Black Panther Movement and Huey P. Newton* by Bobby Seale and this would lead to the formation of a new gang based on the Black Panthers in the US. As he said:

> The true story is the King Cobras at that time was led by a guy called Nari Felix ... He was doing time, and he picked up a book called *Seize the Time* about the Black Panthers. Meanwhile I'm out here in the Niggs picking up the book, you know, in regards to my studies. So he comes out of prison and says 'Oh, let's unite' ... we said, oh yeah sure, we'll combine under the Black Panthers.

The Ponsonby Black Panthers were the start of Will's political journey: he understood from his own experiences that Pacific people faced racism, unemployment, poverty and lacked knowledge about how to get support in the New Zealand welfare and legal systems.[14] He wanted to challenge these issues and fight the systemic racism he saw in society but knew that a traditional gang model, particularly when violence was involved, might not be the answer. As he tried to encourage his friends and fellow gang members to become involved in political struggle, things came to an abrupt head:

> We had a party, and these other guys put one of our sisters on the block.[15] And we who ended up being the Polynesian Panthers, we looked at each other, and said, 'This is not the Panthers'. And so we walked out and set up the Polynesian Panthers, because of what happened, and the feeling of that's not us ... We left

and went down to Fred Schmidt's house. He was the first chairman, because we used his room as our meeting place. In that group was Paul Dapp. He was Chinese Māori. And so we said, 'Okay, Paul, you'd be Minister of Defence because you know karate.' So he was Minister of Defence … all the roles that the Black Panthers had, we filled them … The guys took their roles seriously and they started enacting all the programmes that we did: so under the information programmes, we had homework centres and under defence we had karate classes and teaching our little kids how to stand up for themselves … Fred said, 'cos he was a seaman and most of the time away, he couldn't carry on as Chairman. So I became chairman.[16]

The newly formed Polynesian Panthers quickly grew, attracting young Pacific men and women, and rural Māori who wanted a new kind of society and were prepared to use passive resistance and if needed, military tactics, to challenge the status quo. While their immediate focus was community-based, their aims were political and focused on changing the racist policies of the state.[17]

THE DAWN RAIDS AND COMMUNITY RESPONSE

By 1973, Norman Kirk's government was focusing on crime and immigration as touch points for voters. In March 1974, police raids took place on homes of Tongan families in Onehunga suspected of being overstayers. Churches were also raided by police with dogs and the shame suffered by the Tongan community was intensified as overstayers were publicly dragged to police stations.[18] Tongans were not the only group who were targeted by the police; those stopped and questioned on the street were often racially profiled by police as anyone who looked Pacific, which included Māori, New Zealand-born Pacific people, and those who had legal rights to settle in Aotearoa.

The relationship between Māori and Pacific peoples was a varied one; the two groups were frequently treated the same by Pākehā because of the colour of their skin. Māori were struggling to fight their own battles over tino rangatiratanga, loss of land and language and increased urbanisation which resulted in alienation and isolation, particularly for young people. Hone Harawira, who worked closely with the Panthers through his role in Māori activist group Ngā Tamatoa, said 'I never thought of myself as being Māori and them being something else … we were all brought up to be who we were … we were just all brownies …'[19]

The Polynesian Panthers. From left to right: Fred Schmidt, Ta Iuli, Paul Dapp, Nooroa Teavae, Semi (Sam) Vete. Courtesy of Nigel Bhana photo archive

Will and the Panthers recognised that Māori oppression was also oppression of all minority migrant groups. Moreover, they argued that visa requirements and immigration legislation came from Pākehā governments, rather than from the Indigenous people.

> Our argument has always been that Māori were never on the beach when our wakas arrived asking us for papers. To us in Polynesia, visas and permits is a pālangi concept.[20]

There was a desire from the Panthers for indigenous sovereignty but they believed this would be achieved through acknowledgement of unity through diversification not uniformity.[21] As primarily New Zealand-born Pacific youth, the Panthers remained committed to valuing their Pacific identity, culture and values in all the work they did.[22] Will talks about the way his father came to understand the similarities between the struggles of Māori and for the Pacific communities.

> When I got sprung for being [protesting] up at Bastion Point, my dad said, 'Why for you go there? You're not Māori'. He knew I was involved with some of the people up there so I said to him, 'Dad, how would you feel if you lose your land?'

> Dad comes from the traditional Island viewpoint: you can't lose your land; the land is your land. I said, 'Dad, these people have lost their land' and showed him how the land had shrunk from iwi. Three weeks later Dad and his church drove a truckload of food up to Bastion Point. Nothing was said, but for me, Dad understood.[23]

The election of Robert Muldoon and a National Party government in 1975 brought change. Muldoon's election campaign had strongly emphasised the problems of Polynesian migration to New Zealand and used racist cartoon ads which showed brown people getting off the plane, stealing jobs and health services, getting into fights at pubs and making New Zealand cities a less desirable place to live.[24] By 1976, Muldoon's government had reintroduced dawn raids, like the ones seen in 1974, largely with support from the New Zealand public.[25] Usually striking in the early hours of the morning, police would descend on homes in Auckland, Wellington and Christchurch, with dogs and batons. They pounded on doors, shone bright lights in through windows, and forcibly searched houses for suspected overstayers. People were dragged from their beds and taken into police custody, many of them still in their nightclothes. Women and children were no exception and the cultural indignity of being seen by strange men with no clothes on was particularly shameful for Pacific women.[26] During this time, the Polynesian Panthers were instrumental in helping those who had been detained. They developed a legal aid book which instructed people on their rights if confronted or held by the police and this resulted in many from the Pacific community reaching out if they were in trouble.

> Because of our legal aid book and the community starting to know who we are, if they got picked up they were allowed a phone call. So we would get a call and that's how it would start. We were also living in the area and so we would know all the neighbours … I think that's why they came to us, because we weren't putting on the usual shame.[27]

Another crucial action taken by the Panthers at this time was the use of their military wing to apply specific pressure to government ministers. This involved dawn raiding National Party politicians directly involved in organising or supporting the raids on Pacific homes and churches: Bill Birch (MP for Franklin), George Gair (MP for North Shore) and Frank Gill (Minister of Immigration).[28]

> Henry Nee Nee who was our Panther Youth leader (that was all our Panthers who were still at school) came up with this idea – why don't we dawn raid the

ministers? So we thought, okay! We chose three ministers and had three squads; Paul Dapp would appoint a Panther each and it was up to that Panther, whoever you recruit that's it. So if we do ever get caught by the cops, because you don't know anything … so that's how our MW [military wing] would work. So we worked it out that we would go and do the same thing, raid them. We let our investigators go and do some homework on where they were staying, and the investigator for my squad, which was going to raid George Gair, he came and said, 'He's at Unit 1 at this address'. So we all go to these addresses at the same time across Tāmaki Makaurau … so we all hit at the same time and here I am outside Gair's home with a microphone, 'We are members of the Aotearoa Liberation Movement. You have 24 hours to prove that you are allowed to stay in this country.' And we shone the lights in the window. Lo and behold, the place that I had was the wrong address and we could see the guy pulling across the curtains and because I'm tall, in the background I could see a girl fully naked running into the toilet. So he came out said, 'Gair's in Number 3' but being street savvy and we were doing a crime here, split, don't hang on and do it again! Luckily Tigi's crew and the others, they were successful. Next thing you know, the Minister's on the radio complaining calling for the police to track us down. The cops came round asking where we were on such and such night, I said, 'What do you want to know for? Am I under arrest?' 'Nah nah we just want to know.' 'Well if I'm not under arrest, then see you later.' So the cops were getting really pissed off. And then a bit later, they stopped the Dawn Raids.[29]

MEMORY AND SHAME

Kaufman argues to 'live with shame is to feel alienated and defeated, never quite good enough to belong. And secretly we feel to blame. The deficiency lies within us alone. Shame is without parallel a sickness of the soul.'[30] Māori culture uses the word whakamā to describe a feeling similar to shame: one of embarrassment, of paralysis, of stigma. Tainui Stephens argues that: 'Whakamā is not guilt for something you did, but humiliation for who you are. It's a deep hit to the core of your being. You are inferior, disgraced, disadvantaged: and you know it. It has an acute memory.'[31] This concept of whakamā is closer to the lasting experiences of Pacific people who lived through the Dawn Raids.[32] At the time of the raids, shame was a pervasive emotion for those questioned by the police. Will believes that people's relationship with religion amplified their feelings of guilt for overstaying visas. 'It's shame because you've broken the law, you're brought up in a Christian life to not break the law even if the laws are anti-Christian. Shame is still there [today] although not as bad as it used to be when overstayers wouldn't even leave the house.'[33]

Historically, there is an incredibly close affiliation between Pacific society and Christian faith.[34] The spread of Christianity throughout the Pacific region resulted in an entanglement of religious and cultural values; so much so that it can be difficult to distinguish under what influences societal attitudes and beliefs came to be formed. For Pacific people overstaying their visas in New Zealand, the pressures of trying to provide a better life for themselves and their families were often mixed with feelings of guilt and shame for knowingly breaking the law. These feelings were frequently exacerbated by a strong Christian moral code that not only amplified individual shame but also allowed them to pass judgement on others in the community who were known to have broken the law.

> Being an extended family, collective sort of people, if one of your family is an overstayer or has broken the law, you'll see shame if Uncle has done a crime and he's gone to prison. It's the whole 'don't rock the boat, we're lucky to be here' sort of thing. Whereas us in the Panthers, we were saying, 'Hold on, we were born here, we have the right to be here'. Being shameful of someone who has done a crime, I think, is based on our faith and our belief in the Bible. Because in the Bible it says you don't break the law. Some of us would argue that it was written for Palestine and Israel and Persia but this is Aotearoa and the law in Aotearoa is not the same. We'd have to spend a lot of time arguing that especially to faifeaus [ministers] because they were influential. Some of us, like Wayne [Toleafoa] decided to go into the clergy to try and work in the system to change that attitude.[35]

Will argues that a culture of shame and fear was ingrained into new Pacific migrants to New Zealand.

> The guys that we helped and worked with were always fearful. Beside the fearfulness and the pressures they had to endure – they didn't realise that you had to pay to live in a house for example – beside the worry of trying to live a good life without getting into trouble, that's the pressure that they were under.[36]

In addition to the worries of migration, Pacific people overstayers also faced judgement from their own communities who had legally settled in New Zealand.

Will 'Ilolahia with members of UB40. From left to right: Earl Falconer, 'Ilolahia, Norman Hassan. Courtesy of Will 'Ilolahia personal collection

> Being shameful of being an overstayer is still a thing. The trouble with our people, they get their permit, they become New Zealand citizens and they look down on those who are overstayers. I try and remind people that Aotearoa is part of Oceania so we shouldn't need permits.[37]

Reaching out to those members of the community who were legal migrants was not a guarantee of help for those less fortunate.

> The thing we tried to put across especially to our community was that we're here legitimately. I used to go and talk to these faifeaus and say, 'You know there's overstayers, you don't stop them donating money to the church and that kind of thing, help them out!' But they were like, 'Oh no, they're breaking the law' and again I come back with, 'That law is not the law of Aotearoa, it is the law of the pālangi, the white man'. I continually had to keep talking to people about this, even people you'd think would have a brain in their head, continually because the

> shame was really strong. Especially if they were related, it was like 'keep it tight, don't tell anybody' … it was hard for us to get their families who were legitimate to put their names on the forms and say, 'I'll sponsor these guys'. So there was this big battle and it was only when people started to understand what we were doing and they'd come and see us. And we'd say, 'This is our country, we're New Zealand born and my cousin's come over here and now you're telling him he's an overstayer? No.'[38]

The concept of whakamā or shame was not simply limited to those who had broken the law by overstaying their visa. The nature of Island communities meant everyone was somehow connected to an overstayer, even if only through reputation or distant family or church connections. Whakamā can be collective and some attempted to overcome this feeling by distancing themselves from those they believed were causing trouble in their new homeland. Will remembers his time fighting for overstayers as a challenge, both personally and as part of a threatened community.

> It was hard. The thing that makes me happy is the results that have come out of that but it wasn't easy. You know, a lot of our enemies were our own people. They were like, 'Don't do that, don't rock the boat' and even though we had things for the community like homework centres and Christmas parties, we still got a lot of flak. Now because we've become 'famous', people are saying, 'Oh, Will, you did great work' and I'm saying under my breath, 'Where the fuck were you? Why didn't you come and stand with us?' It wasn't easy.[39]

REMEMBERING AMIDST FORGETTING

Indigenous researcher Linda Tuhiwai Smith writes that 'the remembering of a people relates not so much to an idealised remembering of a golden past but more specifically to the remembering of a painful past, re-membering in terms of connecting bodies with place and experience, and, importantly, people's responses to that pain.'[40] For Pacific people who lived through the Dawn Raids, both as victims and as those fighting state policies, the memory of those times is a painful one whose legacy remains in the present. Migrant families still fight for residency and many generations still struggle with the traumatic aftermath of the raids. This can include fear and anger towards the police, being afraid to sleep alone or answer the door, or silence around discussing the past with family members.[41] Their Pacific bodies, their Pacific identities, were the things that made them targets and a remembering of this past is, as Tuhiwai Smith describes, one where 'the story and the storyteller both serve to connect the past with the future, one generation with the other, the land with the people and the people with the story'.[42]

The Dawn Raids have only recently begun to enter into the narrative of New Zealand's official history. In 2021, New Zealand Prime Minister Jacinda Ardern formally apologised to Pacific people affected by the Dawn Raids on behalf of the New Zealand government. Her apology included performing a traditional ifoga, where an offender is covered with a fine mat and waits to be forgiven.[43] The government also agreed to provide financial support to Pacific students, in the form of educational scholarships, and to facilitate teaching about the Dawn Raids in New Zealand schools. Will argues these actions are not enough and do not recognise the suffering of overstayers.

> Really the overstayers of that time should have been given pathways to residency. We're not saying amnesty but a second chance to get themselves sorted, especially those who have been here for 10 or 20 years and been living by the book, no trouble. The only trouble they've got is doing the traditional thing of visiting an island and staying there! So in regards to the Dawn Raids, we're pissed off that it hasn't turned out to be what it should be. The five million dollars designated to go towards scholarships … are they going to kids who are descendants of overstayers? The overstayer issues should be for overstayers.[44]

The stories told by those who were falsely accused and victimised during the Dawn Raids are just one example of multiple betrayals by the state. Only recently have Pacific voices begun to speak publicly, many from the community still reluctant to share their stories, held back by feelings of whakamā and shame. Oral history is one way of giving voice to those stories but it requires careful negotiation and an understanding that for these communities, the past, present and future are irrevocably intertwined. Shame is embedded into social memory. The way the Pacific people were treated by the police, the attitudes of the Pākehā community, the censure from their own people and families and the knowledge that these actions took place under the auspices of the New Zealand government has taken its toll. There are so many stories that are yet to be told, even within families, about this part of New Zealand's history but the formal apology has opened a tentative acceptance that this is a vital part of our story as a nation. Drawing on the work of Māori scholar Alice Te Punga

Somerville, Bonnie Etherington argues that '"re-remembering" is crucially important for decolonization efforts, as colonial projects thrive on the suppression and subsequent forgetting of the oppressions they have enacted on Indigenous peoples. Furthermore, "re-remembering" ensures that young people enact and maintain an active, agential understanding of their history and how it applies to their present.'[45] For Pacific people, re-remembering the Dawn Raids involves not just reflecting on the past but thinking about its impact on their present, and their future as part of New Zealand society.

Thinking back to that time, Will reflects on the part the Panthers played in trying to right a wrong.

> We have the saying: 'Once a Panther, always a Panther' so even though we went in our own lives and did our own work, my Panther principles are always still there. It's only now that we start to realise actually how much we've done. There are so many stories. I'm rapt that our story is in the history books so that the young ones can understand that it wasn't rosy, that there were times when people like us, like Ngā Tamatoa, and all the different groups, stood up and made a stand. Now and then I feel the pain from batons and that, but I see my mokos and my kids doing well in their work, the pain subsides. I feel thankful that I stood up.[46]

Recording oral histories from Pacific people who experienced the Dawn Raids is a challenging process; time and trust are needed for people to feel comfortable sharing any part of this story with the public. While Will's role as a member of the Panthers and as a public figure allows him to reflect on the important activist and advocacy work done by Pacific people at that time, whakamā still haunts many in the community and its aftermath is felt in their relationships with the state. This chapter signifies one small step forward for Pacific voices to reclaim our past, to honour our present and to look forward to our future.

5

'A peasant farmer': Narrative identity and a sense of belonging

ANNA GREEN

'Identity' is one of the most widespread contemporary concepts in both popular and academic writing, autobiographies and oral histories. But what do we mean by 'identity'? The term is notoriously ambiguous and elastic.[1] In this chapter I will take a simple definition: that identity constitutes 'our own self-understanding in relation to others'.[2] And perhaps the crucial environment in most cultures and societies, where we first absorb or start to develop our sense of our identity in relation to others, is the family. Indeed, the New Zealand Families Commission, while recognising the diversity of families, identified 'the psychological "anchorage" of adults and children by way of affection, companionship and a sense of belonging and identity' as one of the essential, core functions of the family.[3] There is a rich body of work by social psychologists into both the transmission of family stories and the expression of narrative identities, which has informed my own research.[4] A narrative identity is a 'person's internalized and evolving life story … to provide life with some degree of unity and purpose.' Researchers in this field argue that the construction of narrative identities that formulate a meaningful story for one's life led to higher levels of well-being.[5]

In contrast, historians have generally been rather wary of family stories and genealogical history. One reason for this is a greater emphasis in family histories upon continuity between past and present rather than the historians' conventional preoccupation with change over time.[6] Secondly, historians have often preferred written historical evidence generated during the time under study over memories of the past recalled many decades later. Finally, New Zealand quantitative demographers have argued that family histories cannot give us any 'meaningful data' about the interior, subjective dimensions of family life in the past.[7] But there has been comparatively little investigation into intergenerational family memory, or critical interrogation of these common perceptions. For example, apart from a handful of recent autobiographies and memoirs we really do not know how the majority of those descended from colonial settlers think about their family past.[8] Do they have much knowledge about, or interest in, their earliest European settler forebears? Have family stories about the interior world of the family been passed down the generations? And in conclusion, would they describe a settled sense of belonging in New Zealand or express a more complex diasporic European identity?[9]

With all these questions and critiques in mind, in 2016 I began a large oral history research project with settler descendants. The goals of the research were to gain insights into the interior world of the family in the past, record the knowledge and stories that had been passed down the generations, and explore the connections being made between past and present by those whom we interviewed. Members from 60 multigenerational families, initially approached as part of a random national sample of the General Electoral Roll, were recorded by four oral historians.[10] Each interview comprised three parts. The interviews began with a personal autobiographical narrative, followed by a broad question intended to elicit a self-directed narrative about the family past. We then concluded with a small number of specific questions ranging from historical interests to the choice of national identity terminology. It is impossible to encompass the complexities and nuances of 150 interviews within the length constraints of a single chapter; these are the subject of a forthcoming book. Here a single interview with one man, Des McSweeney, has been chosen and his recorded interview provides valuable insights into the construction of a narrative identity by a settler descendant. Although he belonged to the eldest generation recorded for this research, his narrative reflects common themes shared by many settler descendants across the generations.

Des McSweeney recorded his oral history interview with Pip Oldham in 2016 at his home in Akaroa on the Banks Peninsula in the South Island when he was 90 years of age. The first part of the recording, his personal life narrative, focused primarily on his working life. Born in nearby Christchurch in 1926 as one of seven children, he began:

> My father was a farmer on Banks Peninsula in a small bay called Hunza (Holmes) Bay, which he bought probably in the early 1920s. He was a single man when he bought the farm and he married the girl next door, whose forebears I will

talk about later because they go back a long way as well. In 1939 … there were seven children in our family and I can distinctly remember my father saying after the 1938 election, when Labour was returned to power, 'We are moving to Christchurch for the education of my family, because the future is in the cities'. And so, in 1939 we all moved to Christchurch. But my father retained the farm and had we not moved to Christchurch I would probably have spent my life as a grader driver in Pigeon Bay or a worker in the cheese factory. But because of his foresight we all went to Christchurch and thus had access to secondary schooling.[11]

As Des's time at St Bede's College came to an end he remembered having 'vague ambitions' to be involved in farming but was persuaded to take a two-year diploma at Lincoln Agricultural College. This was followed by teacher's college, where he added an extra year to become a 'nature studies specialist'. Eventually, after teaching in schools for some years and further part-time study, Des returned to teach at Lincoln, with spells overseas, in rural development and extension studies. At this point Des deliberately drew the relatively short factual account of his working life to a close, saying that 'I should complete this life story by saying that I retired in 1986 to a small farm about 100 acres in Akaroa, so I came back to my roots':

> My interest in nature evolved, because of my deep interest in farming …
> I achieved my lifelong ambition when I was 60 years old, which was to be a farmer but … I describe myself as a peasant farmer because I, other than having a quad bike, I still do everything by hand, I shear my sheep with blades, I chase the sheep and do all those ordinary things that my father did 80 years ago.

This brief conclusion to the life narrative part of the oral history interview is a pivotal moment in the narrative. Des describes becoming 'a peasant farmer' as a form of closing the circle, in terms of his own ambitions as a young man, returning to the Banks Peninsula and continuing the farming life of his father and earlier generations.

Des then turned to the story of his forebears and started with his Irish paternal grandparents.[12] 'We knew the Irish very well', he said, 'because of my Irish grandmother who was through and through Irish'. Des's Irish paternal grandparents, Bill and Margaret, independently migrated from the same village in County Cork in 1878 and 1882.[13] Both families had a large number of children and many were sent or migrated overseas during the latter half of the nineteenth-century. What did Des make of this Irish ancestry, and how did he frame this part of his oral narrative?

My father's parents were both born in Ireland, in a little village called Knocknagree, and they left Ireland, they were both brought up in the same village but they migrated to New Zealand in the 1870s and 80s. We subsequently went to Knocknagree, this little village, and I called in at the pub, one of the many pubs in this little village, and said my name is McSweeney, is there anybody else … 'Oh', they said, 'you'll want to be talking to Millie' or whatever her name was. So we got in contact with them and they were my relatives. And even after a hundred years they still remembered, and we have been in close contact for many years. They took me to see the blacksmith's shop because my grandfather was a blacksmith and his father was a blacksmith before him, and so on. So my father's background was totally Irish.

Why did they come in the 1870s? Because 20 years before that was the Great Famine. That was before the Celtic Tiger arose, and when we visited in the early 1970s it was still a very poor country. And my brother, my farming partner, subsequently went to Knocknagree and came home and said, 'The wisest thing my grandparents did was migrate to New Zealand', because he saw the poverty that was there. We went to Cork and we looked down at Cork harbour from which those emigrant ships sailed. And I had a vision of my grandmother … boarding this ship as a single woman to come to Christchurch.

First of all, this account demonstrates a strong connection between past and present in Des's mind. The comments about the 'Celtic Tiger' suggest that a counterfactual imagination may have strengthened the brothers' response.[14] When Des made the reference to the more recent rapid economic growth in Ireland, he and his brother may have assumed that had they been born in Ireland in the 1920s the economic trajectory of their lives would have been very different. Secondly, the story of standing above Cork harbour imagining his young grandmother boarding the ship to come to New Zealand could have led to an emotional diasporic identification with Ireland, as it has in other accounts of American and Canadian settler descendants returning to visit the country and place of family origin.[15] However, this story is almost immediately followed by less happy memories of this grandmother and a reflection upon his father's critical attitude to Ireland and Irish history.

Des remembered this grandmother well and described her as a 'caustic, unlovable woman who'd had a hard life'. His daughter recalled Des's description of his grandmother as a 'real tartar', who locked him inside the house when he was ill so that she could go to church.[16] When Pip asked what Des meant when describing his grandmother as 'totally Irish' he replied with the following story:

> Yes, I can remember on Guy Fawkes night in Christchurch when I was staying with my grandmother [in 1936], there's a knock on the back door and a little child peeps up, 'A penny for the guy'. And my grandmother called out, 'I'll give you a clip on the ear, my boy, out of here'. And, of course, if you understand Guy Fawkes, one of my teachers at St Bede's described him as the only man who went to the House of Commons with a good intention [laughter]. So my grandmother, you know, still had the baggage of Ireland with her.[17]

In contrast, Des said that his father, tolerant of all religions, rejected the 'old animosities'. Even though he would have 'been aware of the 1916 uprising in Dublin, he wouldn't have a bar of anything Irish. He said they were a disruptive, rebellious group of people and he would not belong to any Irish association in New Zealand.' In terms of the wider context, historians generally concur that the Protestant-Catholic fissure was less entrenched in New Zealand society than elsewhere.[18] The refusal by Des's father to take up Irish political and historical causes surely influenced the perceptions of the third family generation in New Zealand, as did the memory of the 'caustic' and deeply religious grandmother.[19] While Des knew where his settler forebears came from and had visited their village in Ireland, neither the warm reception in Knocknagree nor the 'vision' at Cork harbour generated a strong sense of personal identification with Ireland.

Des also remembered this grandmother's cold response to her daughter-in-law, Des's mother. Both families, by this stage, were farming on Banks Peninsula, but in contrast to his paternal Catholic Irish grandparents, his mother came from an Anglican family with German ancestry. Des's maternal great-grandfather arrived in Lyttelton from a German settlement called Hahndorf, founded in 1839 just south of Adelaide in Australia. Des did not know what compelled his great-grandfather to leave the dissident Lutheran German settlement, and any knowledge he had was the result of later research: 'My mother, who knew her German Hahndorf grandfather well, all she could tell me was that he spoke with a German accent'. She passed virtually nothing on to her children about her family history even though, as Des remarked, 'she knew the stories but I had to dig them out of her'. Reflecting on why he learnt so little, he said 'it's quite strange, not an intentionally closed book, I think it was a case of let the dead pass, bury the dead, they didn't want to know. They were much more interested in the here and now and the future.' This was not an uncommon experience among the wider oral history cohort, who attributed limited information or stories about their earliest settler forebears to a range of causes, including wanting to forget a difficult past, more interest in the future than the past, or a reluctance among adults of earlier generations to talk to children.

As with so many of the family oral histories, it is memories of grandparents that provide the most insights into the subjective dimensions of family life in the past. In the case of Des's maternal grandparents, his grandmother died when he was a child although he remembered her as warm and affectionate. But thinking about his maternal grandfather elicited the comment that he was a 'hard man':

> I knew him well as a child, but he had not gentleness about him somehow. He was hard on his livestock. You judge a man, or at least farmers judge a man by how he treats his livestock. And I can remember him beating his draft horse, you know, to make it pull harder. Whereas my father was a much more gentle person and behaved towards animals in a different sort of way …

Many memories of grandparents in these oral histories are perceptions from childhood, when children often feel a close affinity to pets and animals. This may explain why others with farming origins in this oral history cohort also recalled episodes of either harshness or kindness towards the working horses.

Changing his name from Pache to Peach, Des's maternal great-grandfather eventually acquired 60 acres on an 'inhospitable little block of land called Wild Cattle Hill … the bleakest part of the Banks peninsula' in the 1880s. Despite having little information passed down about the German side of the family, Des joked that there were so many Peaches in the graveyard at nearby Port Levy that it 'looks like a stone fruit orchard'. The family remain mystified why this great-grandfather chose Wild Cattle Hill farm, and later in the interview Des commented that:

> … my daughter went to Hahndorf and looked around this beautiful settlement, at the gateway of the Barossa Valley, the vineyard of Australia, and asked the question: 'Why, in the name of God, did my great-great grandfather choose Wild Cattle Hill instead of the Barossa Valley?' [laughter].

A little later in the interview, Des brought out a photograph taken by his mother of Wild Cattle Hill farm that he had chosen to reproduce and frame for his family. The photo triggers a flood of detailed description with an unexpected conclusion:

Wild Cattle Hill, Peach Homestead on Banks Peninsula, early 1900s.
Photographer: Elsie Peach, Des McSweeney's mother. Reproduced with permission of Des McSweeney and Ann Jarman

I had it done as a Christmas present for my immediate family and the frame I had made locally out of local tōtara wood harvested on Banks Peninsula. The photograph is of the Peach Homestead at Wild Cattle Hill. And I'm looking at the first little cottage that my great-grandfather John Frederick Peach [built]. He was born in Germany, which is now part of Poland, and was on a whaling ship and jumped ship in Lyttelton. He went chopping down the trees and finally got enough money to buy, I think it was a 60-acre farm in the bleakest part of Banks Peninsula, right at the top of the hill, between Pigeon Bay and Port Levy. And there's the first house that he built, just a slab-sided cottage [right of picture, to which a two-bedroom annex was added in 1920]. And that's the homestead which my brother and I demolished in derelict condition … And we have rebuilt that in a little cottage on our farm, which serves as a museum.

After the oral history recording had finished, Des drove Pip up to see his farm and the family museum. Pip recalled in her field notes written the same day:

The post on the right in this photo is the tōtara fencepost that was relocated from Wild Cattle Hill to Akaroa. Photographer: Pip Oldham. Courtesy of The Missing Link Family Memory Project

When we had packed away Des showed me an image in the McSweeney history, 'Willie comes courting, Wild Cattle Hill about 1921' and asked me to remember the fence post behind Willie. The picture was taken at the farmhouse of Wild Cattle Hill dairy farm – the gate and hole in the hedge not visible in the image. Well, Des got me to hop in his car and drove me up the valley to his land. Our first stop was a small mustering station to show me the tōtara fence post that he has moved there – I took a photo to show its scale – a huge solid 6 x 6 post, much larger in real life than the old photo suggests. Then we got back in the car and drove up the road to where Des has erected the little 'museum' building from the timber dismantled from Wild Cattle Hill. I took a photo of him sitting on the kauri deck.

Although Des had not inherited any possessions from the earliest generation, commenting that they 'travelled steerage and had nothing', the determination to preserve the fence post, and the small building from Wild Cattle Hill farm in which to house the family archive, are a powerful testament to the emotional and sensory

Des McSweeney on the veranda of his family museum, Akaroa, 2016.
Photographer: Pip Oldham. Courtesy of The Missing Link Family Memory Project

attachment he feels towards these objects. While many of those we interviewed cherished inherited family objects, Des was the only one to reassemble the cottage his earliest forebear built, and dig up and reinstall a fence post from his great-grandfather's farm.

The last part of the oral history interview included a number of specific questions we asked of all our participants. The first concerned an interest in history, and Des expressed a much greater level of engagement than most. At the time he was reading about World War II and 'the futility of war'. Asked what history he was taught at school, he replied:

> … bloody useless stuff … I know a lot about the Crusades, the causes and effects of the Napoleonic Wars, but I'd never heard of the New Zealand Wars, I've never heard of the history of Japan, of the Pacific Rim. Even though I enjoyed it, and I still enjoy reading history, I lament that I don't know anything like as much as I should about our near neighbours.

What then did Des formally respond when asked 'What is your preferred way of thinking and talking about yourself?' He replied that he wrote 'New Zealand European' on his travel documents and went on to reiterate that, 'I do not think of Ireland as my homeland. Britain is the source of my culture, my education, my whole knowledge of world events is dictated by my knowledge of England'. But he felt that while the links to Britain would not disappear neither would they grow. His descendants' lives would, he thought, be much more influenced by the increasing diversity within New Zealand society and the events and cultures of the Pacific Rim.

Returning to the contrasting perspectives and questions about family memory in the introductory paragraphs, what can be learnt from Des McSweeney's oral history? Throughout the recording, it is apparent that Des had thought about what he wanted to say and, perhaps aware of his age and how long he might be able to sustain the interview, he spoke decisively and without many pauses. This is why very few questions are included with most of the excerpts above; early attempts by the interviewer to ask a question were largely batted aside. This oral history, I believe, is very much the story he wished to tell – about his life, his family's past, and what these meant to him. He described himself as a 'missionary', trying to 'convert' his family into knowing their 'rich history'. He felt that, like his wife, he was a 'guardian of the treasure'. In this sense Des fits the description of a generative adult, providing 'psychological anchorage' for the next generation through the transmission of family stories and a sense of belonging.[20]

His narrative certainly contains strong elements of continuity, especially the circular framework for his own life history. This is evident in his discussion around the return to his 'roots' on Banks Peninsula to go farming, and the parallels he drew between his lambing percentages and farming practices and those of his father 80 years earlier. During the interview he wore a jersey knitted by his wife with the wool from the first sheep shorn on his farm. In this context, material objects are deeply significant as sensory links that connect his past and present. Des inherited very little from his earliest forebears, but his decision to dig up the fence post, dismantle the derelict building his great-grandfather had built, and reinstall them on his own farm is another powerful statement of continuity. These are the foundations for a narrative that enabled him to articulate a life story with a degree of coherence, meaning and purpose. But equally Des was also very aware and open to the wider contemporary social and cultural changes in New Zealand. He was not nostalgic about the national past and expressed a positive Pacific-oriented outlook for the future of the country and the lives of his grandchildren.

While his forebears did not talk a great deal about their past and earlier generations, there are some insights into the subjective, interior worlds of the family, as there are in every oral history recorded for this project. These brief glimpses are often observations through the eyes of a child, and reflect the connection between emotion and the senses in sedimenting long-term memory. The stories about the 'caustic' religious grandmother and the harsh grandfather who abused the plough horse reflect this emotional and sensory nexus and illuminate family relationships and behaviour. The later memory of his father placing the education of his children above all else, despite the difficulties this created for him farming on Banks Peninsula, provides interesting insights into both the immediate impact of Labour's promise in 1938 regarding the provision of secondary education and his father's vision of the future for his children.

Finally, Des did not express any form of diasporic identity with Ireland, although he recognised the seminal influence of British culture upon his life in New Zealand. Indeed, he specifically stated that Ireland was not his homeland. This he shared with the oral history cohort as a whole, where diasporic identification with a place of family settler origin was vanishingly rare. Indeed, while nearly all those recorded for this research expressed an interest in their European family origins, this appeared to be driven primarily by intellectual curiosity rather than emotional attachment. When asked what he perceived as a pivotal turning point in the family history, Des replied with the decision by his forebears to leave Ireland. This again corresponds with many other interviewees who also made explicit reference to the choice their ancestors had made to leave the land of their birth and their respect for that decision.

If identity constitutes 'our own self-understanding in relation to others', the others in Des's life narrative are the three generations of forebears that preceded him in New Zealand, and this orientation is reflected across the oral history cohort. Des had made an immense effort to retrieve and pass on to his children and grandchildren the family history revolving around that decision to come to this country and their subsequent lives here. The significant others in Des's narrative identity were his New Zealand family forebears, upon whose lives and memories he built the connections between the past and present that anchored him in time and place.

Note: Des McSweeney died in 2019, and I am deeply grateful for his contribution and permission to publish. I also thank the Marsden Fund of the Royal Society Te Apārangi for making this research possible.

6

'She would always be there': The (im)material life and home of Miss Marion Steven

NATALIE LOOYER

How a house is lived in can tell you everything you need to know about people, whether it's the choice of wallpaper, the mess in the kitchen, the silence or shouting over meals, doors left open or closed, a fire burning in the hearth.—Hermione Lee, *Lives of Houses.*

If home is where the heart is, does it follow that to know a home is truly to know the person who resides there?[1] In our ways of remembering, what parallels do we draw between people and the places they inhabited, or the material culture that surrounded them?

Place is an important mnemonic device in oral history, especially when remembering individual people and the homes they filled. In my research into Miss Marion Steven, a pioneering scholar, teacher and collector of classical antiquities at the University of Canterbury from 1950 to 1977, I interviewed family, friends, former students and colleagues. They all turned to recollections of Marion's richly characterful home in suburban Christchurch when telling their stories. Their intense visual and sensory memories of Marion and her home greatly enhanced my understanding of Marion's enduring legacy. Not only was Marion's home a recollection of times spent with her, but the home's physical characteristics also became emblematic of how Marion was remembered as a person.

Miss Marion Steven (1912–1999)[2] was an academic Reader in Classics at the University of Canterbury, and during her career, she formed many lasting friendships with colleagues and students.[3] Nowadays, she is best known as the founder of the James Logie Memorial Collection, an assemblage of predominantly Greek and

Roman artefacts, which is so named in memory of her late husband, James.[4] The collection resides on public display at the UC Teece Museum of Classical Antiquities in Christchurch and is an integral part of the university's Classics programme. While I was a Classics student at Canterbury, Marion had something of a mythical status in the department. Little was officially recorded about her, and existing department members' knowledge was scant, except for some stories of Marion cycling to the university from time to time with her treasured ancient vases stashed in a shoe box in her front wicker basket. Intrigued, I set out to interview a selection of her family, friends, colleagues and students in order to build more of a biography of the Logie Collection's fabled founder.

My research findings proved fruitful and enchantingly vivid. I got to know of Marion's kindness, warmth, peculiar characteristics and ceaseless hospitality through those who had been a part of her life. This was most apparent in the ways that my interviewees spoke of Marion's house at 21 Andover Street in the suburb of Merivale. They recalled her vast collections of 'things' – detective novels, reference books, crosswords and cereal box figurines. The interviewees all described the draughty, tumbledown house and the warmth of Marion's fireplace, where she would teach her guests how to make paper coals. Marion and her home shaped each other over time, as Marion implanted her identity upon the home and, in turn, came to be identified by it.

MARION AT HOME

The following excerpt comes from one of the first interviews I conducted for the project, with Marion's niece, Jane.

> She had a great gift for hospitality, as did [James] Logie. And [guests] would come to her house, always did. I mentioned when I was showing you downstairs that I ought to have done what Marion used to do for visitors, which was put a kettle in the bedroom, a tray with a glass of water on it. She didn't fill the kettle, because the bathroom was right next door. But the idea was that you could make yourself a cup of tea. She would have coffee-making facilities, too. And then she'd have a selection of books that she thought you might like to delve into if your eye happened to catch them. And so she did that for anyone who visited, whom she liked. She wasn't interested in impressing them, she just – they were a part of her community.

She was having a party, one of her legendary parties, and it was school holidays so my twin sister and I were staying with her, and she said, 'We're going to have some stifado', which is apparently a beef and wine stew. You and I are going to have that tonight, Natalie, and it reeks of garlic. She invited every academic that was slightly peculiar, I think, in Christchurch, and all her artist friends, and that party rocked! The whole house hummed. And I must say it was a fire risk because she didn't turn the lights on for her parties. She got long candles in empty Chianti bottles and she would put them on every windowsill and ledging. And she loved the fact that the soot from those wretched candles would darken the walls. She loved dark walls. She said, 'It's cosy and no one will see the dust'. And so the guests arrived and the candles were lit and the red wine flowed and flowed and flowed! And the stifado came out and, as children, we watched this magical occasion of all these so-called adults behaving in delightfully unconventional ways. She was a marvellous hostess … she had the gift of hospitality.

She had in her kitchen a great big pegboard and she'd pin things that she liked, such as little witty quotations or cartoons or crossword puzzles. I can't remember whether they were just the completed ones or ones that were haunting her and she wanted the answer to. Certainly, yes, it was a very interactive sort of kitchen. I don't think she did much cooking. She was too busy doing things on her pegboard and not washing up … It was a bit of a scruff of a kitchen, too, especially the newspapers that she spread on most surfaces. She said, 'Well, when it gets a bit untidy I just take the top layer off', which was a very pragmatic way to do housekeeping. She wasn't a great one for dusting or sweeping.

She kept one room 'good', as it were. And it was a remarkably formal, cold room compared to the others. I never liked it. I loved the rest of the house because it had that cosy sort of lived-in, rather batty feeling. I mentioned that the walls were fairly discoloured from all the long candles. But she also always had fruit that had a marvellous scent, and so the smell of grapes or whatever fruit was in season was right through her lounge.

She had a peculiarity on the walls. She once wanted to show her slides and she didn't have a screen, so she called in a house painter to paint a great rectangle in white paint on her sooty wall. And that was her screen from then on. So she was rather indifferent to appearances in her lounge as well. And the floor plunged down. 'Oh yeah', she said, 'I need new piles.' And so if you were in the dining room dining, things tended to move on the table, shift downwards, because it really was quite a lean … the ceilings were – the plaster was falling off with a 'whump' now and then. But it was still an incredibly welcoming place. People enjoyed being there. There was an atmosphere of calm and a kind of gloomy serenity. She didn't like glaring sunlight, she really did not, in her house. She wanted it restful and slightly dull.

I travelled to Dunedin and stayed with Jane, whose hospitality likely rivalled that of her aunt. She did not quite provide tea-making facilities at my bedside, but I do remember a small stack of books left in the room for guests. And Jane indeed made me a delicious pot of Greek stifado for dinner that evening, with the required lashings of garlic. During my time with Jane, it seemed that her hospitality was part of her way of telling the story of her aunt. She wished for me to feel Marion's warmth and hospitality.

Marion's disregard for household upkeep crossed over into the way she presented herself at times. Jane spoke of her aunt's 'scarecrow' appearance when they attended the theatre together; Marion would dress in long socks up to her knees, a tattered raincoat and a floppy gardening hat. In her eulogy for Marion at her funeral in 1999, Jane informed those in attendance that Marion's raincoat would often double as a dressing gown over her pyjamas. But Marion was practical. Perhaps most symbolic of this practicality was Jane's retelling of Marion's engagement to James Logie in 1950: when Marion's mother called around to see her daughter's new engagement ring, Marion pointed into the kitchen towards her new Westinghouse refrigerator. 'We thought it would be more useful', Jane quoted her aunt as saying.

Jane's recollections of her aunt are great examples of how the home acts as a mnemonic device for remembering Marion's personal character – the dark walls and candles, the scruffy kitchen, the scent of fruit, all representing Marion's hospitable nature. The characterful qualities and anecdotes that Jane provided were reiterated in other interviews with Marion's family and peers. Richard and Alison, past colleagues of Marion, recalled the house's ramshackle appearance, its coldness and sooty walls:

> **Richard**: If there's anything I remember about that house, is it could be freezing cold in winter, absolutely.
>
> **Alison**: It was a really weird house, and it was quite a cold house. It had very high ceilings. The kitchen opened into the sitting room as I remember. Really, really high ceilings. Bedrooms upstairs, and really cold.

Jane's sister Ann also remembered the coldness of her aunt's house, as well as the many books that lined Marion's walls:

> Marion had a fabulous house that she decided was going to be pulled down eventually, so she decided it didn't require any maintenance. But nevertheless, it had lovely high ceilings, and was a very gracious house. It was two storeys, but despite the size, it wasn't all that huge. Her bedroom had floor-to-ceiling bookcases. The stairwell had floor-to-ceiling bookcases. Her main lounge room, which we as children were not supposed to go into, had floor-to-ceiling bookcases … Upstairs, the house was somewhat interesting, in that the front porch room, which is the one I normally stayed in, had sliding windows that didn't actually seal, so in winter you got the winds of Christchurch, which were freezing cold! By that stage, I was coming down from Wellington and I really did feel it. It was cold. But the bed was always very, very warm and very comfortable.

Robin, who knew Marion during the early stages of his academic career, remembered his colleague's detective novels and the crossword puzzles plastered to her walls.

> **Robin**: She was an avid reader of detective stories. She had a huge collection in her house in Andover Street.

Interviewer: How big?

> **Robin**: How big? Oh, walls lined with it. All upstairs. It was a double-storey house, and there were books up the staircases just crammed. And going right back there was Margery Allingham, Dorothy Sayers, Josephine Tey, just heaps and heaps of them, you know, the traditional classic English detective stories. Agatha Christie, of course, Ngaio Marsh, of course, who's a Christchurch woman, anyway. So she was fascinated by that. And she did the most fiendish crosswords … And when she finished them, she would paste them to the walls of her house. I remember that.

Marion's niece Gael remembered Marion's curious collection of cereal box figurines:

> … she ate a lot of cornflakes … she used to get the little toys, plastic toys, out of them. And she had the most amazing collection of these creatures … And as I say, it was almost a – not an obsession, but I don't know how you'd describe it, actually. And also, she would collect good cartoons, and there was always something interesting. It was the first place you sort of looked, was on her noticeboard in the kitchen. It was always, 'What's on there? What's new?' [But] I

think I was just fascinated that someone so intelligent could get off on these toys. She had an amazing collection!

Marion was a collector by nature, having dedicated much of her career to collecting and curating the Logie Collection of antiquities, but she was not materialistic in the traditional sense and she was certainly not overly precious about her things – as the legend of cycling around with her ancient vases attests. Nor was she overly concerned about the upkeep of her home. But, like anyone, Marion surrounded herself with things that comforted her, stimulated her intellect, or held significant meaning. Perhaps in this way, Marion collected people, too, as she nurtured meaningful relationships with those close to her. This can be seen in the number of interviewees who recalled spending time by Marion's fireside making paper coals:

> **Anne (a former student)**: … staying with her in the winter, I remember her sitting, rolling up newspapers, to make what she called 'paper coals' for the fire. Now, this isn't the screwed-up newspaper that you use to kindle a fire, but if you take a sheet of newspaper and roll a strip up like, I suppose, a Swiss roll or something, but really tight, then it will take ages to burn and it will almost be as good as coal.
>
> **Ann**: We ended up having wonderful conversations around her fire. I mean, I can remember many, many incidents of – I'm sure the others have mentioned this – we used to roll up newspapers into paper coals to feed the fire. So yes, that was lovely, staying with her.
>
> **Gael**: One of my first memories of her was rolling newspapers. So she'd get the newspapers – she obviously had lots of newspapers – but they would all be rolled and then into whirls, if you like, and that would be for starting the fire.
>
> **Alison**: Like sitting by the fire at her house … She showed me how to make paper coals … I still make paper coals. Every time I make them, I have this memory of Marion at the back of my head.

The paper coal itself was clearly a powerful memory hook that connected my interviewees to the feeling of warmth they felt under Marion's care. While her house was physically cold and showed all the signs of dilapidation, her guests' experiences of sitting with Marion by her fireplace, in conversation and actively creating physical warmth by way of a repetitive, ritualistic activity were symbolic of their memories of her personal warmth and hospitality.

These times spent with Marion in her home meant different things to my interviewees. Marion's family members remembered parts of their childhood and early adulthood staying with their aunt. Jane's twin sister Sue, now living abroad, emailed me some of her memories, all of which centred around Marion's house. 'Marion was huge fun as an aunt and her large and then rather ramshackle house was the perfect vehicle for entertaining visits. I cut my teeth reading-wise on her huge library … and cut my shins with my sisters and the other cousins sliding down the stairs on metal tea trays. She didn't mind the noise and lack of safety one bit.' Times spent with Marion were moments when her young family members were free to be themselves and were given space to grow under their aunt's mentorship. Marion offered the same mentorship to her colleagues and students who stayed with her and experienced her hospitality, as she provided gentle guidance in the early stages of their careers. Edwin, a past student of Marion, recalled keeping in touch with her after finishing his studies. He and his wife Patricia would call on Marion when visiting Christchurch. In our interview, Edwin poignantly stated, 'In fact, thinking about it now, we assumed Marion would always be there. And nothing could possibly be wrong in Christchurch with Marion there.'

The significance of the excerpts above lies not in the repetition of stories between interviewees. The apparent coldness of Marion's home indeed suggests that guests would likely remember making paper coals to warm the place up. Rather, it lies in the fact that they came largely unprompted and were often seamlessly integrated into recollections of Marion's character. Marion's home became synonymous with the way Marion's family and peers felt in her presence.

MATERIAL CULTURE: HOUSES AND MEMORY

The importance of houses and memory is by no means a new avenue of thought when writing biographically. In the preface of her book *Lives of Houses* (co-edited with Kate Kennedy), Hermione Lee opens with the statement, 'The writing of lives often involves writing about houses. Bringing a house to life through observation, familiarity, memory, or excavation can be a vital part of narrating the life of an individual, a family, or a group.'[5]

This is evident in the configuration of many museum spaces; the use of material culture in recreations of the interior space of a home help to tell stories about families, cultural groups, or individuals. The home interior setting allows a museum visitor to physically transplant themselves into the surroundings of the storyteller or narrative. For example, the 'Immigrants' Stories' semi-permanent exhibition at Te Papa, Museum of New Zealand, displays living room-like spaces, showing the kinds of possessions that travelled with migrants, or the ways that migrants made homes for themselves in foreign lands. Likewise, the Oranjehof Dutch Connection Centre in Te Awahou Foxton includes a recreation of a migrant Dutch family's huiskamer (dining room), displaying a Dutch-style table dressing, a grandfather clock and trinkets on sets of shelves. And Canterbury Museum exhibits the famous Pāua Shell House, displaying a recreation of Fred and Myrtle Flutey's living room with their huge collection of pāua shells and other homely possessions.

Another common type of museum experience is the preservation of artists' and writers' homes. The homes of Jane Austen, Frida Kahlo, Mark Twain and Claude Monet are but a few examples that are open to public visitors around the world. In New Zealand, the homes of Katherine Mansfield in Wellington and Ngaio Marsh in Christchurch were converted into museum-like landmarks after their deaths in 1923 and 1982 respectively. More recently, the former home of suffragist Kate Sheppard was restored and opened to the public in suburban Christchurch.

This very idea of opening her home to the public had been presented to Marion, too, as Jane recalled:

> She had a colleague called Dale Trendall who said to her, 'Marion, you've got a rare collection of books in your house'; there were detective books and first editions of New Zealand literature and a huge number of history books on New Zealand and a massive library apart from that. And Dale had said to her, 'Have you thought about making your house some kind of memorial to a certain kind of academic mind and a pioneering woman?' And when she told me this, my heart sank because the house was such a scruff of a place. It was falling down! And I thought, how can I honour this?

Jane was able to honour her aunt by donating Marion's extensive collection of detective novels to the University of Canterbury Library. Besides the Logie Collection, however, this was the extent to which Marion's homely possessions made it onto public display. While not an artist or a writer as such, Marion, as an academic, had become a person of intellectual significance within her community. Had her life and her achievements around the Logie Collection been more widely publicised following her death, there may have been some interest in preserving her home in a way that mirrored the preservation and museum-like purpose of the homes of

Katherine Mansfield, Ngaio Marsh and Kate Sheppard. But this was not to be, and instead Marion's home was demolished soon after her death.

In terms of oral history and memory, my interviewees often brought visual and sensory memories into the narrative of their experience of Marion and her home. Paula Hamilton notes, 'we would expect all kinds of references to the senses in interviews, both as part of the communication process and as an act of remembering'.[6] Visual memories of Marion and her home were plenty – her unusual dress sense, her sooty walls – but my interviewees called upon other senses in remembering too; the smells of garlic in Marion's stifado dish and the fruit in her lounge, and the comfort of her bed despite the coldness of the house. Even the memories of rolling newspapers into paper coals recalled a sensory act involving physical touch. Therefore, my interviewees' senses helped them to rebuild an affirmative narrative of Marion by way of delightful smells and feelings of warmth and comfort.

In '"Unpacking" the stories', Anna Green illustrates two visually striking characters from a series of Frankton Junction oral histories: Police Constable Francis Bonnington, a large man with heavy boots and a reputation for using them on local misfits, and Catherine 'Coffee and Bun' Hill, a local spinster. Green states:

> Oral accounts of the past are full of figurative language, such as metaphors, where meaning is conveyed through visual images. Let us take the example of Bonnington's boot, which acts as a powerful symbolic marker of authority and preservation of order.[7]

Coffee and Bun, on the other hand, was remembered for her dowdy and sometimes 'frightening' appearance, this representing 'the opposite of the images and values that the storytellers generally wish to convey of Frankton Junction – that it was a place of respectability and conformity'.[8]

For those who remembered Marion, visual and sensory memories of her house and the happenings within it were the symbolic markers of her hospitality, her warmth and her practicality. But like Coffee and Bun, Marion's peculiarities were made more memorable by the way she transcended norms. Marion was ungendered in many ways; she was childless, having lost her husband young, and she seemed unconcerned with her own physical appearance. Jane alluded to this paradox of Marion in her funeral eulogy for her aunt, stating:

> My aunt Marion was a puzzle. She could detect a spelling mistake at a thousand paces, but she couldn't seem to see the dust under her nose. She had a deep and

sensitive appreciation of aesthetically fine things – I've heard her describing with passionate delicacy the figures on a Greek vase and the way the folds of their garments fell – yet her house at 21 Andover Street is a conspicuous scruff of a home in upmarket Merivale.[9]

Reflecting upon my interviews and Jane's comment above, I sense that public audiences would not connect with Marion's home in the same way that audiences do with artists' and writers' homes whose works are more widely known. Instead, the charms and peculiarities of Marion's home were alive in my interviewees' memories because they were fused with their personal experiences of, and relationship with, Marion. With the absence of Marion, her home may just have been a 'scruff' of a place and not much more.

In Emma-Jean Kelly's biography of New Zealand archivist and broadcaster Jonathan Dennis, Kelly demonstrates the ways in which Dennis's friend and filmmaker Peter Wells achieved a preservation of the interconnection between Dennis and his home through film. Wells captured the sights and sounds of the interior of Dennis's home, with Dennis present in the space, in the days leading up to Dennis's death. Kelly describes the film as 'a library of sounds, which, decontextualised, mean nothing. But attached to the name Jonathan Dennis, they are filled with memory for those who knew him and had spent time with him at his house.'[10] My interviewees' memories of sights, smells and sensations within Marion's home were likewise filled with context. Visual memories of books stacked everywhere, crosswords plastered to the walls, and the white-painted square on her lounge room wall recalled Marion's intellectual, peculiar, practical character. Memories of smell were remnants of Marion's hospitality. The coldness of the house yet the warmth of Marion's fireplace took my interviewees back to the physical experience of being in her company. The visual imagery captured in Wells' film serves as an extension of the memory of Jonathan Dennis for those who knew him, in the same way that those who knew Marion used visual and sensory memories of being in her home to remember her.

The memories of Marion's family members, colleagues and students who stayed at her home were centred around particular stages in their own lives, be it their childhood or career beginnings. My interviewees found meaning in the ways that Marion and her hospitality served them at those times. But fundamentally Marion's home was an embodiment of Marion herself. In his book, *Stuff*, Daniel Miller discusses the ways that couples negotiate spaces; one person might have more influence over the style, décor and material of different rooms within the home.[11]

Marion, however, had no one else with whom she negotiated her space. The rooms were completely shaped by her way of living and, to an extent, decorating. Over time her home may have shaped her too, providing a moody, comforting haven in which she could retreat into the 'life of the mind'.

Near the end of the interviewing stage of my research, Elizabeth, a friend of Marion, made email contact with me to express her delight at hearing about my project. When I asked Elizabeth for some memories, she recalled Marion as being 'far from materialistic' and spoke of her home with great nostalgia. 'How we chuckled at the peeling wallpaper.' Elizabeth concluded her anecdotes with, 'Not long ago I drove along Andover Street to see the old house. It is gone.'[12] For Elizabeth, her memories of Marion were integrally linked to the place where Marion was perhaps her greatest self, and so the desire to drive past Marion's old house was a way for Elizabeth to reconnect with Marion. My interviewees revisited her house through oral history, taking themselves back to the physical place where aspects of Marion were present in every detail.

Giving interviewees the opportunity to talk around a subject is key to building memories. When I embarked on my research into Miss Marion Steven's life, I did not specifically ask my interviewees about her home. It was something that came naturally in their ways of remembering Marion. The unprompted way they described their memories of her home with an emphasis on her material and cultured surroundings gave me an opportunity to reflect on my own method of questioning in oral history interviews. It was a reminder of why it is important to ask about places or objects in order to unlock ways of remembering subjects (whether they be individuals, events or personal experiences) in more dynamic and intimate ways. Giving my interviewees the freedom to talk about Marion's home and the things within the home enabled a richer exploration of her personal character. Marion shared her famed collection of antiquities, her books, her knowledge, and her conversation with her friends and family, all the while sharing the warmth and welcome of her home. Thus, memories of Marion became inseparably connected to the material culture of her life.

7

Writing Anglo-Indian stories

ROBYN ANDREWS

Anglo-Indians have been making their home in New Zealand since at least 1869 when Mrs Frederica Hay, an Anglo-Indian of Calcutta, arrived in Dunedin with her husband, Robert Hay. They had just married in St Paul's Cathedral, Calcutta, before travelling and settling in New Zealand where they went on to have a family of 11 children. A number of their descendants, knowing of Frederica, now identify proudly as Anglo-Indian. Since Frederica arrived, many other Anglo-Indians have come to New Zealand. Some arrived well before Indian Independence from Britain in 1947, and many came after it, carried by the wave of Anglo-Indians migrating to English-speaking Commonwealth countries. Yet this minority group barely features in the history of South Asian migrants to New Zealand.

This relative invisibility of Anglo-Indians, in both historical and contemporary accounts, contrasted with my personal experience of meeting many Anglo-Indians in New Zealand and hearing, on my research visits in India, of still others. This anecdotal discrepancy inspired me to embark on a project aimed at building a more balanced, inclusive, and historically accurate picture of Anglo-Indians in New Zealand.[1]

The stories of the Anglo-Indian community illuminate the experiences and challenges they face living within a particular social group. The type of individual and intimate experiential material offered by personal stories is just not obtainable through other means, such as archives, policy documents and quantitative research-informed reports. Oral histories can 'people' these accounts – breathe life into the statistics and factual documents, convey emotion and opinion, adding an extra dimension to help us understand what it was like to live in a specific time with a particular identity. In addition, oral history can aid the rediscovery of invisible or forgotten experiences and stories, make the silences audible and challenge assumptions about lived ethnicity and identity. Oral history connects the individual to wider societal structures (encompassing religion, class, ethnicity and gender) – demonstrating how the personal and wider society intersect to produce life experiences. The following oral histories present the history of Anglo-Indians in Aotearoa New Zealand, and in turn, the social history of the country as it has changed towards and in relation to these people.

THE PROJECT

Since 2015 I have been engaged in an oral history project aimed at recording personal histories of Anglo-Indians in Aotearoa New Zealand. I have captured the stories of past experiences transmitted orally through families and across generations and from these I have compiled a collection of individual stories that reveal overarching trends in the experiences of this minority community.

While I am not Anglo-Indian, I have been involved with the community for more than three decades, initially through my sponsorship of Anglo-Indian boarding school students[2] and then through a comprehensive ethnographic study in Calcutta (now renamed Kolkata). My research relationship with the community has continued through ongoing projects, such as this one, in both India and the Anglo-Indian diaspora.

For this project, I carried out more than 50 oral history interviews with Anglo-Indians who had migrated to New Zealand or whose ancestors had. The interviewees were aged from their mid-twenties to early-eighties, and with varied links to and identification with the Anglo-Indian community. They included a number of Frederica Hay's descendants. In their case, my interest has been both what they know of Frederica and what it means to them to be descended from their Anglo-Indian great-grandmother.

By telling their family story and those of others, a number of specific Anglo-Indian concerns and experiences are demonstrated. For example, because the Anglo-Indian migration story is largely untold and undocumented, their individual identity is often mistaken or misunderstood. In some cases, a sense of grief or pain is attached to the experiences of their ancestors; the memories of those family members who were some of the earliest Anglo-Indians in New Zealand. Another contribution the stories reveal is the growing trend for Anglo-Indians to investigate their ancestors' lives, often leading to trips back to India – the past is influencing their future in direct and obvious ways. Anglo-Indians in New Zealand can feel isolated, but when they hear about the experiences of other Anglo-Indians, they know they are not alone. On a personal level, oral histories have great value to the individual.

WHO ARE ANGLO-INDIANS?

Anglo-Indians are a culturally distinct minority of mixed Indian and European descent who are defined in the Indian Constitution in this way:

> An Anglo-Indian means a person whose father or any of whose other male progenitors in the male line is or was of European descent but who is domiciled within the territory of India and is or was born within such territory of parents habitually resident therein and not established there for temporary purposes only. (Section 366 (2))

One particular characteristic of an Anglo-Indian person, relevant to this chapter, is a 'culture of emigration'[3], based on more than half the population having left India for English-speaking Commonwealth countries since Indian Independence.[4] Socially and culturally Anglo-Indians are generally more 'Western' than 'Indian': they are Christians, primarily they speak English as their mother tongue, and have western names. All these factors help them to settle easily in their chosen destinations,[5] many taking pride that they are able to assimilate seamlessly with the communities they move into. In addition, there are many who could 'pass as white', aiding their assimilation further, although, potentially making them invisible migrants.

ANGLO-INDIANS IN NEW ZEALAND

Anglo-Indians have been migrating to Aotearoa New Zealand since the mid-nineteenth century, sometimes more easily than at other times depending on the social mores and immigration policies in effect. For example, while Aotearoa New Zealand never had an explicitly 'White New Zealand' immigration policy (as Canada and Australia did until the early 1960s and 1973 respectively) it did, until 1974, have a racially discriminatory policy determining entry.[6] It was not until 1986 that 'national origin' was formally abolished as a factor in an immigration policy that aimed 'to enrich the multicultural social fabric of New Zealand society',[7] and this has been followed by further changes over the decades since.

According to the 2018 New Zealand census, most of the 381 people who reported identifying as Anglo-Indian lived in the Auckland region (58.3 percent).[8] The residence location statistic concurs with my research findings, but the census population number is much lower than is likely to be the case. In interviews, I asked Anglo-Indians how they identified in the census and approximately 25 percent said they had ticked 'other' and wrote 'Anglo-Indian' – which is the only way to be recorded as Anglo-Indian. The rest selected Indian, European, or New Zealand European for a range of reasons, some of which I will come back to. Turning now, from statistics to individuals.

THE STORIES

In this section, I introduce three Anglo-Indians: Frederica (through, and along with, her great-granddaughters), Christine, and Parvati. While I collected stories first-hand from both men and women, the stories recounted in this chapter are told by women. Men are referred to through the women's stories though, and later on I draw on comments made by men where they best articulate a point.

I selected these particular stories as they offer a range of experiences and cover many of the key ideas found in the broader project. As such, they are critical in understanding the experiences of an otherwise largely invisible social group. A key theme concerns the subjective perceptions of being Anglo-Indian (or descended from Anglo-Indians) in New Zealand. As is illustrated by the stories, this has changed over the generations in response to the social context in which each generation lived, for example, from potential shame when 'whiteness' and eugenics-influenced notions of purity of descent was valued, to pride in their 'mixed' heritage as part of a multicultural nation. Frederica's story reveals social change from 1869 to 2016. Christine's story spans a shorter period, from 1949 until 2016, and includes her parents' life in Aotearoa New Zealand. Parvati tells of her life from 1955 when she arrived on her own to be fostered by an Aotearoa New Zealand couple, until just after she had made a significant trip back to India.

FREDERICA HAY (NÉE COVENTRY) AND HER DESCENDANTS

While I initially thought of this story as Frederica's, it is as much the story of her great-granddaughters who also identify as Anglo-Indian, or at least as descended from an Anglo-Indian. One of the great-granddaughters, Lynne, explained that she first heard about Frederica through her mother:

> I distinctly remember it; my mother had just made me a brand-new dress. She was a beautiful sewer, and it was a little bit ethnic looking. It was unusual fabric and she tried it on me and said: 'You look like an Indian Princess. Did you know your great-grandmother was an Indian Princess?' My mother never ever used language like that. She did not tell us what little princesses we were. Pink was not allowed in our house. I've never heard her say that word again. She said: 'Your great-grandmother was Indian,' not Anglo-Indian, Indian. So, I always assumed she was full-blooded.[9]

Another of Frederica's great-grandchildren, Tina, said:

> Because I am the baby of the family, some of my memory recall would be partly through the others and may be different from the others as well. I have a very, very clear memory of playing with these exotic pieces of jewellery that mum had, and I remember asking her where they were from, and she said: 'India. My grandmother's, she was part Indian.'

Lynne: Did she say part Indian? Or did she say Indian?

Tina: Umm … No, she said Indian. That's me saying part Indian.

Lynne: Yeah.

Tina: Actually no, because we didn't know back then. We thought she was full blooded, that's me … And just a few times she mentioned that her great-[grand]mother Frederica was of a high caste or nobility in India. And so, we were quite intrigued by that. She didn't elaborate to me, or I was too young to understand. So that's my earliest memory.

Lynne: I just thought as a seven-year-old, this was the most exciting, exotic thing that could happen. And related to a princess! Who thought? And she did say at the same time, do not tell anyone. She said that … because our great-grandfather was quite a wealthy man but instead … and this is in her words and not mine, they ostracised them from society.[10]

I also asked another great-granddaughter, Jennifer, when she first knew of her link to India:

Yeah, well I may have asked after something, perhaps I may have asked of Robert Hay or something because I still remember this day when: 'Why the hell didn't you tell us?' I said: 'You know I've always been asked where I come from?'[11]

Frederica's great-grandchildren have carried out their own research to find out more about Frederica, mainly through signing up with the genealogical database, Ancestry.com, along with visits to the Early Settlers' Museum in Dunedin and through a cousin's visit to the British India Office in London. They have also visited an archivist in Kolkata and viewed church records there. They have in their possession a number of personal items brought from India, such as the jewellery Tina mentioned, and stories from their mothers. The stories they shared were tantalising in their exoticism, brevity and speculative nature, and they longed to know more.

What they do understand is that 'fitting in' to Aotearoa New Zealand's society was not easy. They told me, for example, that after Frederica arrived, she settled in Dunedin where she 'was ostracised … because of her mixed blood'. At the time she arrived in 1869, Aotearoa New Zealand was very much a 'white settler' country that too often discriminated against people of colour. The sense of social exclusion that her great-granddaughters report being directed at Frederica had repercussions through several generations of her family. And meant that 'my mother told me not to tell anyone, which I did not understand at the time. Because it sounded so exciting to me, as a seven-year-old. Of course, our generation thinks it is the most interesting part of our family ancestry.'[12]

It is evident that Frederica's great-granddaughters share no sense of their mother's generation's feelings about being of mixed descent. Tina, for example, said that when anyone asked about her ethnicity she would always talk about her Indian side. Also, Lynne told me she had recently enrolled in a night school class and in the ethnicity section of a form she had written 'Anglo-Indian', very proudly. She added that this was not such a change from what she might have done earlier – before they knew the type of Indian their great-grandmother was. She said that in the past she would have said she was of 'Indian origin', rather than specifying Anglo-Indian. As Tina said: 'I always identified with it [being Indian] actually and was very proud of it. If people ask me, I would say that first, and then say the other parts.'[13]

I was interested in this self-identification and how it might play out in their lives. I had heard, for example, that one of the cousins had made a trip to India over 20 years ago. And all claimed to be attracted to 'everything Indian' too, as Lynne describes:

> I was thinking about what effect it had on me, and you know, in terms of what it triggered later on. And that memory of a seven-year-old ... That absolute wonder of this exciting, exotic ... I just loved it. And how it played out later ... If ever I saw a movie like *Gandhi* ... I'd be attracted to things Indian, or *Passage to India*. I'd go to those movies because of the subject but I would be peering into the background. I would be watching everything that was happening. And even reading the books, that's probably more recent. I always loved Indian stories, things happening in India, and hearing the life, and what it would have been like in my grandmother's, and great-grandmother's time.
>
> And then when I was at Teacher's College and I did a higher diploma in Arts Education, dance was my major. We had to choose a dance form as part of our major and I chose Indian dancing so that ... there was always that attraction, always that awareness and interest.[14]

These conversations offer a stark contrast to Frederica's experience of being ostracised: rather, they celebrate their Indian connection, claiming that culture as part of their identity, and taking all opportunities to immerse themselves further in their Indianness.

They are motivated to find out more about their great-grandmother and go to great lengths to gather what information they can. This impetus was summed up by one of them who said:

> What is at the heart of the matter for me now, about the longing and urgency for more knowledge about Frederica is that I feel if we don't do the work on this it will be lost. It is not enough that this generation of Frederica's great grandchildren just acknowledge her like our mother's generation did. What is different with our generation is we proudly celebrate this wonderful racial diversity in our family and in this way, we honour Frederica and her mother. We sort of reclaim her as our own. We also long for more information about her and her mother's life.[15]

In pursuit of more knowledge, two of the cousins, Tina and Lynne, expressed an interest in going to Kolkata with me at the end of 2018. As well as looking for further information about Frederica, Frederica's father and mother, they were also fascinated to be in Kolkata because they know that genealogically, it is a part of who they are. They were keen to see the buildings their ancestors had spent time in, for example, St Paul's Cathedral where their great grandparents married, and which is still in daily use, as are so many other buildings from the era Frederica lived in the city.

The stories offered by Frederica and her great-granddaughters are difficult to obtain via traditional sources or archives, but here we find out significant insights about changing social values towards being of mixed race in New Zealand and the work required by Anglo-Indians to fit in at different historical junctures together with how that impacts on a social group's identity over time.

Their stories demonstrate the value placed on material objects in order to understand lives lived in another age, and illustrate the power to influence choices made decades later, such as a travel destination, as part of their search for an identity.

CHRISTINE ATKINSON (NÉE PALMAN)

The next story is Christine's. Before coming to New Zealand, she lived for her first few years in Mussoorie, a hill station town in the foothills of the Himalayas with vistas of a distant, always snow-capped, mountain range. By the late 1940s, Partition[16] had left its terrible scars and India had gained independence from Britain. The insecurity felt by many Anglo-Indians about their future propelled Christine's young parents to apply to migrate. They were successful and arrived in Auckland by ship in March 1949 when Christine was four years old. Once there, it was not smooth going, particularly for her mother. They must have questioned their decision about whether migrating was a good move for the family when the reality of being in New Zealand severely challenged their expectations.

In India, the family had enjoyed a refined English-influenced lifestyle that included having servants to carry out the domestic work. One family member, Christine's grandmother, had her midwifery expertise recognised when she was summoned by Indian royalty. Christine said that she 'would regale us with tales of her nursing training in Calcutta India, being called in to attend the Ranis in various Rajah's Palaces and bring them safely through their childbirths, and of becoming a highly experienced Matron of hospitals [in India] in later years.'[17]

Christine recalls the huge adjustment the family had to make on arriving in New Zealand where, until her father found employment, they had stayed in boarding houses. She recalled that:

> [Because there were no cooking facilities at the first boarding house they stayed in] all they could get for us to eat was baked beans or spaghetti on toast at a local dairy. We must have lived on that; I don't know what else. It was awful. And, I

mean, Mum and Dad were used to better things. Mum used to cry. It was just too much for her really. And Dad was trying to cope with us, and cope with Mum being so upset.

Then we went to this next boarding house in [named street]. And that was even worse than the first one. We couldn't believe it; it was very rough. And it was full of black-singleted workers. I don't know where they must have been working; the freezing works or somewhere. They seemed uncouth … But they were kind. Mum used to say that they were very kind to us.[18]

Christine's father, like many Anglo-Indians, was a trained and experienced teacher. As Christine says, 'Dad's influence was huge, a gifted teacher of English, mathematics and geography'. He had taught in prestigious English-medium schools in India and within a few days of arriving in Auckland he called into the Education Department offices and very soon afterwards secured a teaching position. This meant the family could move out of boarding house accommodation and into their own home.

As well as the change of living arrangements being an enormous relief for the family, other events helped them settle in. The following year, Christine's maternal grandparents came to New Zealand to support the young family. Anglo-Indian friends from India, whom they had encouraged to migrate, also came to settle in New Zealand. Before long they established a very active social group that met often including, for example, to attend New Year's dances, and picnics together in the summer. Having other Anglo-Indians close by made all the difference to the family's sense of finding a way to belong in their new country. Another arena that assisted their settling was their involvement with the local Catholic church. As Christine says:

One of my early memories is of being on my dad's bike whilst he cycled to Mass at [named church]. Our Dad was an inspiring Reader of The Word and also began the Church choir there. He had an extensive knowledge of Scripture and Church Liturgy. I remember well those days of singing in our dad's choir as an eight-year-old along with my beloved late sister, Margaret, five years older than I. These are memories I treasure.

She has continued an active involvement with the church. A bonus of her church connection is that she has met more recently migrated Anglo-Indians. She says: 'There are a couple of ladies at church that are obviously Anglo-Indian, and they're later immigrants. So, we always get a hug from them, and a hello, because we have something to say to one another [laughs], which is quite nice.'

This type of connection and recognition of similarities is in contrast to her experience with many of the people she meets. These encounters demonstrate some of the assumptions people make about migrants. Christine talks about how others identify her and how she identifies herself, saying:

> They don't know where to put me. They honestly do not know. When I go up North, they think I'm Māori. If they look at me around here [in a South Auckland suburb], they think I'm part of the Indian society here.

> I say I'm European now in the census because I don't know what to say, 'cause I don't want to be confused with the Indians here. I'm different, as I have a strong European background as well.

I asked Christine if she, or her family, had faced discrimination:

> Ummm … well … my father did. My Dad used to go and have his hair cut in [named suburb], and the barber was quite rude to him one day, and it was basically 'cause he was dark-skinned. He was quite rude. My father was mortified. When he was this well-spoken, beautifully-spoken man. He used to be asked to speak at weddings and things like that, and always read at Mass, and he was actually quite upset.

> And I guess, in small ways, I have come across it. And have chosen not to get involved with people who are like that. I just ignore them or keep away … but I've felt it. Little things, but, well that's their problem, not mine [laughs]. But you have to get a little bit of a thick skin at times. On the whole I find 'Kiwis' very open and welcoming though.

Christine says that it's only recently that she feels she would like the chance to go back to India. She had not wanted to earlier, mostly because it held such painful memories of family separation.

One of her sons spent a few days in Mumbai, and she delighted in reporting, 'He loved it, he absolutely loved it … And I was quite emotional about it. I thought, "Oh my goodness: the first of our family to set foot in India." I didn't think I'd feel like that, but I did.'

Another son, David, a medical practitioner in Whangārei, is researching and writing their family history. As Christine says, 'he is very interested, he always strongly identifies with his Anglo-Indian heritage. He's quite proud of the fact.' Since I interviewed Christine, David has also visited India, and said he loved the experience, particularly being able to go to places he had heard of through talking to his mother.

PARVATI ERIKSON

Parvati, or Nancy as she was originally named, is the daughter of a British tea planter and a local Bengali woman. At the age of two and a half, she was left at a Presbyterian orphanage, Dr Graham's Homes, in the hill town of Kalimpong, West Bengal. It was her home for the next 10 years. She has no memory of her birth mother or father but says:

> When I was a little girl in the nursery, I can remember seeing this woman coming towards me, and she was wearing a white sari, and her hair was done in a bun … and all I could think was, 'Oh, what a beautiful lady'. And that lady came straight over to me, and she got on a knee and gave me a hug and a kiss. She put some sweets in my hand, stroked my face, then walked away.[19]

She recalled that when she was 10 years old the Homes' 'Aunty' first discussed her moving to New Zealand: '"Do you remember Mr and Mrs Dick?" I said, "Yes". But I didn't really, I just said yes. And she said, "Well, they would like you to go to New Zealand and be their little girl."'

In 1955, aged 12, she left Dr Graham's Homes to move to New Zealand to live with her new family in Remuera, Auckland. She recalls arriving at a home with views out to Rangitoto: 'It was just such a beautiful home, with white cotton runners on the floor at the entrance.' She says despite being brought up in a Western manner in the children's home, moving to New Zealand was a 'huge shock'. The way she was treated accounted for much of that. While she spoke warmly of her foster parents and the way they treated and supported her, her experiences were not all positive. Parvati first attended a local intermediate school, which she remembers fondly, unlike the two very unhappy years at her all-girls high school.

> I had an Australian teacher, and she took one look at me and disliked me on sight … I learnt about what they called colour prejudice, in those days. She used to make fun of my accent, because it was very strong. And again, I was the only dark one, there were no Indians or Māori. She was a nasty lady. I used to do everything to try to make her like me because I didn't want to be abandoned

again. So, I was always this bright happy girl. I couldn't understand why she didn't like me! But it was so bad that she stopped correcting any of my work. She used to throw my book across … and this happened for two years, and I couldn't tell [my foster parents] anything, because of course I didn't really know them. I'd only been in the country for two years. And an adult is not going to listen to a child. In the Homes a child was seen and not heard. So, I grew up with that. I grew up very respectful of authority. So, I couldn't go and tell them that this is what's happening to me.

Parvati left school as soon as she could and worked as a hairdresser then as a receptionist, and then moved to what she describes as her most exciting career. She told me about applying for the job:

So, I went for my interview with TEAL[20] as an air stewardess. I looked around, and I saw all these beautiful girls. And in talking with them I thought, 'What am I doing here?' They'd all been to university, a couple of them were models and all that. So, it was not very long that I realised I didn't have a show in hell of becoming an air hostess. [When I was interviewed] I just shrugged and I said, 'You know, you don't need to ask me any more questions.' They'd asked me, 'How does an aeroplane work? Where do flights go to?' And I had done no research. But they asked, 'So, where were you born?' and I told them, 'In Assam. But I was brought up in an orphanage in a place called Kalimpong.' 'Where's that?' [They asked.] 'It's Darjeeling. You know Darjeeling, very fine tea.' There was a map of India. 'There is Darjeeling up there, and you go all the way up India, and there's Darjeeling up there. Dr Graham's Homes is right there.'

She couldn't believe it when she was offered a job. Her foster mother called to tell her: '"Dear, dear! You've got the job!" I said, "What job?" she said, "With TEAL. You're a hostess!"'

I was 22. And so I went through the training. We were trained at Māngere. And I was first on the Electras. And then when the DC8 started we trained on the DC8s, and I was on the second flight to Los Angeles and Honolulu. So, my work was just, ahhhhhh. They had these gorgeous TEAL uniforms with a hat and everything.

She worked with TEAL until an injury meant she could no longer meet the physical demands of the role. She later married and had her own family. It was more than four decades after leaving the children's home in India, and encouraged by her 'Kiwi' husband and two adult daughters, Parvati responded to her eternal longing to find her family. In doing so, she discovered that the woman in the white sari had been her mother and that she had died shortly after their meeting.

She also found out that some relatives on her paternal side of the family were living in New Zealand. The quest then was to find her mother's family, and the brother who she learnt was still living in Assam. So, in 1996 she set out on a four-month journey to India, first of all, reuniting with her brother: 'I've been away from India for 42 years, and when I met my brother, of course, all he could say was, "Hello, Sis", when I first saw him.'

Parvati told me she was given her Indian name in 1995 by a close Indian friend. At the time she was finding out about her Indian maternal heritage. She says she wears the name with pride, in respect of her mother, adding that 'Nancy' had never felt right. Her sense of identity with India is unmistakable.

THEMES REVEALED

These three stories highlight a range of experiences, some unique, but others more widely shared. The circumstances of their arrival, for example, are specific to each, but other experiences once settled are markedly similar. Some of the key themes to emerge reveal the way Aotearoa New Zealand's social norms have changed over the years. This is reflected in the subjective experience of identifying as Anglo-Indian, which has changed from one generation to another within families: rather than being a matter of shame and pain, and as much as possible hidden for decades, later generations are enthusiastic in their claim to an Anglo-Indian identity. The compilation of such stories, sometimes intergenerational, over a wide span of time, attests to the possibility that Aotearoa New Zealand is significantly more multicultural and inclusive than has been portrayed earlier. This perception has led in turn to changes, from the sense of discrimination faced by early Anglo-Indians, to the embracing of their 'difference' or even 'exoticism' nowadays. While 'misidentification' still occurs, the inherent racism of the past has mostly been replaced with a genuine curiosity about Anglo-Indians and their origins. In addition, this changed social value has led, in a number of cases, to Anglo-Indians or their progeny embracing their historical antecedents and their identity to the extent that they seek out the country of their forebears.

In the following section some of these themes are explored in more detail. I draw on the three stories, and in some cases on material collected from other Anglo-Indians who were also part of this project.

PASSING, EXPLAINING AND MISIDENTIFICATION

A key aspect of being an Anglo-Indian person in New Zealand is that they are not easily identified. Some are 'white' enough to pass as Pākehā, although in many cases they are not 'white', and being non-white has mattered. While in the early years, there is no doubt this led to racism, discrimination and negative stereotyping, differences in ethnicity are now more often experienced as the opportunity for inquisitiveness and questioning.

Many of those I interviewed told me about feeling frustrated, and at times exhausted, by having to constantly explain who they were. Mostly they said they did not feel invisible, rather they felt they stood out from 'the norm' in the way they looked and sounded. Christine and Parvati expressed this on their own behalf, and Frederica's great-grandchildren refer to it. This frustration was also expressed by others, as captured below by a woman now in her early sixties, who came to New Zealand with her family in the late 1960s and who later completed doctoral studies:

> I'm always asked where I'm from, and then I'm asked how I learnt such good English. And when I converted to Christianity.
>
> When I was a teenager, I used to string people along. I got so sick of the questions, which I found insulting actually. I wouldn't just go up to people and ask! So, I would reply, 'Where do you think I'm from?' And if they said, say, 'Egypt?' I'd say, 'You're right!' And as for the question, 'Where did you learn such good English?' I would say I learnt it on the boat over here. I got so sick of having to explain it all. I'd just make stuff up.
>
> But once I was in my thirties or so I would tell people: 'I'm Anglo-Indian', and then if they genuinely seemed interested in knowing more, I'd explain. But only if they had time! [laughs][21]

Most Anglo-Indians I interviewed said they regularly fielded questions about 'who they were'. They explained that the reason people asked that question, was their appearance (a cast of features combined with skin tone) and their accent. People could not identify their 'look', nor could they accurately place their accent. As the quote above indicates, offering the explanation that they were Anglo-Indian was not always straightforward either. This led to what I refer to as 'explanation fatigue'. As they would say to me: How many times do we have to explain who an Anglo-Indian is? Why we speak English so well? That we were born into Christian families, and that our name is our 'real' name?'

As Anglo-Indians have a European antecedent on their father's side, their family name is invariably 'European', and their given names mostly are too. The usual expectation of someone with this type of name is that they are 'white'. The mismatch between a person's name, and how they look could also be problematic for some New Zealanders who ask the question, 'Yes, but what is your *real* name?' Parvati had solved this 'problem' by taking on an Indian name, although her motivation was less about conforming her name to her 'look', than about taking a name she identified more comfortably with.

As Christine and many others reported, along with being misidentified as 'Indian' they were sometimes misidentified as Māori. Another woman I interviewed described her mother's greeting to the country:

> She said that when they first came here, when they first got off the ship, someone came up to her and did a hongi! Of course, she didn't know what that was about! They thought she was Māori. People assumed that she was Māori until they talked to her. Because she spoke, well, a bit like the Queen. A very nice English sort of accent. We used to tease her about it sometimes.[22]

A man who came to New Zealand in the 1990s via the United Kingdom where he grew up told me:

> I was working in a role in the public service sector in New Zealand, I ended up working for the Ministry of Māori Development. And in the early days, people naturally assumed because I was working in the Ministry of Māori Development, I was Māori. And it was only when I started speaking that they all got confused [both laughed]. I remember one comment was, 'Oh you've been away too long in London, bro. You've picked up the accent'. I was never a Māori in the first place. So that was quite funny.[23]

Those I spoke to have mostly been more amused than unhappy at this mistaken identity and reported little racism and discrimination. This form of misidentification, as part of the indigenous community of the nation, is not something I have come across in research on Anglo-Indians in other of their preferred destination countries, for example, Australia and Canada, which also have indigenous populations. As such, this form of misidentification seems to be unique to the Aotearoa New Zealand experience.

For all the policies and strategies in place, racism in Aotearoa New Zealand has typically targeted Māori and other non-white residents. In Frederica's time especially, migrants from China, India and other Asian countries, who had been making Aotearoa New Zealand their home since the 1800s, had a history of facing racism and discrimination in the country.[24]

PRIDE IN BEING ANGLO-INDIAN

The change from one generation to the next in terms of pride in being Anglo-Indian kept coming up in the oral history interviews. For example, in response to my question, 'What characteristics do you associate with Anglo-Indians?', Simon, a second-generation young man responded:

> A search for identity, I suppose that's what I've noticed. With people like me, looking completely New Zealand European. And they find out that granddad might actually be part Indian, and he kept his secret his whole life, and now they're suddenly, 'Oh, I'm actually connected to this whole culture.' I think there's that, again, from my generation I've noticed, (I don't know so much about the ones coming out from India now), those young white New Zealanders who suddenly find out, they seem quite, 'Oh wow, I didn't realise this.' For some, it's just a novelty factor, but for others, they obviously want to get back more in touch with their roots.[25]

This generational change in relation to their identity was one of the most significant themes in my research. It was evident in Jane McCabe's New Zealand-based work too. McCabe, a historian with an Anglo-Indian ancestor on her father's side, carried out research in New Zealand on a group of migrants she called Kalimpong Kids, also drawing on oral histories as part of her research. She comments in the abstract of her PhD thesis that 'The silence that significantly affected the next generation of Kalimpong families in New Zealand reflected major stigmas in the early twentieth century around race, illegitimacy, and institutionalisation. The willing involvement of descendants in this study attests to a fundamental shift in attitudes regarding all three in the space of one generation.'[26]

Simon added that he didn't know if the same would be said about Anglo-Indians just arriving in New Zealand, which highlights to me the value of the approach of talking to people about their own family's different generational attitudes towards their identity. They are able to trace the difference in social mores from within their own family. Those whose family members came to New Zealand some generations ago were able to offer a much longer perspective, even with less detail and some inaccuracies that might have crept in.

ROOTS OR 'DESI' TOURISM

One of the outcomes of embracing their identity is the desire to travel back to India. For Frederica's family it is evident several generations on, with her great-granddaughters having made descent-oriented visits to India; in Christine's case it is her children along with her growing interest; and for Parvati the visit to India was about trying to find her own family. Others I spoke to were also making plans to go to India or had been already. They are all contributing to a growing phenomenon referred to by some scholars as 'roots tourism'.[27] In so doing they are demonstrating the continuing connections between past and present in human thought and practice by 'remembering the past, thinking about the present and planning the future'.[28] They are also demonstrating the value of oral histories, which can highlight significant places and memorialisations, thence enabling revisiting by successive generations.

*

In 1869, when Frederica and Robert arrived in Dunedin to settle there, her name, Frederica Hay, on a passenger list, would not have hinted that she was Anglo-Indian or any other type of Indian. This feature of Anglo-Indians, their European names, probably accounts for them being overlooked in histories of Indians in New Zealand because they rely on the use of names to search for historical data. Oral histories, on the other hand, 'flesh out' the experiences of those named people. Given that there were such early and ongoing arrivals it is particularly important, nevertheless, that information is located and disseminated so that Frederica and other Anglo-Indians may be recognised as some of New Zealand's earliest migrants from the Indian subcontinent.

An additional factor leading to Anglo-Indians being overlooked in New Zealand's migrant story was the potential social stigma of miscegenation in identifying as the descendant of a 'mixed blood' parent, or grandparent, particularly for those who might be able to 'pass' as European. Of course, now many New Zealand residents proudly identify as being of mixed descent. A result of the changed social value attached to such ethnicity is that more people may identify as Anglo-Indian, or of being descended from an Anglo-Indian, than in the past. In the meantime, though, their past inconspicuousness has left a legacy of being misunderstood (ethnically) and overlooked.

The stories I focus on are from both migrants and descendants of migrants, from interviewees who were able to look back over their own lives and previous generations of their families. They illustrate what oral histories can offer in terms of subjective assessment of particular identities that have changed over time as a result of wider social changes. Through this, they offer a commentary on some of the ways in which Aotearoa New Zealand's social norms have changed. It is my hope that this project will fill a knowledge gap and lead to the understanding of another aspect of the nation's multiculturalism.

Note: I acknowledge the generosity of all the Anglo-Indians involved in the project for their time and for trusting me with their own stories and, in a number of cases, their families' stories. I am also very grateful to the Asia New Zealand Foundation, who provided the grant that made this research possible.

8

'I felt I was master of my own destiny'

MEGAN HUTCHING

War is a collective experience, as is the commemoration of such conflicts. Parades of former servicemen and women on national days that remember war, and memorials, such as those held at tombs of unknown soldiers or national cenotaphs, all provide a time or place for communities to acknowledge what their citizens who served in the military have experienced during times of conflict.

But, as Roberto Rabel reminds us, while wars may be resolved and remembered collectively, they are experienced individually.[1] This chapter uses an interview with a man who became a prisoner of war during World War II to illuminate the often-ignored experiences of ordinary people who were in uniform and to remind us that combat is not the sole defining experience of war.[2] Prisoners of war, while still in uniform, are also permanently out of action. I show how, and discuss why, the narrator tried to claim back some agency in a situation over which he had very little control and no idea of when, or if, his incarceration would end – for prisoners of war do not know when their war will end and how long they will be in captivity.

First of all, some background. When I recorded this interview in 2002, it was part of a commissioned series of interviews done for a large project, primarily with women and men who had served in uniform during World War II. I was working at the Ministry for Culture and Heritage and the interviews (and subsequent publications) were made as part of my role as a public oral historian.

I am not a military historian, but I was eager to record the interviews for this project as I felt that an oral history approach would add nuance to the experience of war. I wanted to examine the effect of taking part in war on the individuals concerned instead of concentrating on military strategy, accounts of battles, advances and retreats, and technical information about military materiel, which are the focus of standard accounts of war, intended as omniscient overviews of the military action. In a reflection of this top-down view of how wars are conducted, when the project was first mooted there was some pushback because a few people felt that it could not be done as most of the officers who had served at the time were no longer alive.

Interviews that concentrate on strategic decision-making and combat experiences reflect a very narrow concept of war. Most time in uniform is spent out of action. Most servicemen and women are what is called 'other ranks', that is, not officers, and are not in frontline units. I was certainly interested in recording information about the military service of my interviewees, and their reactions to their experiences, but also the events that are usually unrecorded by conventional historians because they are so ordinary that they are taken for granted. Much of the wartime experience has to do with getting on with other people, training, meeting civilians, coming to terms with loss, sightseeing, and dealing with the chores of everyday life, such as washing, eating and drinking, more than active fighting.

The project began in 2000 at the suggestion of then Prime Minister Helen Clark, who realised that the number of those who had seen military service during World War II was getting smaller and smaller. She was also influenced by reading Maurice Shadbolt's *Voices of Gallipoli*, which spoke strongly to her about recording the experiences of 'ordinary' service men and women.[3] The History Group of the Ministry for Culture & Heritage has its roots in the War History Branch of the Department of Internal Affairs, set up to write the official history of New Zealand's involvement in World War II. The interviews for the project that I was involved with, while not official histories, did have the imprimatur of government-sponsored, public history.

William (Bill) Flint, whose interview I have chosen, was born in Invercargill, New Zealand, on 27 January 1919. He enlisted the day after war was declared on 3 September 1939, aged 20. After training in New Zealand, he went overseas in January 1940, arriving in Egypt a month later as part of 18 (Infantry) Battalion in the 2nd New Zealand Division.

In March 1941, the New Zealand Division was sent to Greece to help protect that country from Italian forces and a possible invasion by the Germans, which happened not long after the New Zealanders arrived. (At the time Germany and Greece were not at war.) The Division was chased down through Greece by the Germans. Bill was separated from his unit and along with an assortment of other troops made his way to the Greek port of Kalamata, from where he hoped to be evacuated to Egypt, where the New Zealand Division was based. This was not to be, and he was taken prisoner by German soldiers.

The things that we remember most vividly are those associated with some emotion, and when I interviewed Bill in February 2002 about his experiences in Greece over 60 years earlier, it felt to me as if he was there again. It was an almost perfect encapsulation of Paula Hamilton and Linda Shopes's description of:

> the dynamic nature of remembering, gaps and silences in the transmission of memory, the collapsing of past and present in individual recall, and people's sense of 'living in time' or historical consciousness.[4]

Bill recalled how he felt when taken prisoner [Ernie is a British soldier who he had teamed up with on the journey to Kalamata].

Interviewer: Can you remember how you felt?

Bill: Yes. It felt bloody awful. Excuse my French. That's mild. It's the heart-sinking sensation of the world. The only thing that kept us, or kept me on my toes, was the fact that I was almost certain they were going to shoot me, and I didn't want to bow the knee or anything. I still wanted to poke my chin out. You know, we did have hatred of them. You're not supposed to have hatred but it was sort of built into us. And that's all I could think of: the game's up. They're going to knock us off. And, and it was pretty terrifying for a while.

They herded where I was into an empty section. We were massed up there, several hundred of us, and every time the Germans made a move ... and there were lots of them moving and they all had, they were heavily armed ... we thought this was it. And it was quite touch and go, I think. And the feelings – it was almost indescribable. The horror of ... it wasn't the fact of being defeated or being a prisoner so much, as the ... I don't know what it was, it was just, sort of, angry, sort of, that it had happened to ... Why me? Sort of thing. And it was unavoidable ...

Oh, Ernie had said to me when we found we were going to be prisoners, he said ... I said, 'I'm going to make for the hills.' Oh, that's right. See how it comes back? I said, 'I'm going to make for the hills.' And he said, 'Oh no. I'm a married man with two children in England and if I'm captured, the Red Cross will notify my wife. She won't know that I'm a prisoner unless I get captured and the Red Cross ...' He knew all about it. I didn't. And, I, that's right, I think he told me that he was a tram conductor in civvy street, in England. But that swayed me into this frame of mind that I owed it to my parents – it wasn't a cop-out because I would have, if he hadn't told me that, and I hadn't believed that it was a good idea, and I thought, Well, I'll have plenty of chances once I get … Oh, he said, 'I'll wait until they're notified and all the rest of it, then I'll consider escaping.' That was, that was how it went. I don't know what happened to Ernie, but that convinced me.[5]

The above excerpt vividly conveys his feelings at the time of capture, but also his absolute determination to escape, perhaps the result of a certain feeling of shame associated with having been taken prisoner of war. Bill was captured very early in the war and may have felt that he had not 'done his bit' because among some former servicemen after the war ended there was an attitude, usually only articulated obliquely, that men who were taken prisoner subsequently had an easy life in prisoner of war camps while others were still fighting and placing their lives in danger.

Bill recounts that he was thinking of escape as soon as he became a prisoner: 'I'm going to make for the hills.' The extract lays the foundation for what is a picaresque version of Bill's experiences as a prisoner of war in Greece. The interview that follows is a disjointed, loosely connected set of humorous anecdotes where he leads, escapes, manages to extricate himself from difficult situations, and triumphs over adversity. The recording is around three-and-a-half hours long but we did not get past his time in Greece – there were three more years of being a prisoner of war in Germany that we did not even touch upon.

Picaresque novels are normally comedic or satirical in their tone, offering a humorous look at the corrupt world around them. They are often episodic, choosing not to dwell on plot but instead jump from one misadventure to another. The stories are told in the first person from the point of view of the adventurous 'hero'. The hero does not follow society's rules and lives outside society's norms – just as Bill did when he was evading capture in Greece.

His narrative fits almost perfectly to the picaresque pattern: 'including a loose, episodic structure; a rogue-hero (the picaro) who is on the move and goes through a series of encounters with representatives of a hostile and corrupt world; a first-person narrative; and a satirical approach to the society in which the adventures occur'.[6]

The structure of Bill's narrative fits snugly into the picaresque genre of storytelling, as does his explanation that he felt master of his destiny – despite being in the most perilous of situations in a dangerous world. At the end of the interview,

Bill had not completed his story as a prisoner of war but had spoken about a lengthy period on the run in Salonika (now Thessaloniki) in northeast Greece, always fearing identification by the Greek police. In his account, this period was also a time of dalliances with young Greek women, good food, and learning the Greek language. He concluded the discussion of this period by saying:

> The strange thing about, you get to the point, I got to the point, I believe, where I felt that I was master of my own destiny. I was so inured with doing the right thing and sticking by it and, and, for so long, that I believed in my own destiny, that I was just about infallible. I did really. I certainly had no fear. Only purpose. And I forced myself to believe that there was no dilemma that I couldn't get out of. Excepting a firing line ...[7]

As Alessandro Portelli tells us, oral history is not only a source of information regarding the events of history, but it can also be used to discover the interviewee's attitude towards those events, in other words, how people rationalise and make sense of the past. During his narrative, Bill began to depict himself as being in charge of the situations he found himself in and as rather a hero. As the interview progressed, the themes of escape and being in charge became more obvious. He talked about his many near escapes and how he dealt with being on the run in northern Greece, usually portraying himself as the star of his story. After he escaped the first time, he recalled how he lived with a Greek doctor in her apartment in Thessaloniki. Her flat was the only one occupied by a Greek; the rest were occupied by German officers, and he recounts how they would greet and carry on conversations with the Germans every day. At one stage in the interview, while we were still talking about his time on the loose in Thessaloniki, I asked him if he was scared. He said he was not, and when I asked him why, he replied, 'I'd had so many frights, they were out of fashion. You had to be very self-confident ... I used to pretend I owned the place. You had to act a lot.'[8]

When he was recaptured in Thessaloniki, he was quite casual about the violence done to him when he was interrogated but very proud of the 'huge file' of information about him held by the Gestapo.[9] It was when talking about this time that he mentioned feeling infallible and unafraid. 'I forced myself to believe that there was no dilemma I couldn't get out of. Excepting a firing line.'[10] This pretty much sums up Bill as he presented himself in his interview. And it was this attitude, of course, that enabled him to keep escaping over and over again.

Listening again to the interview, I wondered why Bill framed his account this way. It was certainly due to personality but was also a way of giving himself agency in a situation where he had very little. The transition from being a soldier to being a prisoner is deeply confronting and it is well known that most soldiers do not contemplate being taken prisoner. As a result, when it happens, they are in a state of shock and disbelief at their sudden disempowerment, as Bill so powerfully recounts in the extract: 'And the feelings – it was almost indescribable. The horror of – it wasn't the fact of being defeated or being a prisoner so much, as the – I don't know what it was, it was just, sort of, angry, sort of, that it had happened … Why me? Sort of thing.'[11]

For that reason, I think, he was utterly determined to escape right from the beginning. When he was taken prisoner, he felt he owed it to his parents to surrender initially. He was not being a coward but, rather, a good son because he knew his parents would be informed of his situation.

His emphasis on being determined to escape may also have been influenced by popular perceptions of the prisoner of war experience in books and films produced soon after the war ended, such as *The Great Escape* and *The Wooden Horse*, which both emphasised the heroism and derring-do of officers who made a mass escape from German prisoner of war camp Stalag Luft III.[12] Escape narratives tended to be the focus of prisoner of war accounts and it may be that Bill is fitting his experiences into that popular perception. As military historian Paul Springer has written, the 'public has an almost insatiable demand for military history, but only military history of a certain, glamorous, heroic flavour'.[13]

Bill was not a great frequenter of the Returned Services Association. He had not had the opportunity – or the desire – to tell and retell his story to other returned servicemen at reunions and commemorations, year after year. Bill was neither a member of the community of prisoners of war (the majority) who did not continually try and escape nor was he a member of the community of the Returned Services Association. He was, in the classic picaresque way, outside these social groups so he had not experienced the give and take of reminiscing with others over a beer down at the clubrooms when other people's memories get mixed up with your own, and things that you have subsequently read or seen on the television or at the movies become part of the larger narrative of your, and your friends', experiences. Similarly, he had never written about his wartime experiences.[14] In this interview he had the opportunity to recount his story and to cast himself as a 'glamorous' hero.

In the context of how Bill told his story, some phrases that also interest me are: 'Oh, that's right. See how it comes back?' and 'That was how it went'. In themselves these are nothing startling – you can imagine anyone saying this sort of thing while they were being interviewed. What is thought-provoking is that very few of the men and women I interviewed for this project said such things. This is also what makes Bill interesting – he is actively remembering as he tells his story, and as more things come to mind, he relates them. When reading the transcript of his interview, this habit makes it more disjointed, but Bill was, I think, consciously trying to make sense of his memories and experiences in a considered and logical way.

Addressing how Bill's account fits in with what I hoped to achieve with these interviews, and the role of public historians in adding nuance to the commemorations of war, I would suggest that how people remember the past when they are interviewed does not necessarily reflect public memory. This is why oral history interviews are so helpful in investigating public memory.[15]

In recent years, on Anzac Day in New Zealand, large numbers of people have turned out to the dawn parades and other commemorative activities. Television and other media platforms are full of programmes about World War I and World War II, and each year significant numbers of books on this theme are published. Most of these portray war as a collective experience. With public commemorations, people are taking part in activities that are framed in general ways so that everyone can participate.

In New Zealand, perhaps one reason that public participation in commemorations of war has become so popular is that it is no longer necessary to engage with the mourning, the psychological and physical damage of these wars, because the number of people who took part in them grows smaller and smaller each year. The passage of time has lent a distance to the rawness of the emotions that were engendered by the wars. This means, perhaps, that they have become safer to contemplate.[16]

The holding of commemorations has perhaps become safer, too, if one feels that such events are a manifestation of the symbolic way in which a nation-state can help its citizens feel part of a collective national identity. Everyone's contribution can be acknowledged and, to a certain extent, 'celebrated'. A result of this is more ritualistic ways of commemorating the war, such as the Tomb of the Unknown Warrior at the national war memorial in Wellington, and the use of the patriotic rhetoric associated with memorials of this type, terms such as 'sacrifice' and 'dying for your country'.

To me, this way of depicting the contribution of men and women lacks nuance, and contains no examination or understanding of what it was they were actually involved in, that is, the extreme violence of war. There is often a somewhat celebratory association between war and nationhood; war and manhood. One problem with this is that people such as conscientious objectors who actively opposed the war or people who recall unpleasant (and therefore unheroic) aspects of it do not fit into these narratives of a collective past. Graham Dawson and Bob West have suggested that by publicly representing experience we are generalising its significance and so it is important to offer 'forms and general interpretive categories by means of which people can locate their own experiences in terms of wider social patterns. Popular memories work in just this way, struggling to generalise meanings in such a way as to pull together and give a shared form to a multiplicity of individual and particular experiences.'[17]

This is where the value of oral history interviews with people who experienced war becomes apparent. Such interviews provide an opportunity for the remembered particulars of personal experience to be compared not only with the official histories produced by the War History Branch but also with the more general accounts of World War II. The role of public oral historians in interpreting the past for a wider audience is important as a means of challenging stereotypes and a tendency towards unthinking nostalgia. An individual's memories, as recounted in interviews, can be used to add nuance to public memory of events and can lead to 'new discourses' or 'alternative frameworks', which in turn offer the possibility of oppositional accounts that challenge 'official memory'.[18]

Bill's way of dealing with the humiliating 'bloody awful' experience of having been taken prisoner was to constantly try and escape, and so his narrative is centred around the theme of escape. In that way, he dealt with the attitude of those ex-servicemen who had not been taken prisoner and who were often heard to say disparaging things about former prisoners of war at the local RSA (to the extent that many of the group refused to keep up their membership). As Matthew Johnson writes, 'Captured soldiers did not fit within the popular notion of men triumphing in battle.'[19] At the same time, he was fitting his experiences into the popular conception that placed the prisoner of war experience in a narrative of it being the prisoner of war's duty to escape. He owed it to his parents to let them know he had been captured, but he owed it to himself to escape capture. His account is a means of making sense of his experiences in a way that mitigated the disempowerment he felt when transitioning from soldier to captive. By casting himself as the hero of his story, in charge of a situation where he was in fact quite powerless, and by using the theme of escape in that account, Bill was rationalising his time as a prisoner of war and fitting those experiences into the popular conception of a World War II narrative.

9

The kitchen: Insights from a 1950s domestic workplace

HELEN FRIZZELL AND **PIP OLDHAM**

Oral history work is done between individuals, the interview subject and the oral historian, with the intention of being useful to a wider audience. Many oral historians use the framework taught by Judith Fyfe and Hugo Manson to explore an individual life within their family, as well as a local and national context.[1] As a result, oral histories can support broader narratives of periods of history. Close study of an account of a single person reflecting on their personal and social context is also a reminder of the sheer diversity of individual experience and can reveal the complex interplay between the collective and the personal.

Histories of domestic life in the 1950s can produce a range of narratives about marriage, family life, gender roles, work, houses and homes based on an understanding of common experience. But these can only ever serve as high-level proxies for individual lives. As if to emphasise the gap between the representation of such a collective history and individual, lived experience, the details of domestic lives in the past have often been missing from historical records. With Judith Fyfe and Megan Hutching, we set out to explore the subject of domestic life in the period 1940 to 1960 using recipe books as a starting point for topic-based life history interviews. We called the project *Mrs Schumacher's Gems* after a recipe in one of those books. Helen Frizzell interviewed Phyllis Aspinall.

*

At first sight, the life of Phyllis (1922–2018) fits within the expected social and gender norms for her time. She was a farmer's wife, mother and unpaid worker. She is described in one obituary as 'Aspiring Station matriarch' and 'an outstanding contributor to rural life'.[2] For her time at the station, she is particularly remembered for catering for hundreds of people: shearers, farm workers and visitors. The picture that accompanies her oral history at the Alexander Turnbull Library, speaks to her domestic prowess. It shows Phyllis surrounded by her preserves. But these representations need context. When they are combined with her oral history interview, we get a better understanding of who Phyllis was. Not a farmer's wife but better thought of as a chief executive in her own right, with all the intellect, skills, drive and personal attributes we credit to highly paid people (often male) in other places. The oral history provides context on the division of responsibility and labour between Phyllis and her husband and how that was negotiated (or not), family relationships and expectations, and how Phyllis processed her situation emotionally (often an elusive aspect of the historical record). This information about Phyllis can't be found on the printed page. It emerges in words and tone from her recorded interview. This is the power of oral history.

*

Mount Aspiring Station is an isolated high-country farm in the Southern Alps. It is by the confluence of the east and west branches of the Matukituki River right on the edge of Mount Aspiring National Park. The nearest town, Wānaka (or Pembroke, as it is sometimes called) is 50 km (or 30 miles as Phyllis describes it) away. The Macphersons, who were crofters from Scotland, built homesteads (in 1878) in the shadow of Homestead Peak (where Phyllis lived) and (in 1899) in the lower West Matukituki valley. Mr Macpherson and his children left the farm after his wife tragically died crossing the river to get back to the homestead after going to Dunedin to cast her vote in the 1919 general election. John (known as Jack) Aspinall, purchased the station in 1920 and moved to the 1878 homestead with his new wife, Amy, an English 'war bride' who had arrived in New Zealand in November the previous year, 1919. Amy and Jack farmed there until Jack's death in 1942. Their son Jerry, who was 20, took over from Jack and farmed with his mother until 1952 when he married Phyllis. Amy left the farm at that point.

Nowadays the station homestead is Glen Finnan, located on the Wānaka side of the river, making access easier, but when Phyllis and Jerry were first married (the

Phyllis Aspinall in her kitchen, 23 February 2010. Beside Phyllis are buckets of apples for bottling or making apple cider vinegar. Photographer: Peter Henderson

period Phyllis talks about in the extract below) the homestead was on the alpine side. The riverbed was half a mile wide and could be treacherous, increasing the physical isolation of the location. The area has extremely high rainfall; after rain Phyllis could see 50 waterfalls from the homestead. The ground stayed frozen in winter. In spring and autumn conditions underfoot were often 'squishy'.[3]

A picture taken in 1967 of Phyllis's son working in front of the homestead gives a sense of the environment while Phyllis was there. An earlier traveller in the Matukituki valley, Maud Moreland, described it like this:

> It was a forbidding, desolate place; great bare mountains ran up in rocky pinnacles and serrated edges on either side. The bush, along the base, had been swept by some forest fire, leaving only a few scattered groups of beech. Though the sunshine was flooding over everything and the sky cloudless, the entrance to that gorge always to me had the same dread look, and a sentence kept running in my head: 'Through the grave and gate of death we may pass to our joyful resurrection.'
>
> The ground, too, was stony and barren, and cut up by torrents that tear their way from the mountains; and in many places tumbled boulders and tree-trunks gave us plenty to do to get the horses over.[4]

The following description from the *School Journal* gives a sense of the size of the farm and the outside work but not the domestic work of the station:

> Mount Aspiring Station is 23,100 acres and carries 2750 sheep and 650 cattle, mostly Hereford, which are raised for beef. The sheep are Merinos, which produce a very fine wool. They were once a popular breed, but today they are found mainly in the high country, where their toughness helps them to endure the cold alpine winters.
>
> There is always work to be done on the station – fencing, mustering, dipping, shearing. It is hard work and it is made much harder by the ruggedness of the land. But, for those who are not afraid of loneliness and hardship, there is no life like it.[5]

Neither Amy nor Phyllis came from farming backgrounds. We don't know enough about Amy's life to know what it was like for her arriving in New Zealand after the World War I and going to live in this remote part of the country, working in a domestic role in the farm business. We know that Phyllis had only been to

Mount Aspiring two or three times before she went there to live although she had read about Mrs Macpherson in Maud Moreland's book, which, along with the description quoted earlier, includes a poem with the line, 'The nearest woman's face may be a hundred miles away', a vivid summary of the social isolation from other women.[6]

Despite her lack of familiarity with the physical surroundings at the station, Phyllis was under no illusions about her role. As the third farmer's wife at Mount Aspiring she was taking up an established role for which expectations had already been set. In taking over from her mother-in-law Phyllis came into an existing workplace, house and kitchen with clearly articulated expectations from her husband. Among other things, she was to provide a continuous supply of meals to family, farm workers and visitors. Visitors included stock agents, rabbiters, deer cullers, government employees, climbers, and university students. Modelling his idea of Phyllis's role on what his mother had done, Jerry told her he 'wanted everyone who came to the door to be offered a cup of tea'.[7] One summer that amounted to a hundred people. There is no sense that Phyllis had a choice about what she would do on the farm, and there are clear indications that she did not enjoy personal autonomy even in the domestic sphere for which she was solely responsible.

Turning now to an extract from the interview with Phyllis Aspinall. Helen Frizzell asked Phyllis to describe the station homestead.[8] The house and kitchen Phyllis talks about were built after the 1878 station building was largely destroyed by fire in 1920, shortly after Amy Aspinall arrived at Mount Aspiring. This is the first kitchen of Phyllis's married life. She is speaking about her mother-in-law's kitchen. The second kitchen came in 1955, when Jerry and Amy (who was still involved in the farm business) agreed to some modest but important changes, and the third was in 1969 when Phyllis and Jerry moved to the newly built Glen Finnan.

Helen: So, Phyllis, the … house you were going to [after your marriage], we were looking at a photograph of it yesterday.[9] Describe that house for me?

> **Phyllis**: Well, you might say it faced the front because the road did go along there, but I didn't think it was the most practical approach. For instance, in the winter, although we had sunshine outside for four hours in a day, if you opened the front door, there was a little place on the wall high up where the sun shone for 10 minutes or so around 11 o'clock in the morning. And that was the sunshine that came in the living room in the winter. And it was cold, and

damp. The kitchen got some sunshine in the afternoon. But one of my other sons was telling me yesterday that in the old days, they'd put the kitchen in the darkest place nearest the wood supply because the kitchen would be warm even if nothing else in the house was. So, it wasn't an easy house to maintain. And you would air things with great difficulty because some houses had a rack high up in the kitchen where you could hang things to air or dry. But the roof in the kitchen was so low, you had no hope in the wide world. And at night, you would drape clothes – garments – around the kitchen to finish drying. They'd been out on the line during the day … but you could only get enough dried that way to use the next day. It was a very tricky thing to keep clothes dry. And they got wet so often with what they were wearing anyhow, in that climate, it was a high rainfall area. So, it was a real challenge to keep the washing in order.

So, the kitchen was on the dark side of the house then?

Yes, at the back. Mmm. Yes.

How old was the house when you got there? How long had it been there?

The original homestead had burnt down just after Jerry's parents had got married and gone there in 1920. And the replacement was there when … she came home with a baby early in 1922. And it was, shall we say a modern, well more up-to-date house than the original one, but it was what I call a face, with a door in the middle and a window on either side. And … it was four bedrooms: a bedroom each off … the living room and kitchen. And I think that was it. Oh then, later on across the back yard, there was a shed building which was better built than the house and on the front of it there was the wash house and it got a lot of sunshine, it was nice. And on the back – no, no it didn't, it was a shaded room. The back was the storeroom, at the back of the washhouse, which meant quite a hike from the kitchen to get round to the storeroom, if I wanted a teaspoon full of brown sugar, or something like that. And as well as all that, there was a great big beech tree beside the storeroom side of the building, and a tank that supplied water to the laundry. And if the tank happened to get overflowing, it fell over the path and that meant that you got soused going around to the storeroom. So, life was hazardous.

What was kept in the storeroom?

Well, all supplies. All the ingredients for baking with were there. And hanging from the rafters was a row of sleeping bags, I think the mice couldn't get at them

William Aspinall in front of Mount Aspiring Homestead, 1967. Photographer: Helen Buttfield.
Courtesy of Phyllis Aspinall

that way. But they didn't buy things in bulk. You didn't buy a case of … raisins, or a sack of oatmeal or of flour. We didn't use them at that pace but you'd get a 50-pound bag of flour, and 70-pound bag of sugar at a time. They were kept in the storeroom. Mice got in there freely. I remember one time … I ran out of flour. I was careful usually and as soon as the last container of something was used, I'd write it down on my shopping list. And I remember one time I had run out and I happened to look in a bag in the storeroom and there was a 50 pound of flour with a … dead mouse lying in the bag on top of all the flour. I was profoundly grateful more flour came back that day that I could send [it] straight away up to the hens.

Vermin were a problem though?

Yes.

Did they get into the house as well?

Oh yes, yes, badly. But in the storeroom, I had to keep everything in tins or containers. And it was a matter of as soon as it came you put it into something safe.

Did you keep any food supplies in the kitchen?

Well, I had a bit but I didn't quite understand … there were several cupboards in the kitchen. Jerry's father was versatile. He was a jack of all trades. And one of the cupboards was about chest high and don't ask me why, but all the cleaning stuff was in there. The floor polish … and a wee primus that you could boil a kettle quickly on were in there, and the whole cupboard was quite redolent of all this cleaning stuff. Well, I didn't see any reason why that had to have priority in the kitchen over the food and … the food supplies. In the kitchen there were the dishes and the china and a whole lot of the stuff that only went to the woolshed. The shearers' teapot and the mugs that went down to the woolshed. Well, they could have gone in the storeroom to my way of thinking and the food in the kitchen. But mice had access to every shelf in the kitchen.

So … from your point of view that wasn't very practical.

No.

Did you make changes?

> Well, I had to put up with that until 1955. We renovated the kitchen, and I had a whole wall of cupboards in the kitchen then, and that was mighty because … we could use it intelligently after that.

You were inheriting an existing system. What was that like for you?

> I found it very hard to accept because Jerry's mother didn't have my mother's approach to … well she didn't use her brains about what was sensible to do. I'm not too sure what guided her.

So, you couldn't just make changes, like moving everything from the storeroom in and moving other things, right?

> No, well because of the smell of the cleaning cupboard. There was no way you could take that away. And the pots set, some of them sat in the bottom of the pot cupboard in the kitchen. But the sink on the top of that pot cupboard leaked. So you had to wash every pot before you used it. But the main pot cupboard was in the back porch. And most of the pots were there, but the front of it had the door on it, but the back was open, and it was no rare thing to find a cat sitting in a pot. So, you had to wash everything, just about. I mean everything from there had to be washed before you could use it as well.

And could you have moved the shearers' stuff out and to somewhere else?

> Ah, yes. I did put it … in a room they called the pantry but I don't know why because it wasn't one. But that cupboard wasn't really very … well, the shelves where I would have put those things were low down and … they were fairly deep cupboards. And it wasn't practical, shall we say, to use them.

I'm just trying to get a sense, I guess, of how easy it was for you, coming into an existing setup that had been there for years, to put your own stamp on it, to make those changes?

> Mmm. I was very grateful to have a new kitchen and I spent a considerable amount of thought on planning it and it really worked very well.

So, what changes did you make?

Well, we made it bigger. It was … fairly small. And because Jerry's mother was short, she was five feet tall, and the kitchen sink was her height. And the range, it was an enamelled range and she was very proud of that, rather than having … a black one. But it had a sort of balcony on the front. And the theory was you put wood in there … about 15 inches long, the pieces. And while the wood in the actual firebox burned, the wood on the veranda balcony on the front would get dry. But that was only theory. And in the winter, it was … very difficult indeed. I'd put a roast in the oven in the morning and if I was very lucky, it would be cooked by night. But it was more likely to be tomorrow night when it was ready. And we mostly had to have things like stew and soup. And I'd have to make shortbread and fruitcakes in the autumn when I could still use the oven and let them sit, because of the temperature … well, you could only cook things that took slow cooking.

And this was all because of the wood?

Yes. And Jerry, he never had time to bring wood in, in March when things were dry. It was always April that he could do it, so he said. Well, if they were going to cook, they would bring home wood from the riverbed, or they'd find an empty carton or a … wooden box or something. And they'd bring that home and use it. And they'd nurse their fire so that … they could cook much more readily than I could when I had to throw things in the oven and had so many other things … to do as well.

When you're talking about 'they', who are you referring to?

The men.

The men were cooking elsewhere?

No, if I was away anywhere, and they had to cook … they could cope. And they would say at me: well, they could do perfectly well … when they had to do it. But that was because they could bring dry wood home from the riverbed or wherever. And they'd nurse it. But I was doing so many other things that I'd put the wood on the fire and expect it to behave itself.

Where were you getting the wood from? Were you dependent on them bringing it in?

Yes. The woodshed was out just over the fence from the house. It was there but they would bring tree trunks and suitable wood, only it was wet, home in April once … everything was damp outside.

So, really for you, dry wood was pretty important?

Yes. Yes. …[10]

So, this was your coal range [wood range] then?

Mmm.

Was there anything else to cook on other than that … when you first arrived?

Well, there was an open fire if I wanted but it was in the living room. And you could make an awful mess with an open fire so I didn't ever try.

So, you were stuck with this coal range [wood range] that may or may not work, depending on the wood?

Well, it worked after its fashion.

The Aspinalls of Mount Aspiring are well known. Jerry Aspinall wrote several books.[11] Phyllis's family have contributed to a book about Mount Aspiring Station.[12] Phyllis herself was well known through her extensive community and local involvement. She appeared on the radio and in print and a number of tributes were published when she died.[13] These primary and secondary sources tell us something about life on the farm, but they disclose little about the day-to-day realities of Phyllis's domestic life, the small details that contribute to the larger context.

In the interview for the Gems project, where there is a deliberate and sustained focus on her personal experience of domestic life, Phyllis adds another dimension to what is known about life at Mount Aspiring Station and knowledge about the domestic lives of farmers' wives in the 1950s. Hearing Phyllis speak adds nuance and helps us understand Phyllis as a person. Through listening to what she says and does not say and how she speaks, we develop a fuller picture of the situation that the two women who preceded her at Mount Aspiring faced. We hear how Phyllis processed and responded to events and experiences, and the dynamics of her relationships with her husband and her mother-in-law. These things may (or may not) be known or understood by family members and friends, but they are less readily accessible from standard research sources. First-hand information of this kind, showing gender roles and expectations, the value and significance of women's work, the position of women and their bargaining power in domestic situations, is scarce. Phyllis provides this.

Studs Terkel tells us, 'It's what a person says, and how they say it, and where they're saying it to – to you, to the past, the future, the outside world' and he reminds us about the importance of the indirect silences and non-verbal clues.[14] These clues are there in Phyllis's interview. As Anna Bryson and Séan McConville say, what is told in the interview is only part of the story; how and why that information is presented is often equally, if not more, revealing.[15]

At times Phyllis pauses, evidently thinking about what she is going to say. There in the room with Phyllis, Helen Frizzell was conscious that Phyllis was going through a process of deciding what she could or should say. Listening to Phyllis speaking on the interview recordings (as opposed to reading the transcript) there is a perceptible distance between what she first thinks of when asked a question and the reply she gives, a gap between what she really felt and thought and what she is willing to commit to the record about the topic. In this respect Phyllis is similar to the women Jane Moodie writes about in 'The moral world of the Waikite Valley'. In the life narratives of the women she interviewed she found most criticism of husbands was usually mild, brief and often told as a joke as convention demanded that women shield their marriage relationship, and particularly its negative aspects, from public view.[16] Despite her reticence and care about what she commits to the record, Phyllis allows glimpses into her relationships and emotional life.

Early life for Phyllis was the opposite of the isolated farm she moved to after her marriage. With no secondary school in Wānaka, where her parents ran the local garage, she went away from home and had three years of secondary education. She 'grieved' the loss of further education when she had to return to Wānaka.[17] Later on she was able to go to university, planning for a career in music, but 'there was no point carrying on' after her engagement to Jerry Aspinall. 'No point' reflects the absolute, non-negotiable nature of her situation and the limitations resulting from gender and social norms of the time.

Phyllis's approach to her domestic life was clearly influenced by upbringing and childhood. Phyllis's father served and was injured in World War I, and the family was impacted by the Great Depression and World War II. In her account Phyllis emphasises her parents' skills and attributes rather than the difficulties they faced or the broader social and historical context. Her mother was 'very competent' in the kitchen and 'shopped intelligently' with the result that Phyllis and her three siblings 'didn't suffer at all – we had nice meals'.[18] Phyllis learnt 'the intelligence of cooking practically and wisely … [and] making balanced meals'.[19] Her father 'believed in efficiency' and 'in having proper equipment for things. Because for the garage, he found that most useful and he was quite forceful about her [Phyllis's mother] having useful equipment in the house, which was very intelligent of him.'[20]

When invited to describe her first kitchen at Mount Aspiring Station Phyllis uses these measures of practicality and intelligence. The location of the house was 'not the most practical approach'. It was cold and damp. It wasn't an easy house to live in or maintain. Her comment that the lack of sun created 'a real challenge to keep the washing in order' tacitly references the laundry aspect of her role at the station. Unlike her mother's well-equipped kitchen, Phyllis was confronted by a workspace that wasn't fit for purpose. It 'wasn't a thoughtfully planned room by any means'. Ingredients and kitchen supplies were kept elsewhere, cupboards were filled with stuff for the woolshed, the bench leaked and vermin were a problem.[21] The hike to the storeroom for a teaspoon of sugar entailed possible 'sousing' en route. It was imprinted on her mind that to go there and back was 56 steps. In short, 'life was hazardous'.

Helen Leach describes the kitchen as the site of major changes including work patterns, kitchen layout, fuel types, attitudes and customs. But she acknowledges that domestic kitchens exist in the private realm of the home and her research, reliant on printed resources, could not give even coverage to the diversity of kitchens that existed here in the twentieth century.[22] Phyllis's criteria for a kitchen (and how to operate in it), are thoroughly consistent with ideas current in architecture from as early as the 1930s. The proper arrangement and plan of a kitchen were considered part of the training of a modern architect.[23] Yet architectural ideas or design did not come to Mount Aspiring until the Aspinalls employed an architect to design the new homestead in the late 1960s.

There is little indication anywhere of how the Mount Aspiring homestead and its outbuildings came to be constructed as they were. We can only guess what the fire of 1920 meant for Jerry's parents, especially Amy, and under what conditions the rebuild took place. Given the location and the severity of the weather, time is likely to have been of the essence and materials limited to what was easily to hand. We don't know what role, if any, Phyllis's mother-in-law Amy had in the design of her workspace (Phyllis's first kitchen), except that the kitchen sink was built low because Amy was only five feet tall.

Perplexed by the existing setup, Phyllis outlines practical improvements to storage that would have made her job easier. Yet she 'had to put up with' the kitchen for five years before any improvements were made. In her first exercise of personal agency, in 1955, they put a 'whole wall of cupboards in the kitchen … and that was mighty because we could use it intelligently after that'. For her third kitchen Phyllis 'spent a considerable amount of thought on planning it and it really worked very well'. The language is simple but the import of these changes cannot be underestimated. Her voice resonates with the significance and satisfaction; it was finally an opportunity to exercise complete agency over her working conditions through the design. Asked what she requested in that kitchen Phyllis replied, 'convenience, I suppose, and efficiency, and space to store things wisely', directly reflecting both the features of her first Aspiring kitchen that she had to manage and her own criteria for a kitchen.[24]

At a time when homes in towns and cities were lit with electricity and increasingly equipped with refrigerators and electrical appliances, in Phyllis's first kitchen electricity was supplied by a small hydro generator from one of the waterfalls nearby and was only available for lighting. Phyllis cooked on a wood range. This worked after a fashion, but she details the difficulties involved in using the range for both cooking and drying laundry. She needed a supply of dry wood, which was at a premium in the wet climate, and she was reliant on 'the men' to bring the wood. Jerry didn't have time, 'so he said', to collect it in March when it would have been dry. This put Phyllis at the mercy of wet wood and having to find creative and intelligent ways to get by and keep the wood stove going. She couldn't nurse the fire because of all the other demands on her time. Supplying dry wood for her was not a top priority for the men, yet they 'could do it perfectly well in her absence'. The situation is a vivid reflection of how Phyllis thought she was viewed on the farm and the priority placed on her needs.

Having grown up on the farm and running it with his mother in the 1940s, Phyllis might have thought Jerry would be better attuned to the demands of her role and her needs. Writing about this period in *Farming under Aspiring*, Jerry notes that it was his job as a lad to keep a supply of dry wood and 'without wood-shed facilities this wasn't always easy and at times my popularity wasn't of a very high order', but he does not appear to connect his own experience (as wood supplier to Amy) with an appreciation for the demands of Phyllis's situation and her expertise. He says, 'It was very hard work and a great challenge bringing up and teaching our family of four … and feeding hungry and sometimes ungrateful men' and of Phyllis's role, 'with the dedication and determination endowed by her parents she set to work to make a success of her new career and husband'.[25]

Family relationships, present or absent, close or extended, form part of the broader context of a life. We know that Phyllis was relieved that Amy Aspinall moved off the farm when she and Jerry took it over. Phyllis mentions her mother-in-law during the interview but avoids offering direct comment about her or her role at Mount Aspiring. There are signs that there was feeling on both sides. Jerry Aspinall expected Phyllis to replace Amy on the farm; she would do what her mother-in-law had done before her, follow the same routines, use the same equipment. And while her mother-in-law was no longer at the homestead, she remained in the farm business and carried an element of financial influence over Phyllis's life. Her views on provisioning informed what was to be bought and what was expected. Phyllis's knowledge from Amy that she had to use what was there 'burdened' Phyllis's life.[26] When the kitchen was improved in 1955, Phyllis would not have had an improved heat storage range but for the fact that her mother-in-law wanted the wood range.[27] Amy, on the other hand, was determined that Phyllis should not have what she herself had lacked.[28]

A matter-of-fact way of talking about her own circumstances and what she inherited carries through Phyllis's interview. In common with women of her generation, she accepted her lot, but how she felt comes through. In her characteristically understated way, Phyllis tells us that the reality of Mount Aspiring was 'a bit different from what your imagination tells you, doesn't it? Always'.[29] She empathises with (the crofters) Mrs Macpherson and her circumstances raising her children in an isolated place and connects emotionally with her in a way that is absent in how she talks about her mother-in-law. Commenting on the school inspector's criticism of the Macpherson children's manners Phyllis is forthright, 'my heart rings for her'. But she regrets mentioning her admiration for Mrs Macpherson when she visited Mount Aspiring for the first time.[30]

A later generation of people reading the history and hearing Phyllis speak might be puzzled by Phyllis's focus on Mrs Macpherson and wonder why Phyllis gives Amy's experience so little space in her account. Perhaps a clue is how much acknowledgement Phyllis had of her own role and expertise. She was in no doubt that Jerry valued his mother's contribution, but Phyllis's experience of personal acknowledgement seems to have been different.

While looking at Phyllis's recipe books Helen Frizzell asked about the inscription by the author in *Entertaining with Graham Kerr*. He wrote, 'I have heard many wonderful remarks about your delicious food, and long for the chance someday to pay you a visit. Would you please accept this small volume as a mark of my respect for your interest in the subject that I hold so dear?'

Phyllis said of this, 'The inscription is very precious.'[31] And she explains:

> And he [Graham Kerr] didn't know – well he does now because I told him – what a kindness he did me because if people were visiting us and commented upon the quality of the meal they had or the variety or whatever in Jerry's presence, he would invariably say, 'Oh, if you want a decent meal, you should have come when Mum was here', and I felt a bit irate about that. And my friends learnt not to say anything. So I minded that too. So when this inscription came from him, of course, I showed it to Jerry straightaway, very proudly. He never once said it again. And so until I wrote and told him Graham Kerr didn't know what a kindness he had done me. And my golly I valued it.[32]

This short statement is telling. Phyllis minded that she was always compared to her mother-in-law, and minded Jerry's silence, and she valued Graham Kerr's praise. 'My golly' she did.

The interview with Phyllis provides a closer focus on the domestic side of life at Mount Aspiring than other sources. Perhaps more importantly it is a working example of social expectations around gender roles and, usefully, a vivid insight into the emotional life of a woman fulfilling a gendered role in a rural setting in the 1950s. This understanding is hard to find except in an interview like this. It is moving to hear the importance of personal agency to Phyllis, and the significance of having her skill and expertise valued objectively. These windows into Phyllis's emotions provide a powerful way of connecting contemporary audiences with the lived past. Through the interview, women of later generations have an opportunity to hear about the daily life of a woman born in the early twentieth century, consider what has changed and not changed since Phyllis's time, and ponder what she would make of their own lives and the role of women's work and gender relationships in the twenty-first century.

10

Revisiting consent in oral histories of sex work

CHERYL WARE

One of the strengths of oral history is its capacity to engage with individuals' personal memories and private reflections, making space for topics and voices that have previously been silenced. Oral history allows researchers to enrich understandings of the past by challenging and complicating existing historical narratives. The topics interviewees feel comfortable discussing at any given moment – and the responses they receive from the interviewer – offer telling reflections on the historical context in which the interview takes place. This was certainly evident during interviews I conducted for my Marsden-funded project on histories of sex work in Aotearoa.[1] The interviews took place in 2021. In the preceding years, discussions about consent and sexual violence took centre stage with the international '#MeToo' and 'Time's Up' campaigns. These movements not only provoked more open discussions about the sheer prevalence of sexual violence, but they have also triggered critical reflections on what constitutes consent, and importantly, what does not.

This chapter examines the significance of oral history in offering new perspectives on histories of sex and consent, especially in regard to sex work. It features interviews with two Pākehā cisgender women who worked in the sex industry in the late-1980s and early-2000s. The interviews offer insights into how the narrators remembered and interpreted their experiences of defending their rights over their bodies amidst evolving cultural narratives about what consent entails. Taken together, the oral histories challenge historical narratives that emphasise how the liberation movements across the late twentieth century transformed public attitudes towards sex and sexuality. They demonstrate how these changes played out in the lives of individuals in pre- and post-decriminalisation contexts. An examination of consent in oral histories of sex work offers deeper insight into women's endeavours to assert their rights over their bodies in late-twentieth and early twenty-first-century Aotearoa. It reveals how public debates about women's bodily autonomy, reducing stigma and discrimination, and protecting sex workers' human rights resonated with some of the individuals at the heart of these discussions, and how they reflect on their experiences several decades later.

The interviews followed a 'life story' approach, which traces an individual's progression through childhood, education, and into their working lives. Life story interviews aim to uncover the narrators' interpretations of the key influences in their lives, the obstacles they faced, and the contexts in which their narratives are set.[2] I also drew on a series of questions I had prepared for the interview, which focused on their memories of growing up, becoming aware of sex work, engagement with mentors and sex worker networks, and their experiences with the police. Upon reflection, questions specifically about consent were notably absent from my list. Nevertheless, when I returned to the recording, I noticed my emphatic verbal responses to interviewees' reflections on consent, which I likely accompanied with head nodding and other affirmative physical cues. My subconscious responses perhaps confirmed that I was especially interested in these topics. They might have also elicited more open and extended reflections on consent than the narrators may have otherwise offered. In this regard, narrators' emphases on consent illustrate how oral history interviews are co-creations between the interviewer and interviewee.

Oral history plays an important role in moving towards a more nuanced understanding of sexual violence and consent. Scholarship on sexual violence in late twentieth and early twenty-first century Aotearoa primarily focuses on more conventional interpretations of rape as forced or coerced. Historians have highlighted the achievements of women's liberationists in exposing the prevalence of sexual violence in New Zealand society, especially that perpetrated against cisgender women, and shattering victim-blaming rape myths.[3] They demonstrate how liberationists resisted the silence attached to sexual violence through public marches and the establishment of independent Rape Crisis Centres in the late 1970s and early 1980s.[4] These historians paid due tribute to the success of feminist activism in shaping reforms of rape laws in 1985 and instigating significant changes in public attitudes towards rape complainants. Scholars have also focused specifically on sexual violence against women in the sex industry. Australian political scientist Barbara Sullivan's analysis of court cases in New Zealand, Canada and Australia traces a cultural shift from sex workers being legally constructed as women who were 'always consenting', to sex workers launching successful rape prosecutions. Sullivan attributes these changes to 'feminist activism, rape law reform and improvements in social attitudes towards women working in prostitution'.[5] Yet such social and legislative reforms did not always translate to a wider recognition of women's body autonomy, especially for those in the sex industry. Indeed, Grace Millar's assessment of historiography on women's lives highlights the limited scholarship on the 'vast majority' of sexual violence that is not reported to police, 'let alone tried in a court of law and discussed in the media'.[6] It is these unreported cases of sexual violence with which this chapter is concerned.

Kaupapa Māori scholars have taken the lead in raising concerns about the limitations of definitions of sexual violence that exclusively focus on forced or coerced sexual acts. Leonie Pihama et al argue that these definitions, which are located within dominant Pākehā frameworks,[7] fail to adequately convey the context of sexual violence for Māori 'not only as a form of physical violence but also as a cultural and spiritual transgression that impacts both the individual and the collective well-being of their entire whakapapa line and whānau'.[8] Rather, they argue that for Māori, sexual violence is also understood in relation to the 'violence perpetuated upon whānau, hapū and iwi through colonial invasion'.[9] Scholars have conducted valuable investigations into the prevalence of sexual violence as an impact of colonisation, which created an environment where one's right to grant or deny consent has been denied.[10]

It is also important to recognise the distinct ethical considerations associated with conducting oral histories of sexual violence and sex work. Discussions of sexual violence can trigger painful and raw memories, and lead to what Penny Summerfield describes as 'discomposure'.[11] Numerous scholars and practitioners have also identified the limitation that oral historians are neither trained to identify the signs of trauma nor provide the emotional follow-up that therapists offer.[12] While narrators might find comfort in sharing their stories, the risks associated with doing so must also be acknowledged. On the other hand, narrators might be silenced by concerns they would encounter unsympathetic listeners and are perhaps more likely to anticipate such negative responses given that sexual violence against sex workers is often regarded as inevitable.

The ethical issues historians encounter are certainly not limited to conducting and interpreting interviews. Oral historians are attuned to the possibility that the stories they engage in might be taken out of context and exploited in ways that cause harm to the interviewees. Melissa Matutina Williams' engagement with Māori oral histories offers a particularly powerful assessment of the potential dangers of publishing oral histories. She argues that empowering stories can become disempowering when used by others to perpetuate negative stereotypes or to determine what is best for Māori communities.[13] Sex worker activists in New Zealand and elsewhere have raised concerns that opponents would use narrators' adverse experiences to undermine the legitimacy of the sex industry and the agency of those who work in it. The stakes are particularly high considering these stories have been and can continue to be used against sex workers to push for laws that criminalise sex workers and their clients. In this vein, I also must emphasise that I conducted my interviews at a time and in a place where we could speak about sex work on record, without concerns about the legal implications that people undertaking this research elsewhere might encounter.[14] When I conducted the interviews, New Zealand remained the only country in the world where sex work was decriminalised on a national level, and sex workers were protected under employment legislation.[15]

The significance of contemporary discussions about consent, specifically how narrators remember and reflect on the past, was especially clear in my interview with Kate. Kate grew up in a small town in the lower North Island and moved to Wellington to attend university at the age of 16 in 1980. She initially lived in a student hostel where life was 'exciting and heady'. Kate became familiar with sex work through friends who worked in local massage parlours, but 'I had never thought I would be tough enough or cool enough to do it, to be honest'. Nevertheless, after leaving her university course and spending several years travelling overseas, Kate was running low on money and joined an escort agency in December 1988. She moved into parlour work after three or four months and simultaneously resumed her university studies. Kate left sex work in late 1989 following a booking with an older client who 'wasn't very nice'. She explained, 'I was just like "Oh, fuck this!" [Laughs]. And after the job with him, I just got my stuff and went home, and I never went back.' My follow-up question about why the client was 'not nice' became a segue into Kate's in-depth reflections on consent in sex work:

> There are guys that stick in my mind as being not nice. Like, I remember somebody taking a condom off during a job, which is really uncool. Somebody just got convicted of rape for doing that recently in New Zealand, which is kind of awesome. I would never have even thought of it like that myself at the time.

Obviously, I didn't think it was a good thing. I knew it was a terrible thing for someone to have done. But shit, I wouldn't have thought of it as rape. So that's kind of awesome.

Interviewer: It is. And it's also changing more public ideas I guess of what rape is.

Kate: And what consent is and everything, aye? What are you consenting to or not consenting to? It's not consent to all things. It's not consent to all things. Yeah, it's interesting to think about consent isn't it, with sex work? I feel like I need to think on it more and unpick it more. You'd think I'd have done that enough already by now, huh? But I haven't been thinking about sex work that much in the last couple of years, I suppose. But people used to – not people in the sex industry – but people used to say stuff like, 'Oh, a sex worker can't be raped, a prostitute can't be raped'. As though if you have consented to sex work you have consented to all sex, blanket kind of sex. And then the polar opposite of that to me is the thing that the abolitionist people would say, where they're saying that you can't consent to being a sex worker. That all sex work is rape. I feel like I need to draw a picture or something to look at how these ideas work. They're so black and white and they're like the opposites of each other. One is that if you're a sex worker, you have consented to all sex, forever, from everybody; you can't ever say no again. But the other people are also saying basically, what are they saying? That you can't consent, that it's not possible to consent, that sex workers that think that they're consenting are deluded, and that it's all rape. So, it's really problematic. You have to be able to have those dividing lines. Like, if someone wants to choose to work in a massage parlour for whatever reason, there's a real difference, a huge difference, between consensual paid sex and being raped or something. So that's very problematic thinking.[16]

Kate's testimony highlights how recent discussions about consent and sexual violence offered her the framework to revisit and reevaluate her past experiences. Her memory of a client covertly removing the condom during sex, an assault that is commonly referred to as stealthing, is particularly poignant. Stealthing made national headlines in April 2021 – shortly before I conducted the interviews – when a man was sentenced to three years and nine months imprisonment for raping a woman employed in a Wellington parlour by removing the condom without her knowledge. New Zealand media outlets celebrated the conviction as the first of its kind. They suggested the 'landmark case' could lead to a change in legislation that would explicitly outlaw the covert removal of a condom in all sexual encounters.[17] Kate's acknowledgement that she would not have considered the act rape in the late-1980s does not downplay the severity of the assault. Rather, her explicit reference to the conviction highlights how it gave her the recognition she perhaps did not have at the time to identify the assault as rape. Further, Kate's reflection that she knew the condom removal was a 'terrible thing to do' perhaps reflects not only the perpetrator's violation of her boundaries but also his blatant disregard for the risk he posed to her health. The assault took place in 1989, during the height of the HIV and AIDS epidemic in Aotearoa. Sex worker activists were especially vocal about the importance of protecting themselves from the spread of the virus and various sexually transmitted infections by consistently using condoms. They mobilised to provide education and access to safe sex supplies for their peers.[18] The observation that the assault – with potential life-threatening ramifications – was not widely recognised as rape, offers a lens into a complex history of consent and sexual violence. It highlights the kinds of behaviour women who had consented to sex at one point, especially when they worked in the sex industry, were expected to endure.[19]

It is important to consider that some sex workers had been particularly vocal about covert condom removal as a form of rape decades before such cases reached the mainstream press. Sex worker activists were instrumental in recasting interpretations of sexual violence to extend beyond those that solely focused on physical attacks or explicit coercion. They emphasised sexual assault as any act that breached the conditions one set out before or during sex. In July 1990, the editors of *Siren: Sex Industry Rights and Education Network*, the New Zealand Prostitutes' Collective's national magazine, warned readers about 'designer rapists' who paid for services with cheques and then promptly cancelled them. The editors condemned these men as 'blatant thieves and rapists' who 'never intended to pay for your time'.[20] Their emphasis on these men as rapists aligns with anthropologist Sophie Day's ethnographic studies of sex workers in London from 1986–1991. Day highlighted a 'broad "inclusive" definition of rape' among sex workers, which included physical assaults, cheques that bounced, and clients covertly removing a condom.[21]

Our discussion of rape also highlights how oral history provided Kate with a forum to condemn suggestions that sex workers have foregone the right to refuse consent by working in the industry and, conversely, that it is not possible to consent to sex work. Kate's analysis of abolitionist views on sex work reflects a clear departure from the radical feminist ideas she held as a member of a lesbian feminist community with separatist tendencies in the early 1980s. When questioned about her past views on sex work as a member of this community, she replied:

> At that age, I would've thought that sex work was really exploitative and terrible. Well, I don't know, actually; maybe I was young enough not to really know that. But as a radical feminist in the next couple of years, I definitely would've thought that sex work was a terrible thing and that it was really harmful to women, and that it was men paying to maybe enslave women, and force women to do things against their will.[22]

Kate's perspective changed when she became friends with women who worked in parlours, and who described sex work as a lucrative job where they felt empowered. Kate remembered adopting this latter stance when she started sex work several years later. She described having 'a bit of a feminist take on the whole thing. Like, getting heaps of money from these guys and stuff and putting in minimum effort'.

Kate also had experience with being on the margins of the separatist movement. At other times in the interview, she described struggling to reconcile her attraction to men while identifying as lesbian in a community that opposed opposite-sex relations. Kate established a support group for bisexual women when she returned to Wellington in the late 1980s. She described it as 'a funny time' when other women confided in her about their secret sexual liaisons with men and there were signs outside women's dances that read 'bisexuals fuck off'. 'People were quite anti; it wasn't very nice'. While Kate felt protected by having a woman partner, and 'at least I got to be in a lesbian relationship', she was attuned to the existence and consequences of biphobia and ostracism within the community.

Kate's assessment of abolitionist views on sex work not only reflects her defence of sex work as a legitimate occupation but also her opposition to transphobia. She explained, 'And then, of course, that's all tied up with being anti-trans. TERF and SWERF! It's so awful, some of my old friends are involved in that shit now. Some people I was really close to. It sucks.' The acronym TERF (Trans-Exclusionary Radical Feminist) refers to feminists who oppose trans rights and reject any acknowledgement of trans women as women, while SWERF (Sex Worker-Exclusionary Radical Feminist) refers to feminists who oppose sex work as a form of oppression against cisgender women. Her emphasis on some radical feminists' rejection of sex workers' abilities to consent to sex once again highlights her departure from these ideas.

My second interviewee, Frankie, also offers important insights into how oral history can provide new perspectives on changing understandings of consent in New Zealand's past. Frankie grew up in a small town in the central North Island, which she described as 'steeped in this quiet racism, homophobia and sexism'. She remembered having little awareness of sex education or sexuality until the age of sixteen when she met another teenager who identified as bisexual. It was 'a real moment of awakening for me in terms of sexuality' when she realised 'you didn't have to be gay or straight, you could be both and that was okay'. Prior to starting sex work in 2004, Frankie had close proximity to the sex industry through her work at a major adult entertainment club in downtown Auckland from the age of 18 in 1997. The job enabled her to achieve 'autonomy and independence that I wouldn't have been able to have any other way'. She earned enough money to spend her days with her seven-month-old daughter, hire a babysitter overnight, and return home at 3am 'with these really engorged breasts ready to feed her again'.

While she achieved financial freedom, Frankie struggled with patrons' lack of respect for her bodily autonomy, which became a main factor for her leaving the strip club and moving into parlour work. She explained:

> I was having a period of time where I was struggling with dancing. Sometimes you just had enough. You know, when you put yourself on a stage you're there, and you're subjected to criticism, and it can be really hard on someone who's really young. And especially then being naked was considered implicit [sighs] … how do I say this? You may not be giving consent, and we definitely weren't giving consent, but the men consider it implicit consent because you're naked. So, in reality, you're dealing with sexual assault every night. And I found that really hard after a period of time that these men, no matter how many times I said, 'You can't touch me, you can't touch my vagina', that these men would do that. And it's quite shocking. And yes, you could get them kicked out of the club, but they always got a warning first. So, they essentially had an opportunity to grab your pussy before anything would happen. And these guys would do that, and they considered it okay. The worst were the groups because you get men around naked women and the testosterone. I had breast implants when I was nineteen, and that really upped the ante in terms of harassment because once you have them men and women – because they're not, in quotation marks, 'real' – they would just grab them. But you just had men grab you by the breasts, or you'd walk past and they'd slide a hand between your thighs, or I know very few dancers who haven't had someone all of a sudden try to stick his fingers

inside you wherever they can get to. I think a lot of this for me, and whether you include this or not is up to you, but I developed an eating disorder. So, I ended up with anorexia. And I still experienced it. And in my head, it'll be like, 'Do you not see how frail I am?' It was kind of like I was breaking, and I was mirroring this on the outside, and it used to still happen. I found that to be a really tough time. And that was when I was in my twenties. Yeah. And if you asked them, they'd be like, 'No, I didn't sexually assault her!' But it's still what was happening.

Frankie's testimony demonstrates how oral history offers an important space to reclaim agency over her body and to contest suggestions that working in the adult entertainment industry equated implied consent. This was most clear when she described customers' unrelenting sexual assault, through groping and attempted digital penetration. Frankie's emphasis on customers' refusal to acknowledge or accept that their actions constituted sexual assault, despite her protests and visible fragility as a consequence of anorexia, highlights nuances in histories that emphasise progressive attitudes towards women's civil liberties, especially in the field of sex work. Her interview also highlighted the complexities of consent she experienced when she worked in a massage parlour:

I can vaguely remember my first day [in a massage parlour] and being like, 'Oh God, what do I do?' I remember the guy asking me to give him oral sex, and I said, 'No, I don't do that' [laughs]. Like, I didn't even know that I had to [laughs]. I was just so naïve [laughs]. I knew I had to have sex, but I was just a bit clueless, I think. And then everything I learnt, I learnt from other women who were working there. Like the ones who said, 'Check for the condom because some of them will take it off'. Just like the little bits and pieces to try and help protect you because you're really not taught. So, you'd give them a massage, and then you know at some point you'd have sex. For me, there was something freeing about the fact that I was no longer fighting over consent. Like, I'd agreed to have sex with this person. I probably didn't understand certain things, like that I could say 'no'. I knew that legally, we could say, 'No, we didn't want to see someone', but that's really frowned upon when you're working in a brothel. So, you did. There were people I wouldn't see but it was usually because I'd had an experience with them that was concerning, and so then I wouldn't ... NZPC [New Zealand Prostitutes' Collective] are great. I am no longer terrified of them; I think they do amazing work. And there's just so much that you would get from them that you would never get from your managers in the parlours. Like, I've been stealthed, that's happened twice. Just things that were happening that seemed to happen a lot. And it was kind of like, 'the stuff is gonna happen to you', so you kind of knew some things might happen. But now things are changing where it's like, 'No, that is rape'. It doesn't matter if you consented to go into that room with that person, if they take that condom off and they penetrate you, they're raping you. Because you did not give permission for that. If they don't pay you, just all of those things. 'Cause you could be put in some scary situations. If there are red flags, I do not see a client because I work here on my own. I also understand that I'm privileged in the way that I work and the business that I've built that to turn down a client is no problem for me. I'm really lucky in that respect. I really feel for the women and the men out there who are taking bookings with risky people. Just because you've got rent to pay, you've got kids to feed, you've got yourself to feed. You know, it can be a really tough world out there.

Frankie's narrative speaks to the limitations of consent in some massage parlours that prevailed even after most aspects of sex work were decriminalised in 2003. The lack of advice from management and the unspoken policy against declining clients shed light on the external pressures that stopped women from being able to refuse consent. These are, of course, in addition to the financial barriers that meant not everyone was in a position to turn down business.

Frankie's testimony also reflects a shift in attitudes towards sexual assault against people employed in the sex industry. Her comment that 'you kind of knew some things might happen' speaks to how the severity of sexual assault was downplayed both within and outside of sex work. Frankie did not file police reports or tell anyone about being assaulted at the time, including instances when clients removed the condom without her consent. It is perhaps not surprising considering the prejudice against sex workers, and how rape complainants' sexual histories were exposed in court as apparent evidence of their consent. Her testimony therefore reflects her present awareness of the support and advocacy that the NZPC would be able to offer. She had previously described the NZPC office on Karangahape Road as 'the most terrifying place I've ever been to. I was so nervous! And I remember going, "Oh my God, okay, what if someone sees me?"'

I ended all interviews by asking narrators how they would want the history of sex work in Aotearoa to be remembered. Frankie's final reflection highlights how interviews offer space for narrators to contest derogatory stereotypes. She explained:

I guess I should only speak for me; the negative is a fraction of what I experience. I have so many really great experiences. In fact, for me usually a booking that's not that good is just because it was a bit tedious, or we didn't really click so it was a bit harder work. Yeah, none of the really tough stuff. I'm pretty lucky. But what I've found in the time that I've been in the industry is that I've met just so many amazing people, like great morals, great values, highly educated; ones that aren't highly educated are often still very intelligent. You know, maybe haven't had the opportunities. We've all gone into the industry for different reasons. But we're all in it together, and it's just been in so many ways such an honour.[23]

Frankie's assessment of the privilege of working with people in the industry can be read as a resistance against stereotypes that belittle sex workers. It is telling that the qualities Frankie listed – morals, values and intelligence – directly contrast with negative depictions of sex workers that have prevailed since the nineteenth century. She described the curiosity of individuals who, seemingly for their own entertainment, pose questions such as, 'What's the worst thing that's happened to you?' This behaviour underscores the harmful perception that sex industry workers are somehow less entitled to safety and protection. By placing emphasis on her former colleagues, she was perhaps aiming to challenge these perceptions and underscore the severity of the violence they endured at work. While Frankie dismissed such curiosity by concluding, 'We're like that, people are like that. We like to know stuff', her recount also indicated a sense of frustration that clients, friends and acquaintances would enquire about potentially emotionally devastating encounters to satisfy their intrigue. Anna Green has highlighted the significance of emotions when interpreting oral history interviews, which offer insights into narrators' past and present cultural expectations.[24] There is a clear disconnect between Frankie's calm explanation and her admission that 'I used to find that brutal [laughs]'.

Together, my interviews demonstrate that oral history can significantly challenge dominant historical narratives by engaging with intimate and difficult topics. Narrators' raw memories and sensitive reflections illuminate the nuances in histories of sex, consent and gender in Aotearoa. There are important parallels in how Kate and Frankie located themselves in a community of sex workers. They emphasised making an active choice to undertake sex work and the solidarity they felt with their peers. In doing so, they demonstrated how oral history also serves as a platform for narrators to reject the notion that nudity or involvement in the sex industry implies consent, and to assert that sex workers deserve the same protection as people in other industries. Although this should be obvious, the emphasis placed by the narrators on their rights, and on recounting their struggles to protect the boundaries they've set over their bodies, highlights the necessity of explicitly addressing this point. The interviews that feature in this chapter took place at a time when discussions of consent were at the fore. They were also part of a larger project with a historian who has received approval from the NZPC and takes a sex worker rights approach that values and respects sex workers' agency.[25] All these factors have a hand in determining the ways narrators remember and reflect on their pasts.

11

Ted, Margaret and Sue too

DEAN BROUGHTON

My name is Susan. I was born in 1961 and I was adopted. My father was a ship jumper, he would have been here in 1960, I think it would have been, yep that's right, so I was adopted. I always knew I was adopted, my parents who adopted me, Gladys and Bill, always told me. I knew right from when I was little, and I used to think more about who my mother was and whether I looked like her or who did I look like sort of thing.[1]

The opening words in this interview reveal a hidden history. The connection between closed stranger adoption, ship jumping, and compulsory deportation has never been formally identified or written about in New Zealand and this chapter shows how the oral narrative can direct our attention to neglected or silenced aspects of the past. In the preface to *Remembering*, Anna Green and Megan Hutching write 'unless spoken words are published, these accounts of the past are never heard'.[2] Almost 20 years on, Sue's interview shows how some stories from the past will only come to light because of oral history research.

WHY ORAL HISTORY?

The interview with Sue that follows was recorded for my PhD research about 'ship jumpers' in New Zealand. It is particularly interesting because Sue's narrative is the only way I could have learnt about one of the unacknowledged effects of the deportation of ship jumpers – that is, adoption could be a consequence. Prior to the interview with Sue, I had obtained written testimonies of families being torn apart and children left behind but found no mention of adoption. Sue's story casts a new light on what ship jumping can entail when combined with the actions of the government, decisions made by the courts and the police, and society as a whole. Here is an example of how the oral narrative allows us to uncover forgotten and silenced history.

SOME SOCIAL CONTEXT

Ship jumping

Between 1945 and 1970, thousands of British seafarers illegally jumped ship in New Zealand. It was a back door method of entry that avoided normal immigration procedures.[3] Seafarers jumped to begin a new life but risked arrest and deportation.[4] Before 1950, captured ship jumpers received a fine and a one-month prison sentence, but on release were free to remain. Ship jumping increased threefold after World War II and developed into an immigration strategy as seafarers were willing to suffer a month in prison, safe in the knowledge they could stay on release. The government decided to close the loophole and, in 1950, introduced compulsory deportation as a deterrent.[5] From 1951 British seafarers could no longer jump ship, serve a month in prison, then legally remain in New Zealand – instead, they became part of an illegal immigrant group.

Adoption

Closed stranger adoption is part of New Zealand's social history – 80,000 children were legally adopted between 1955 and 1985.[6] While the 1955 Adoption Act did not legislate for a complete break between the birth and adoptive families, in practice, closed adoption meant that mothers waived all rights to their child.

At the time, there was a stigma around having a child out of marriage and unmarried pregnant women were sometimes abandoned by the child's father and did not receive support from their own families. Lack of financial support, in particular, the difficulty obtaining maintenance payments from the fathers was a contributing factor in the high rates of adoption. By the 1970s, with the introduction of a Domestic Purposes Benefit, the widespread availability of contraception, changing attitudes, and an increase in fathers ordered to pay maintenance, the number of adoptions declined.[7]

Access to adoption information in New Zealand changed when the Adult Adoption Information Act 1985 came into force on 1 September 1986. Adopted people over the age of 20 were now able to request their original birth certificate, showing the name of their birth mother and in some cases, that of their birth father. This also meant that they could apply for assistance to make contact.[8]

THE INTERVIEW

Sue is married to one of my work colleagues. He told me Sue's father was a ship jumper. (Oral historians can find their sources in the unlikeliest of contexts.)

Sue is 62 years old and works as a registered nurse, a job that means a lot to her: 'I just always wanted to be a nurse, since I was a little girl and I did and I am. I just enjoy looking after people and caring for people.'[9] Our interview took place in a private room on the tenth floor of my workplace. Coincidentally, the room I chose looked over the Pipitea, King's and Glasgow Wharfs where the ship Sue's father jumped from would have berthed. From this vantage point I could clearly see where the open high wrought iron gates would have been as he walked off the wharves and crossed Custom House Quay to disappear into the city of Wellington, intent on starting a new life.

I began by asking Sue to describe her life in her own words. Following her introductory statement, she began to talk about how she set about finding her birth parents. The excerpt below also provides an interesting insight into the adoption laws at that time.

> So then in 1985 I think it was, when the law changed and um, so it was easier to try and find your birth mother and birth father. So, Gladys said to me, did I want to find out who my biological parents were and so I said, yes, I did. So I applied … I filled out forms and things and they got back to me, and I had to go and see someone and get some counselling before they would tell me anything, really. They gave me a copy of my original birth certificate, which was amazing because it had a name on it, which was me. Donna. I was called Donna and it had my biological mother's name on it, Margaret [surname] but it didn't have my father's, my biological father's name on it. So I was always a bit curious about that to start with and so from there I thought, 'Right, what can I do?' I went to, now where did I go, was it Births, Deaths and Marriages? It might have been, yes. I had to do that because I knew she would probably be married so I (laughs) went off to Birth, Deaths and Marriages. I found her and she was living in Ohakune. I discovered that. Sorry I have skipped a bit. I looked up the electoral rolls and I found she was living in Ohakune. I had her husband's name of course because I had the marriage certificate, and I had a sister and a brother as well.[10]

Sue's delight and excitement at remembering how she felt at the time was obvious, particularly when she remembered how getting her birth certificate made her feel. I asked Sue why she only looked for her parents in 1985 and if she had thought about it earlier. She replied that she 'had kind of thought about it but I, yeah, I think it was all a bit hard, everything was hard, and it was the law that you couldn't'.[11]

Sue went on to explain about meeting Margaret.

> So, I thought, OK, I will write her a letter, so I wrote a letter to Margaret, and I said I was completing a family tree that I – and I believed we were related. And where I was born, which was St Helen's in Wellington in 1961 … I kept thinking if she was going to write back and will I hear anything. And sure enough, I got home, there was the mail and there was a letter from her. And I was so excited. I ran in the house to show my husband and I fell over on the floor, on my hip and I was lying on the floor waving the letter and saying, 'I got a letter from Margaret.' In the letter she said she was happy to hear from me and had been wondering about me, she would love to meet me and all the rest of it and if I could give her a call. So I did that, and we had a good yak and organised for me to go up to see her with my husband. I think it was another couple of weeks away that was alright. So we went up and met her and that was quite an emotional time.[12]

It is at this point in the interview that Sue recalls a negative aspect of meeting members of her biological family.

> My sister was there, and Margaret's husband was there, and they were really welcoming and my sister. I mean half-sister. I found it quite stressful when we met my aunt, Margaret's sister because she had five children and everyone was there and they all – I just remember feeling really self-conscious. They were all just looking at me kind of – like it felt, that felt a little bit uncomfortable. It was these people saying how I looked like Margaret but I never thought I really did look like her. I couldn't really see it.[13]

I asked if there was any talk of her father when she met her mother.

> Anyway, while I was there, I had asked Margaret about my biological father. She was talking with her sister, and they had quite a few photos, family photos and my aunt had a photo of my biological father, Ted, which was really good. It was a photo of him with another couple … They gave me the photo so I could go and take copies of it and all the rest of it. When I saw the photo, I thought, Oh my

gosh, and I thought I looked more like Ted than Margaret, I just wanted to look like somebody in a familiar kind of way. That was quite an exciting moment.

I asked Margaret about some things to do with Ted and – I am just trying to remember. She told me he had lived in England, had jumped ship and that he had been in Mount Crawford [prison], several months, three months, something like that. Yeah, that's what she told me. That they had met, can't remember exactly how they met but I am pretty sure it was in a dance club, because Margaret had been waitressing, that sort of thing and that's how they met and they did, and got on really well, hence I am here. Must have been a fun time.[14]

The *New Zealand Police Gazette* and a social welfare report on Sue's adoption provide some context on Ted's jumping ship and meeting Margaret.

In 1961, British merchant seafarer Charles Edward Martin, jumped ship in Wellington. Charles, commonly known as Ted, was born in England and joined the British Merchant Navy as a steward in the late 1950s.[15] He was 24 when he jumped ship, with four trips to New Zealand on Port Company ships under his belt.[16] Ship jumping was a criminal offence and, as a result, any reported ship jumper was noted in the *Police Gazette*.[17]

On his fourth visit to New Zealand, in 1961, Ted met 17-year-old Margaret in a Wellington club. Margaret had left school at 15 and completed a commercial course but was working as a waitress when she started going out with Ted. Margaret's parents had separated when she was young, and she had experienced an unhappy childhood. Ted and Margaret were a striking couple. Margaret was often described as pretty with dark brown hair, slim build, fair skin and neat features. Ted, with his fair hair and sky-blue eyes, was a handsome-looking man.[18] By early 1961, the couple's relationship had developed and Margaret discovered she was pregnant. Ted and Margaret's discussions about the future are unknown but we do know that Ted decided to jump ship to remain in New Zealand.[19] His new life was short-lived, however, as on 1 March 1961 the police arrested him. Ted spent three months in Wellington's Mount Crawford prison before being deported on 23 May 1961 on the *Port Huon* bound for England.[20] Ted never returned to New Zealand.

In November 1961, at the St Helen's maternity hospital in Wellington 18-year-old Margaret gave birth to a daughter she named Donna. A social welfare report described Susan as 'normal and healthy with masses of straight dark hair.'[21] Twenty-two days later Susan was adopted by Gladys and Bill. Margaret, on her own with no family support and no contact from Ted (who had rekindled a relationship with an old girlfriend in England), believed adoption was the best chance for her newborn baby.[22]

I asked Sue what she thought Margaret's attitude towards Ted was.

> Well, she was little bit, I felt like she was a little bit angry with him still because when he left, when he was deported, he had written to her and – I am trying to remember – he had a girlfriend before he came to New Zealand, before he came away and that's who he ended up with when he went back to England and ended up marrying. I never really pursued a lot of information from her about things because of that. I didn't want to upset her. I was very lucky to have that photo.[23]

Sue then continued with an explanation of why Margaret chose to put her up for adoption:

> Because she was going to be on her own. She never said much about it. I mean she couldn't, she didn't have the money at that time. She lived with her mum and my aunty, her sister and they didn't have a lot of money. They were not well off one little bit.[24]

I asked Sue about her relationship with Margaret.

> It was sometimes good and then sometimes it wasn't. Initially like any adoption when you first find your mother or your father it's like you go through that honeymoon phase and everything is wonderful and then things collapse and sometimes they don't. In our situation, I found things were OK for a while. Like she wanted me to call her 'Mum' and I didn't – I feel she was not my mum. I mean she is and she isn't. I know that sounds awful, cos to her I was still that child … but I found it really hard. And I did call her Mum but not a lot, and when I did it was [for] her not for me. We kept in touch mainly through phone calls and writing letters in those days. It was the eighties. Maybe we saw each other seven or eight times.[25]

> She always wondered about me, always thought about me. The last time I saw her before she died, she was pretty sick with ovarian cancer. She said she called me Donna because that was a popular song at the time, and she used to sing and hear it on the radio and think of me. So that was like, Oh my god. It was the Ritchie Valens one, so the funny thing is now, when I hear it, I think of her. That's quite weird. She passed away in 2014. The same year Gladys passed away. Within seven months. Well, it was a pretty tough year.[26]

TED, MARGARET AND SUE TOO

At Margaret's funeral, Sue met more of her extended family. She then explained how she found her father. She had a photograph and knew his full name and that he had been in Mount Crawford prison so she rang the prison to see if they had any records that could help her. She was fortunate and found someone who could help and gave her some dates and Ted's home address in Kent at the time of his imprisonment.

> So, I thought, I know, I will go to the Wellington library because I knew they had English phone books, and I thought, English people don't move around much. So, I went through the phone books and found a C.E.P. Martin in Kent.[27]

Sue's excitement returned as she discussed her search for Ted.

> I thought I wanted to ring him but thought, How will I do that? My next-door neighbour … was English, and he had a strong English accent. [He] agreed. He rang from here … and he pretended to be a carpet salesman or vacuum cleaner salesman or something like that … he came over one evening and rang the number and said, 'Oh hello, Ted' or used his full name and it was and he made a bit of a spiel about what he was selling and Ted wasn't too interested and hung up. So, I got in a bit of state and thought, Well that was him. What do I do now? I really wanted to ring him back so I thought I would leave it a couple of days, so he didn't link with [my neighbour's call].

> A few days later I rang him and Ted answered. And I said, 'Hi, is that Ted Martin? My name is Sue.' I can't exactly remember what I said at the start but I carried on and said I was building a family tree, I was from New Zealand and your name has come up and then he hung up on me. And I thought, Oh, he knows something here, and so I thought, Oh, I will ring back on the pretence we got cut off or something. I rang back a few times and the phone were engaged, so it was clear he knew something and that he had taken the phone off the hook. I was a bit upset. Because things had gone quite well meeting Margaret, I thought Ted would be the same, and would go OK. So, I just thought that was that then. I thought, I will just forget about it, so I left things, and I left them for quite a few years. This was around 1986 or 1987.[28]

I asked Sue if Margaret knew she was looking for Ted. 'I never said anything, I kept it to myself because I thought she was just a little bit off, so I didn't want to go there. So, I left it at that.'[29]

After waiting a couple of years Sue decided to try again. This time she wrote to Ted.

> [I]t must have been a week or two weeks after that the phone rang and my husband answered. And he goes, 'There's someone who wants to talk to you.' It was Margaritte, who was Ted's wife. She was the girlfriend he had left behind. She was just so lovely and said Ted didn't know about me, but I knew Margaret said he did, and the social welfare report also made it clear he did, plus he hung up on me, which suggested to me he did. Um, but I didn't say anything about that and never have. It was lovely. We talked about Ted, and I found out I had a half-brother and two half-sisters over in the UK and was really happy about it, and she held no grudges. Just lovely. Then she asked me if I wanted to talk to Ted. I did. I can't even remember what – I see now, I must have been a bit nervous. We kind of just had a general chat. We just had a general chat, then we kept in touch, writing.[30]

Sue's life then became complicated and about 10 years later, when she and her husband were travelling to the UK for a holiday, she resumed contact with Ted.

> I ended up writing a letter to his old address and … he wrote back, which was lovely, but the sad thing was Margaritte had died in 2006 … Then my half-sister and I started emailing, keeping in touch and all the rest of it. So, we went over, and I arranged to meet my sister Jenny. She was going to pick us up from the station. She was so lovely and chatty. It was really nice, it was quite strange. We went back to her place. I met one of my half-brothers' wives. She was there, he wasn't. He was still getting used to the fact he had a half-sister and was not ready to meet me. Still haven't met him, mind you. I met my nieces and my nephew, so we had a bit of time, a couple of hours yakking away, getting to know each other.
>
> Then Ted was going to arrive and I just remember the front door opening and closing and Jenny saying, 'That's Dad' and I thought, Ooh what's he going to look like? It was exciting but scary at the same time and I remember I kind of stood to the side so that when he came in I would see him first and get a bit of a visual. And so I sort of did and he walked in the door and he was just so lovely. He said, 'Sue' and he put his arms out for me and I just went there and we had a big hug. And I didn't cry. I thought I might but I didn't. It was a really lovely moment, as it were, and then we sat down and we were talking and just got on really well.[31]

I asked Sue if this if this was different to her meeting with Margaret. She recalled that it was very different because with Ted's family she felt 'more like I was home. I could relate more to them because of my upbringing, which was quite different to the way Margaret lived.'[32]

After meeting Ted and the extended family, Sue visited them again a few times until Ted's death in 2020. I asked Sue if Ted ever said much about being in New Zealand or his relationship with Margaret, but she said he did not talk about that much.

During the interview, I asked Sue if she could reflect on her mother's experience of adoption. Sue quickly corrected me and said, 'You mean Margaret'. I said yes. Possibly there is some connection here to the earlier comments about Sue not wanting to call Margaret 'Mum'. Sue continued: 'I have no doubt it was really tough. She said she … was able to have me for, I think she said, 10 days before they took me away … she did breastfeed me, and I just can't imagine; it must have been awful. I mean … I don't know if it was worse to have your baby taken away right at birth or be able to have your child for 10 days then have it taken away. I don't know which is worse. It's cruel.'[33]

THE ROLE OF ORAL HISTORY

What does Sue's narrative tell us about her relationship to her past? Oral history interviews bring a subjective reality that is sometimes absent from written sources. Portelli argues that 'the unique and precious element which oral sources force upon the historian and which no other sources possess in equal measure is the speaker's subjectivity'.[34] Sue's organisation of her narrative reveals a lot about her view of her history. When asked to begin her life narrative Sue begins with her adoption. She provides little discussion of life with her adoptive parents, a life that provided a stable upbringing and opportunities to succeed. Rather, she begins by describing how she found her birth parents.

The contrast between the fortunes of Sue's two birth parents is noted and is reflected in Sue's gravitation towards Ted and his family. Sue's easy acceptance of Ted is interesting, considering he might be seen as the guiltier of the two parties. Ted was the criminal ship jumper who never returned to find Margaret or ask after his child. Even when Ted denies he knew she existed, Sue is still very accepting. Sue places no blame throughout the interview for either parent, in fact, she expresses sympathy for Margaret. Sue invites little discussion about Ted as a ship jumper. Any talk on that subject was mostly instigated by me.

Portelli describes how some narratives contain shifts in the velocity of narration.[35] An example of this is duration. Sue spends much more time describing difficulties and her feelings about Margaret compared to Ted. She elaborates on the challenges of calling Margaret 'Mum' and recounts feeling uncomfortable when Margaret's family tried to find physical resemblances, but she delights in describing how she thought she looked like Ted. The length of time and tone Sue attributes to each is significant.

Sue's interview provides a new interpretation of the consequences of ship jumping in New Zealand. At first, I thought that was all the interview was about, but it has also provided a new narrative on the history of adoption in New Zealand. Sue's narrative is a rich account of her relationship with adoption and illustrates how she negotiated and interpreted her life as an adopted child.

12

'I remember, I was there': The experiences of children in institutional care

ELIZABETH WARD

In his seminal article 'What makes oral history different' Alessandro Portelli argued that oral sources are necessary for understanding the history of those in society who have little power.[1] This is particularly true when dealing with the history of care institutions. Those who ran these organisations sometimes left behind a considerable amount of documentation which can tell historians much about these establishments, but the financial accounts, minutes and official reports show these from the perspective of those who held power. By recording oral histories with those who lived in the care institutions, historians can provide a balance to the official documents.[2] More importantly, oral histories provide the perspective of those in these establishments who had little power. Understanding the experience of those who lived in care institutions contributes to a deeper, and richer, understanding of these organisations. It provides new angles for interpreting the official papers and gives another perspective for understanding the history of institutional care.

In 2014 I studied the All Saints' Children's Home, an Anglican-run children's home in Palmerston North, a provincial city in New Zealand. The home was opened in 1906 and closed in 1964. Establishments of this kind were once common throughout New Zealand: in 1925 there were 51 such homes.[3] These institutions were nearly always run by faith-based groups and differ from government-run residential homes in that children were more often than not placed in them by their caregivers. Guardianship was often retained by the family of origin. These children have been described as 'imagined orphans', they still had family living, but for whatever reason this family felt unable to care for them at the time they were placed in care.[4] If the Child Welfare Office, the government department charged with the care of children, was involved, it seems to have been on an informal basis.[5] These Homes were for children whose families were experiencing some form of breakdown; they were not places of incarceration or correction.

This chapter will explore the ways in which oral histories with two former child residents at the All Saints' Children's Home can give historians a different perspective on the history of an institution. One of the reasons All Saints' Children's Home was a good residential home to study was that much of the official documentation of the Trust that ran the Home survived. The official documents contain information about the children in the Home, but this is from the perspective of those in charge of the children. These documents may record what those who ran the Home wanted people to know, not necessarily what was really happening.

The two oral histories explored here provide a window into children's experience within the Home. Both interviews reveal common themes, particularly regarding the relationships between the children.[6] They also offer insight into aspects not easily accessible through official documents, such as experiences of violence and corporal punishment.

SOME BACKGROUND TO THE INTERVIEWS

All of my study participants had lived in the Home at some point from the early 1940s until it closed in 1964. The oldest participant was in her mid-eighties, the youngest were in their early sixties. Through advertising in the local paper and word of mouth I was able to find 12 former residents to interview.[7] I interviewed all those who came forward, so no selection process was necessary. The interviews took place face-to-face, apart from one, which was recorded over the telephone. Due to the fact that either I or the interviewees had to travel in order to meet, the majority of the interviews were conducted in one sitting. They range in length from around an hour to over four hours. Some of the people I interviewed were only in the Home for a short period, maybe a year or two, and others spent their whole childhood in some form of care.

Although the interviews focused on a specific part of the former residents' lives, I began by asking the participants about their birth and family circumstances. This proved to be a good starting place as it often revealed the reasons they were placed in the Home. I had prepared a set of questions, which were drawn up as part of the ethics application required to undertake research of this nature.[8] I used these as a guide, preferring to encourage the interviewee to create their own narrative. By doing this, I hoped to understand what aspects of their experience in the Home were most important to them. The questions were only asked when a prompt was needed, as a way of ensuring that similar topics were covered across all the participants equally.

THE PARTICIPANTS

The interviews explored here are with Howard and Christine, two people who lived at All Saints' Children's Home in the years running up to its closure. They were among the few participants who spent more than a few months in the Home and both were resident during the same time period.

The last years of the Home, which are described in these interviews, may not have been typical of the entire life of the organisation. From the late-1950s to the closure of the Home in 1964 the Trust Board that ran the Home struggled to find staff. There were four matrons between May 1961 and the closure of the Home in July 1964.[9] Furthermore, the minutes of the Board show they felt the Home was dealing with more unruly children during this period.[10] In 1963, the Home Management Committee issued its last annual report, which stated that it had been a particularly difficult year because of the number of emotionally disturbed children in the Home.[11] From the official documents it seems that the Home was struggling to maintain staff and order among the children. It is against this background that the two participants describe what it was like to live there.

Howard had been in the Anglican care system since birth. His mother had been abandoned by his father and she felt unable to care for him. He arrived at All Saints' from an Anglican-run infants' home sometime in 1957. He left the Home just before its closure in 1964 and went to another Anglican-run home for boys. Christine entered All Saints' in 1961 having been moved from another children's home which had closed. Her father had placed Christine and her brother in care after their mother left the family. She then transferred to the 'family home' that the Trust opened when the All Saints' Children's Home closed. This was a house and had 'parents'. The 'family home' attempted to recreate a regular family living situation and was viewed by many as progressive compared with the traditional, antiquated institution style of children's homes that had gone before.[12]

Howard and Christine provide narratives that are very personal to their experiences, yet intertwined and deep-rooted within societal culture and the structure of the Home.[13] Their experiences had many common themes which overlap with other narratives about what life was like for those who were children in care institutions.[14]

LIVING AT ALL SAINTS' CHILDREN'S HOME

The building and what it was like to live in evoked strong memories from both participants. Christine commented on the size of the building:

> It was a big dormitory. The girls were in one and boys were across the hall in the other … and I remember all the beds all in a row and the matron and the staff could walk down the middle between the beds …

> It was built for more children, there were probably more children earlier on, there must have been 'cause they were big and empty … it was emptying out for sure.[15]

One question that all interviewees were asked was about the temperature in the house, whether they remember the cold, or hadn't noticed. Christine responded: 'When you're a kid you don't notice the cold. But I know my brother used to get that boiler going and going for the hot water and the warmth.'[16]

For Howard, feeling the cold was a strong memory:

> There was no carpet. I remember linoleum being put in. I remember the smell of it from the sun. It was cold, very cold. When you got into bed at night you got in a position and stayed in that position because just moving slightly was very, very cold. They put in central heating in the dining room. They ran it once or twice and diesel went up or something and they stopped using it.[17]

These memories not only tell us about the form of heating and that it may not have been effective, but they also invoke the senses, which can act as a memory trigger.[18] Howard remembers that the Home had linoleum. He then connects the linoleum to the physical feeling of cold. Not only are we transported to the Home, with the smell of the linoleum as the sun shone on it, we are also told that the linoleum was cold. Howard used smell as memory aid to remember the cold he experienced.

Given the size of the building and the lack of staff, chores featured in both interviews, although Christine had fuller memories of the work the children undertook:

> My brother and I were some of the older children so we had a bit more responsibility, but it was always a fun place … my job was the sandwiches. Every

day after school I used to make 30 lunches for the next day at school. My brother and I talked about it not long ago and he had to do the boiler and get the boiler going for all the hot water and the heating.[19]

When it came to the routine of everyday life in the Home, both Christine and Howard remembered that the children had chores. However, Howard only remembered general things about the chores the children did together, whereas Christine was able to describe in detail what she and her brother did. She displays a certain amount of pride in her ability to do the tasks she was given, and her clear recall shows that the job was important to her and her sense of place in the Home. It has been argued that women tend to produce narratives that show their value in relation to the interdependencies within the groups they belong.[20] Here the pride that Christine displays is not so much in the capabilities she showed, but that she was an important part of the running of the Home – others depended on her. Her account also gives an insight into the way the children may have used the work they were given to generate a sense of belonging and usefulness.

Both Christine and Howard recalled the lack of their own clothing and possessions.

> **Christine**: Looking at some of my clothes I've got on there [referring to photos of herself as a child in the Home which were part of the interview], they were just all clothes that went through the wash …

Interviewer: They would have been donated mostly.

> Of course they were, all the clothes were just in a big bin, I remember and we just all shared the clothes.

Did you have any personal space to keep things?

> Not really, things would be taken a lot and I know my brother had a beautiful teddy bear. I will always remember that teddy bear. It was a big one and he wanted to take it to the Home but my Dad didn't want him to. He did take it to the Home and it just got destroyed and we were both so upset about it. You didn't really have anything of your own … we didn't have much, we lived with almost nothing.[21]

Howard recalls that when he 'was in the Home, they didn't have enough boys' clothes and I remember being forced to wear the girls' clothes, because there was nothing else to wear'. In response to a question about owning his own clothes, he said, 'No never, absolutely not, it was hand-me-downs and what have you ... first up, best dressed type thing.'[22]

The Trust's book of minutes does contain details about the children's clothing and possessions. However, these provide information about the clothing donations and the issues the Trust had with this. What the minutes cannot tell us is how the children felt about the clothing. Both Howard and Christine reflected on the way the clothing was shared and they both had negative memories attached to this practice. For Christine this was about how she looked in the photos, recognising that what she was given to wear was not chosen by her. For Howard there was an added layer in that he was forced to wear 'hand-me-downs' and clothes that were 'for girls'. The comments about not owning their clothes resonates in the context of them living 'in a Home' but not 'at home' with their families.

RELATIONSHIPS WITH OTHER CHILDREN

Moving on to their impression of security and control, Christine recalls:

> It seemed to have pretty good control, the matrons were quite strict, and seemed to have pretty good control. We all knew what we had to do, we all had our jobs to do, we were all disciplined ... I always think we were well fed and well looked after. That's what I always thought.[23]

Howard's memories are different:

> [in relation to a fight he had with another boy] 'Cause there was a structure, ok, he was a bit further up the pecking order than I. When we play fought, I could beat him, but when we had a real dingdong, he always gave me a hiding. And he decided he was going to give me a hiding one day and I had this steel bar and I threatened him with it and I said, '[Boy's name], if you come near me I'm going to hit you with this.' [The boy] wouldn't take no for an answer, he was a fairly determined young guy. He came forward and I just lashed out and hit him with it, 'cause I knew he was going to hurt me if he got hold of me.[24]

And again.

> At Brown House there was a big chunk of coal and he [another boy] was coming up the hill at the back of the building and he was coming up the hill towards

me where the toilets are, and there was a coal shed there in those days and he was going to give me a hiding. I said, '[Boy's name] if you come any closer, I am going to throw this.' I was a damn good shot. I got him right on the – bang he went over backwards …

I recall [mentions a girl], remember the old milk urns, well someone had turned that into a swing. Well, it was her turn and the other girl wouldn't get off and was over a bank. So [the first girl] got up there, untied the knot while the girl was on it. I think she had to be taken to hospital.[25]

When examining the official documents of the Trust, the children in All Saints' Children's Home mostly appear when they are seen as causing problems. The official documents provide very little insight into the relationships between the children in the Home, apart from when the children fought each other. This is where the oral histories provide significant information about how the children connected with one another and how they felt about day-to-day interactions and relationships. Christine rarely mentions other children in her narrative, apart from her brother. We can ascertain from the Home records that there were some long-term residents, but in the 1960s they were increasingly short term.

Throughout her interview the wider idea that Christine wants to convey is that she had a good upbringing in the Home. This could have shaped her memory and response to questions. When interviewing French women about their lives during the interwar period, Chanfrault-Duchet noticed a similar pattern, that the interviewees shaped their narratives according to what they believed about women's role in society.[26] Christine wants the listener to know that she felt well cared for, and she shapes her narrative to fit this. She then extends this to the other children in the Home, although she rarely mentions the other children by name.

However, Howard has quite a different perspective. He wants the listener to know that the Home was disorderly and the staff had little control over the children. His oral history is full of stories about the transience of the children at the Home. There is no hint of stability in the way he describes getting used to children just 'disappearing' and never being talked about after they had gone. Almost all Howard's narrative about other children involves boys, and in particular the way the social order of the boys was established, which he refers to as 'the pecking order'. Within this is the amount of violence that occurred among the boys, which maintained or disrupted the 'pecking order'. He talks about his own role in this, and towards the end of the interview is reflective, but points out that he had to survive among a group of children over whom he thinks the staff had little control. Howard paints a complex picture of interactions between the children, with an emphasis on the ways the children – the boys – sustained an order among themselves, as well as highlighting what he believes was an institution that was poorly run and often chaotic.

ACTIVITIES OUTSIDE THE HOME

In an attempt to give the children what was perceived as a 'normal' childhood, the authorities did make an effort to provide extracurricular activities. Being a Home run by the Anglican Church, Sundays were something that featured in both Christine and Howard's interviews.

Christine remembered that 'Sunday School was a big part of our life, going to All Saints Church … I was trying to think the other day how we all got to Sunday School and I can't really remember but I remember we went to All Saints all the time, every Sunday.'[27] Howard also mentioned All Saints: 'We initially went to All Saints Church, then I believe (a matron) had a falling out with All Saints Church … then we ended up going to St Oswald's.'[28]

The question about church attendance is an example of where the two narratives add substance to each other's recollections and offer a more complete picture to the official papers. Christine remembers that the children went to All Saints and Howard adds to this by introducing the idea that another church, St Oswald's, was where the children were taken for Sunday School. Both of these are probable. All Saints was the church that founded the Home. However, St Oswald's was a church planted by All Saints in the late 1950s,[29] and this church was somewhat closer to the Home.[30] The official records provide a third perspective that ties the two oral histories together. In November 1963 the Matron's Day Book has a note that says, 'all children going to Sunday School at All Saints much better'.[31] This suggests that for some time the children had been split between two different Sunday Schools. Given that Howard remembers St Oswald's as being where he went to Sunday School and Christine All Saints, this fits with the idea that some of the children had been going to St Oswald's and some to All Saints.

The Home authorities also seemed to favour Boy Scouts and Girl Guides as extracurricular activities. In Palmerston North these clubs had strong ties to All Saints Church. Christine was a Brownie:

> We all went to Brownies, then I went to Girl Guides, at the church, All Saints …
> We were definitely encouraged to go to those, which we did, well I know I did.
> And my brother went to Scouts and he did things like that until he left as well.[32]

In response to a question about whether he went to Cubs and Scouts, Howard replied that he did not, but added, 'In saying that, [a matron] was a Cub leader and some of the kids [mentions one] went to Cubs there … but it wasn't consistent, it wasn't for everyone.'[33]

The Trust owned a holiday home near Palmerston North called Brown House where the children were taken for holidays over the summer period. Christine and Howard remember these holidays fondly. Christine recalled:

> We still went to Browns [sic] House every year, we had wonderful holidays, Browns [sic] House was a wonderful place. I remember us older kids going for huge walks along the creeks, right up the back of the hills looking for cockabillies and stuff like that. And it was a great place. We all had to do our work there, we all had to help and we all had to go up and down that back hill at night so we would be tired when we went to bed.[34]

Howard also loved going there: 'I don't know any of the kids who didn't. We used to go for long walks all over the place and sometimes we would break into different groups and one group would contact the other by doing this [makes a loud noise]'.[35]

The annual holidays at Brown House were part of the rhythm of the life of the Home. The preparations for the holiday, the logistics of getting the children to the location and the renovations that were undertaken on the Home's building while the children were absent feature in the official papers. Another aspect that appears in the official papers is that the staff found going to Brown House somewhat onerous. It had no running water or electricity, and the staff felt that it was not a holiday for them; it was much more work than staying in the Home.[36] Yet Christine and Howard's memories express how much they loved these holidays. The official documents cannot give us this understanding of how happy the children were while at Brown House.

CORPORAL PUNISHMENT

The amount of physical discipline given to children is a common theme and memory of children who spent time in care.[37] Christine never mentioned being physically disciplined while in the home, but this was a strong theme of Howard's oral history. 'They used to wallop kids. And a wallop then was more like being shaken ... I lived in a certain amount of fear'.[38] And, referring to the man who drove him from All Saints to the Anglican Boys Home, 'He gave me such a kicking. I had never met this guy before'.[39] Talking about the principal at the school that the children were sent to, Howard noted, 'His concern was that his kids [that is, children from the Home] were turning up hungry, ill clothed and often marked from hidings'.[40]

The fact that Christine does not remember any corporal punishment is in line with her narrative of being well-cared for. Yet, Howard can offer a whole catalogue of ways in which he was beaten. He gives added weight to his testimony by saying that the principal of the school the children from the Home attended was concerned as well.[41]

When it came to corporal punishment, the official documents were almost silent.[42] Yet from Howard's oral history it seemed to be a common way of controlling the behaviour of the children.[43] It is possible that the Trust members, who made the official documents, did not want to record the levels or types of violence used to maintain discipline in detail. Although violence towards children was widely accepted in society during the 1960s, the Child Welfare Office, which was responsible for regulating the Home, was changing its attitudes towards corporal punishment at that time.[44] While it is also possible that corporal punishment was not thought noteworthy as it was so ordinary and 'everyday', those who ran the Home might have had motives for downplaying the extent they recorded violence used to control the children because they relied on government grants and community goodwill to keep the place functioning. It is worth noting that the Child Welfare Office had the authority to close a children's home if they felt the children were being mistreated, and that could have influenced the extent to which corporal punishment was documented.[45]

Portelli's point about oral history providing a voice to those who have little power is particularly pertinent for histories of care institutions. When the historian only accesses the institution through the official documents, they can, at best, discern what those in power wanted people to know. For this reason oral histories are an important addition to the archival material. They provide another perspective on the institution and give a voice to those who had the least power, the children. This leads to a deeper understanding of the institution, the way it was run and what it was like to live in the All Saints' Children's Home.

The daily rhythms, thought too ordinary to record in the official documents, were explained in the oral histories. The chores the children did, how they felt about their clothing and possessions, and physical features, like the temperature of the building, were all discussed. Aspects of the way the children were controlled and punished, which was barely covered in the official documents, and the enjoyment that the children got from the holidays at Brown House, were also revealed in the interviews. One facet that the official papers could not cover was the relationships between the children in the Home. In their interviews, both Howard and Christine provided me with an understanding of how the children interacted with, and were treated by, staff and other children.

Sometimes the oral histories openly contradicted each other. However, when the former residents' memories are understood as providing the meaning of an event rather than a description, this cannot be counted a disadvantage. By using oral history interviews as a research tool, historians can better understand both the events and the meaning of those events to those who experienced them. Such narratives bring a deeper and richer interpretation to the history of an institution.

13

Remembering the making of rural Huapai during the 1910s and 1920s

DEBORAH DUNSFORD

Huapai means 'good fruit' in te reo Māori and is the name of a rural settlement 28 kilometres north-west of Auckland City. However, this place name was not sourced from use by local Māori. It was created in 1913 by a syndicate of investors in the company, Northern Fruitlands Ltd, for a 4000-acre subdivision of plots named the Huapai Estate. The development consisted of small orchard lots and 'bush sections' aimed at city folk wanting an idyllic, orchard life free from the bustle of the city, an investment or a weekend getaway. The Huapai Estate was an early example of the continuing demand for small rural properties close to the amenities of the city. Today, in New Zealand, we call them lifestyle blocks.

Phyllis Fickling was born in Huapai in 1915. She was interviewed in 2000 as part of a book project for a history of the wider Kumeū district (including Huapai), and as a separate oral history project examining childhood experience there during the 1910s and 1920s.[1] In 2000, at 85 years old, she continued to live on the Fickling family property where she had grown up. Her interview showed her to have been a perceptive child observer of her family's day-to-day life, the development of the family land and of Huapai as a whole.

The historiography of rural New Zealand can be described as somewhat slim. Histories have often had a tight focus on a single sector of the rural economy.[2] Written memoirs and biographies have provided significant portrayals of the day-to-day rhythms of farming and rural family life.[3] However, only a very few people commit the story of their lives to paper. In contrast, the invitation to tell someone about their life over a few hours is accepted by many people. Interviewees are guided by questions but are in control of their stories, which can be informative, dramatic and humorous, often with an element of performance because they have been rehearsed so many times over a long life. Oral history reveals the stories of people who may have assumed their lives have been unexceptional and are of only passing interest to others. Theirs are the hidden stories that all too often remain out of the written record.

Oral histories can be seen to have made a significant contribution to our understanding of the lives of rural people and communities in New Zealand from the early twentieth century onwards. Certainly, oral accounts of farming, family life and rural community development have been at the heart of so many of New Zealand's local and regional histories. More recently, Ruth E. Low's accounts of the lives of drovers and shearers in New Zealand have used oral interviews as their primary sources.[4]

DEVELOPMENT AT HUAPAI

When interviewed, Phyllis Fickling vividly recalled her family life at Huapai. She especially recalled the hard day-to-day work of each of her parents, Bill and Emma Fickling. Her mother ran the large family household, which included a number of lodgers. 'For the life of me, I can't think how she managed it all,' was a sentiment of amazement Phyllis expressed repeatedly. Her tone conveyed her pride in her mother's contribution to the family; a pride that had increased as the years had passed.

When Phyllis described the day-to-day work of her father, managing teams of men who were breaking in the land, she painted a portrait of character and of individual leadership during the earliest stage of Huapai's development. In Phyllis's words:

> Mainly what Dad was doing was taking the people that were interested in buying a farm, taking them around, showing them where this place was. He quite enjoyed that and they'd come out on the train, because it was the only way of coming out here, and he'd meet them with a little light vehicle to go out in … He was supposed to have just done the office work and send … the people out to work. But he couldn't do that. He said, 'I can't send people out to work when I'm sitting in a chair. Oh, no, I wasn't built to be sitting in a chair.' And he always looked after the horses. He took the care of the horses 'cause they must have had five or six teams, some of them four, some of them two … We had big stables out the back here.

This Whites Aviation photo dated around 1930 shows the patchwork of shelter belts and fruit trees developed at Huapai in the Kumeu District from 1915. For the first decade, the hard work of clearing the land and planting was carried out by Northern Fruitlands manager Bill Fickling and his teams of men and horses. Kumeu, Rodney District. Photograph: Whites Aviation Ltd. Alexander Turnbull Library, Wellington, New Zealand, Ref: WA-62621-F

At this time, Bill was also breaking in the family's own property at Huapai. Phyllis remembered the sequence of clearing the land that was being replicated across the entire Huapai estate:

> [The family's property] was just bare land, just grew sort of scrubby stuff on it. And then Dad got it all cleared. He had all the stuff that they were clearing, they had all the gear that was used for breaking up the sections around here. A lot of it [the equipment], he owned it. He bought it himself, and ploughed it, disked it

and harrowed it. Drained it first of course … It was pretty wet land and it had to sort of be opened up because it was patted down hard and then there was gum diggers' holes all around it. You had to get all those filled in. They used to dig enormous holes and they'd leave all the tailings of what they'd dug out, just left in a mound, and then you had a frightful, big hole there you could fall into. So before you could stock it with any animals or do anything with it you had to go round and fill all these holes in. And then it was drained and then it was cut up into paddocks …

The establishment years of the Huapai estate ran from 1913 to around 1930. Since Phyllis was born in 1915, her first-hand accounts relate to the latter part of this period from around 1920. However, her memories would include conversations heard and stories told by her parents that related to the earlier years.

The Northern Fruitlands Ltd development at Huapai was accompanied by an advertising campaign in Auckland's newspapers, especially from 1914 to 1920. The purpose of this advertising was to sell the dreams of lifestyle or profit. Huapai was claimed to offer a lifestyle to 'professional men and others who would like to own an orchard within an hour and a half by rail of Auckland, but who may be deterred from investing in the same owing to lack of knowledge of fruit growing, or want of time to give personal attention to same'.[5]

A distinguishing factor at Huapai was the opportunity for buyers to contract Northern Fruitlands to do the hard labour of breaking in sections. This work was carried out by Bill Fickling's teams. In 1915, advertisements referenced the progress already achieved. What had been 'a state of nature was now miles of ditching, roading and shelter trees on the estate, besides some hundreds of acres in various stages of advancement in cultivation'.[6] Purchasers were able to pay for their properties to be developed and managed and were given the expectation of 'a big return on cash invested'.[7]

A first-hand oral account allows us to assess the reality of orchard life behind the company's marketing puff. Phyllis recalled that her father, in his role as agent for the company, regularly found himself treading a fine line between the company's drive for sales and his knowledge of the varying quality of the Huapai sections. It was a point of pride to Bill Fickling that he gave potential buyers his honest advice about a property. His personal principles were informed by his own experience. The first land he purchased at Huapai had proved to be a poor choice and he quickly sold to

Auckland Weekly News *published this image of a group of apple pickers at Huapai on 13 February 1935, 20 years after the district's lands started being cleared for orchards. There is a good crop of fruit although the trees are still small enough for the pickers to pick the crop without ladders.* Auckland Libraries Heritage Collections. Ref: AWNS-19350213-49-04

---

purchase a better-quality section. Phyllis expressed her own pride that her father demonstrated his principles:

> Trouble was, Dad was too honest. If he thought the soil wasn't good enough for what they wanted, he would tell them so. And the company didn't care for that too much. They just said to him, 'Just let them find that out for themselves.' 'Oh,' Dad said, 'I can't do that and let them waste their money on a place that's not going to be viable' … Quite a few that were too wet for orchards … It's all in farm now but, at the time, it would have been a struggle for them. They had no idea. They read the brochures and, of course, it sounded like Utopia. You would be a millionaire overnight sort of style. Most of them came from the city.

CONTINUING CONNECTIONS BETWEEN PAST, PRESENT AND FUTURE

The rural properties developed at Huapai from 1913 can be viewed as early versions of today's modern lifestyle blocks. Then and now, they represent dreams of a life of peace and tranquillity away from the rat race of the city, yet within easy distance of most of its services. They promise an idealised rural world surrounded by space and nature, yet the reality of running even a small property is harder work than anticipated, and the 'dream' is often unfulfilled and abandoned. Oral history at Huapai shows that modern desires to escape 'city life' are not new but have existed across at least a hundred years, with comparable motivations and challenges for those involved. Then as now, the search for a peaceful, idealised rural life, detached from the hustle and bustle of the city, often ends prematurely with the realisation that the rural life sought was far harder than foreseen.

At Huapai, Phyllis's account suggests that buyers with the right experience of working the land could likely make a success of an orchard but there were greater risks for the company's target market of inexperienced city folk seeking the dream of an orchard life or wanting to be hands-off in its development and management. Over time it became clear at Huapai that profits were harder to come by than had been promised by the advertising. By the 1930s, most sections were being used as household orchards or weekend homes rather than productive units. The early advertising's lure of easy money was not matched by the reality of orchard returns. By the early-1950s, of 113 properties planned by Northern Fruitlands, there were just 18 commercial orchards 'representing striking individual triumphs against a general trend of failure and broken dreams'.[8]

PATTERNS OF DAY-TO-DAY FAMILY LIFE AND AGENCY

Phyllis Fickling's interview emphasised the pattern of self-sufficiency and the contributions of each member of the household, as well as the hard work, leadership and agency of her parents, Bill and Emma Fickling.

Fickling's interview is valuable for this close view of her parents' working lives, which can be seen as typical of many of their generation. She had clear childhood memories of the day-to-day operations of their small farm, her father's off-site contract work and a large household that included orchard workers as lodgers. This was prior to the reticulation of electricity and the introduction of labour-saving farm machinery or household appliances. It took contributions from everyone to keep the household and farm running smoothly. Today, it is a given that such work was labour-intensive, yet her oral history gives us a detailed view of actual tasks done and how work was apportioned and managed by her parents. Phyllis's satisfaction with the way she carried out her particular responsibilities is clear in her account. And it gives a sense of the co-operative nature of the entire household and the way accepting responsibility was one of the essential pillars of the Fickling children's upbringing:

> Mum was a good cook and we had good meals … Lots of vegies. And we always had meat of some kind. She'd do tripe and onions and mashed potatoes and cabbages and carrots. You know, masses of vegies, plenty of fruit. And she'd make boiled puddings and rice puddings. We always had fruit. She used to do her own preserving and jams and pickles, all those sorts of thing. The cupboards were always bursting with stuff.

> As we got older, we always had to peel the vegetables and have them all ready for cooking. And as you got older, you took over these jobs. I can remember when I got to about Form Two, I took over doing most of the baking. I used to bake the bread and cakes … You know, it was no problem. Saturday used to be the big baking day. I know she'd spread papers over the sofa and, as the cakes came out, they were taken off a slide and put on there. Because I remember, we were having some youngsters out, kids from the town, you know, that didn't get holidays. Mum used to get them out here in the school holidays for a week at a time. They would go home and tell their people, 'Oh, the cakes, the cakes, whole "sofafuls" of them.'

Her father's role as the 'on-the-ground' manager for Northern Fruitlands gives an insight into how leadership at a local level evolves or is conferred on individuals through their position and personal qualities. It highlights the need to pay greater historical attention to the influence of such local managers and leaders, especially when a district is in the developmental stage. Phyllis's observations of her father and his working life are potentially even more detailed than he might have given of his own life. From an early age, Phyllis appears to have recognised how hard her father worked and how he helped others if help was needed. When interviewed, Phyllis offered a reflective assessment of his strengths and alluded gently to the negative consequences of his approach, saying, 'if they told him a sad story, he was there to try and help them. Now that I'm grown up, I can see how they exploited him quite a bit … A lot of them couldn't afford to pay because it [payment] was forgotten.' She recognised the tension in Bill helping people who were struggling but to his own financial detriment, while also understanding that holding to the personal principle of helping others outweighed such losses. Phyllis's loyalty to the memory of her father is apparent in her words, 'He was too soft,' qualified immediately by, 'It doesn't do you any harm to be that way.'

Bill Fickling was fully involved in the day-to-day labour of his teams and was especially skilled with the horses that were essential for breaking in the land. When Phyllis reflected on her father's working situation, she concluded:

> … it was too tough. He had too many responsibilities. Oh, we hardly ever saw him. He was gone before we got out of bed in the morning because he would look after the jolly horses. He'd get up at 4 o'clock and give them their first feed. He wouldn't give them all of it in one because he said they slobbered over it. So, he'd give them their first feed then he'd take them out down to the creek to get their water and he wouldn't allow them to do their business inside so they had to do that outside. Then he'd take them back into the stable and give them their other lot [of feed]. Then he'd come up to the house and get his breakfast … And the same business happened again at night. As soon as he got them home, he'd water them, feed them, then he'd come up and get his tea … We were in bed by then and he'd go down with his lantern to the stables, turn the horses out, bring them back in and give them their second feed and then he used to get into the feed house … at the back of the stables and he used to get up on the chaff bags and go off to sleep. He'd wake up when it was time to turn them out, then he'd come and have his sleep and be up again at four o'clock. Well, you know, you can't keep doing that all the time. Then, Mum took over the office work, kept the time sheets to help him out … because he was too tired to do any bookwork.

Bill Fickling had learnt veterinary skills while in the army in South Africa and, at Huapai, he provided informal and unpaid veterinary services to neighbours who needed them. His position as a manager meant he was a point of contact for the police when there was trouble or even the potential for trouble from a new arrival in the district. He was a leader within the community at that time due to his position at the company and because of his personal qualities and skills.

REFRAMING EXISTING HISTORICAL PERSPECTIVES

Oral histories often reveal stories routinely omitted from traditional written records including instances of severe economic distress or failure, or stigmatising events such as a breakdown of mental health or a pregnancy outside of marriage. Within the arc of a long interview, people can gain the confidence to speak candidly about such things. And a younger generation speaking about their parents is even more likely to speak openly of events no longer regarded as stigmatising. Here, Phyllis provided an unexpected insight in her account of how her father coped with the pressures of his position. When Bill Fickling became exhausted and overwhelmed by his physical work and responsibilities, a complete break away from Huapai was recommended. In Phyllis's words:

> And anyway, he was just on the verge of a breakdown and we had a doctor friend from town that used to come out here, well, he bought a place out here as well. And he said to Dad, 'If you don't get away from here, you'll have a nervous breakdown.' So, he said, 'I tell you the best thing you can do is pack your bags and go off down to the South Island for a while and get work down there.'

> He [her father] knew cropping because he had done that in his youth. He went down there for four or five months and Mum carried on her own here, looked after the kids. We sold the horses that we could sell … The fellow that took over the management, he managed. He didn't work himself but Dad always did.

> She [her mother] just had to manage. [Siblings] Bill and Hilda were old enough to give a hand. Still had about four horses. They were tough times for them. You just sort of accepted that he was going and that was it, he just went off down to the South Island. Charlie Annett went down at the same time with Dad. They went around together and got work … He came back, he was fitter. And then he just did work. A lot of places had been settled into orchards and they were absentee owners and he would look after their orchards, spray them and prune them, and harvest the fruit … He had four or five different orchards that he did.

The Fickling family's response to Bill's exhaustion extends our insight into how families dealt with such a crisis. Intense hard work and hardship have tended to be seen as the norm in the New Zealand rural historical context during the first part of the twentieth century. Family responses to such hardship have often been depicted at the extremes. The most common was that hardy rural folk simply endured their situation and battled through with stoicism. In the most adverse circumstances, such as during the Great Depression, their ultimate decision might be to walk off their land. In contrast, the Ficklings acted nimbly to their adverse situation, which suggests other families also identified problems and made early, positive adjustments to solve them. Bill and Emma had a pattern of altering their course if their situation demanded it. They moved from Bill's farm job at Whangārei because the climate did not suit him health-wise. When the first property the family bought at Huapai was found to be inferior, they quickly sold it for a better site. And when their doctor friend recognised Bill's exhaustion and the possibility of a breakdown, they took his advice that he needed to get a complete break. He also left the Northern Fruitlands manager job with its overbearing responsibilities and, on his return to Huapai, contracted privately to manage a small number of individual properties, a far less burdensome proposition. The Ficklings did not just battle on against impossible odds or let their situation develop into an overwhelming crisis. In examining aspects of this one family's life in depth, oral history demonstrates the agency and the multiplicity of responses with which rural families successfully dealt with life's challenges.

THE LANGUAGE OF THE PAST

An oral interview brings the unique voice and language of the person and of the time being remembered. Phyllis refers to her younger brother, Bob, as a little 'joker', common slang at the time for a male. Huapai's location is described as out in the 'woop woops', a variation of the 'wop wops', the New Zealand slang term for an out-the-way place. Harvested barley had to be 'stooked up' and described sheaves of barley being stood on end in 'stooks'. These are terms that Phyllis herself had likely ceased using but, in remembering the past, she returned naturally to the terms and phrases of that time. Her examples are all polite slang. There was no coarseness in her choice of remembered language, reflecting the acceptable language within her family and the society of the time. She emphasised her description of her father's micromanagement of the horses, with the polite intensifier 'jolly'. Similarly, her phrase that the horses went out to 'do their business' consciously avoids the coarse words likely to be used today and, possibly, by the working men on the Fickling property out of children's hearing. During the 1920s, coarse language would not have been permissible for a child from a respectable family, and especially not for a girl.

Phyllis Fickling's account of her childhood provides a nuanced understanding of the reality of farming life in Huapai in the early twentieth century. We see the on-the-ground reality beneath sales publicity that promised rapid and easy profits without any physical effort by owners. The Fickling family operated as an autonomous unit, with a high degree of self-sufficiency and a degree of responsibility assigned to all members. Most notably, the labours of both parents, Bill and Emma, were relentless. Phyllis's account reveals her pride in her parents' work ethic and the leadership role Bill played in the district at an early time in its development. While the toll such unrelenting work and responsibility had on her father's health loomed large in her childhood memory, this also revealed the family's rational response to his breakdown. Phyllis Fickling's fine-grained oral history highlights the intensity of day-to-day work within rural New Zealand households in the early twentieth century, and specifically in the developing district of Huapai, in ways that traditional written records cannot. The history and continuity of the ongoing search by some for a small and idyllic, rural property are revealed, together with new models of leadership within rural communities, and recognition of family agency and action in the face of challenges.

GLOSSARY

faifeau (Samoan) church minister

hapori family, section of a kinship group, community
hapū subtribe, kinship group
hau kāinga home, true home, local people of a marae, home people
hui meeting(s)

ifoga Samoan ceremony of apology
iwi tribe, extended kinship group

karakia ritual chant, recite a prayer
kaumātua elder
kaupapa Māori Māori approach to doing things/customary practice
kōrero speech(es)
kuia female elder

mahinga kai garden/food-gathering place
mamae pain/injury
mana power and authority (both), honour
marae village/area in front of the meeting house, communal sacred space
mātauranga knowledge
mātauranga Māori Māori knowledge

maunga mountain
mokos (abbreviation of mokopuna) grandchildren/descendants

paepae where speeches are made on the marae
Pākehā non-Māori person
pālagi (Sāmoan/Tongan) white person
pare kawakawa mourning wreath (for the head), garland of greenery worn by women at tangihanga
pōwhiri welcome ceremony
pūrākau myth, story

rangatira chief(s)
rūnanga public meeting

Tāmaki Makaurau Auckland
tangata person (individual)
tāngata people (plural)
tangata whenua people belonging to the land
tangi mourning ceremony
tangihanga rites for the dead, funeral
taringa areare listening ears
te reo language (usually Māori language)

tikanga custom/correct procedure
tikanga Māori Māori protocol
tino rangatiratanga self-determination
tōpū consolidated, merged, combined, united, assembled
tuku give
tūpuna ancestor(s), grandparents

utu reciprocity

wāhi place/location
waiata song(s)
whakamā shame/embarrassment
whakapapa genealogy/lineage
whakawāhine Māori trans women
whānau extended family
whare wānanga place of higher learning, traditional school of learning
whenua land

NOTES

CHAPTER 1

1. Offa's Dyke is an 8th-century earthwork along the English–Welsh border.
2. George Ewart Evans, *Ask the Fellows Who Cut the Hay* (London: Faber and Faber, 1956).
3. Excellent introductions to oral history include Paul Thompson and Joanna Bornat, *The Voice of the Past: Oral history*, 4th edn (Oxford: Oxford University Press, 2017); Robert Perks and Alistair Thomson, eds, *The Oral History Reader* (London: Routledge, 1998, 2006, 2016); Donald A. Ritchie, *Doing Oral History: A practical guide*, 3rd edn (New York: Oxford University Press, 2014); Thomas L. Charlton, Lois E. Myers and Rebecca Sharpless, eds, *Thinking About Oral History: Theories and applications* (Lanham: AltaMira Press, 2008).
4. Please note that the name Aotearoa is contested, and Aotearoa me Te Waipounamu also includes the name of the South Island.
5. For information about the National Oral History Association see: www.oralhistory.org.nz
6. See: https://mch.govt.nz/funding-nz-culture/ministry-grants-awards/new-zealand-oral-history-awards
7. For further discussion about Māori approaches to oral history and tradition see: Nepia Mahuika, *Rethinking Oral History and Tradition: An indigenous perspective* (Oxford: Oxford University Press, 2019); Te Ahukaramu Charles Royal, 'Politics and knowledge: Kaupapa Māori and matauranga Māori', *New Zealand Journal of Educational Studies* 47, 2, 2012; Rawiri Te Maire Tau, *Pikitūroa o Ngāi Tahu: The oral traditions of Ngāi Tahu* (Dunedin: University of Otago Press, 2003). There are also articles and project reports in the *Oral History in New Zealand* journal (www.oralhistory.org.nz/index.php/home/publications): Cushla Parekowhai, 'Korero taku whaea: Talk my aunt: Learning to listen to Māori women', 4, 1992, pp. 1–4; Charles Royal, 'Oral history and hapū development', 5, 1993, pp. 4–6; and more recently Liana MacDonald, 'Shifting perspectives of the Wairau Affray', 33, 2021, pp. 1–14. See also articles in *MAI Journal* (www.journal.mai.ac.nz), for example Tahu Kukutai, Nepia Mahuika, Heeni Kani, Denise Ewe and Karu Hura Kukutai, 'Survivance as narrative identity: Voices from a Ngā Tiipa oral history project', *MAI Journal* 9, 3, 2020, pp. 309–20.
8. For example, Helen Frizzell and Emily Anderson's prize-winning article, 'Hurunui seismic stories', *Oral History in New Zealand* 32, 2020, pp. 5–13; Ruth Entwistle Low, *On the Hoof: The untold story of drovers in New Zealand* (Auckland: Penguin eBooks, 2014). For an audio podcast listen to Pip Oldham, *Butchers'*

Stories (2018): https://soundcloud.com/iplham/sets/butchers-stories; Chris Brickell, *Mates and Lovers: A history of gay New Zealand* (Auckland: Penguin Random House, 2008); Ann Beaglehole, *A Small Price to Pay: Refugees from Hitler in New Zealand, 1936–46* (Wellington: Bridget Williams Books, 1998).

9   See Cheryl Ware and Linda Bryder, '"We'd just get together … and talk about cancer": Commissioned oral histories and the professional historian', *Health and History 21*, 2019, pp. 47–68.

10 Megan Hutching, 'New Zealand women judges oral history project', National Library OHColl-1033 (2011–2012), and Elizabeth Chan, 'Women trailblazers in the law: The New Zealand women judges oral histories project', *Victoria University of Wellington Law Review 45*, 2014; Megan Hutching, ed. *Last Line of Defence: New Zealanders remember the war at home* (Auckland: HarperCollins NZ, 2007); *Against the Rising Sun: New Zealanders remember the Pacific War* (Auckland: HarperCollins NZ, 2006); *The Desert Road: New Zealanders remember the North African campaign* (Auckland: HarperCollins NZ, 2005); *A Fair Sort of Battering: New Zealanders remember the Italian campaign* (Auckland: HarperCollins NZ, 2004); *Inside Stories: New Zealand prisoners of war remember* (Auckland: HarperCollins NZ, 2002); and *A Unique Sort of Battle: New Zealanders remember Crete* (Auckland: HarperCollins NZ, 2001).

11 See Jaber F. Gubrium and James A. Holstein, eds, *Handbook of Interview Research* (Thousand Oaks, Calif.: Sage, 2011).

12 Yifat Gutman and Jenny Wüstenberg, eds, *The Routledge Handbook of Memory Activism* (London: Routledge, 2023), p. 5.

13 Gutman and Wüstenberg, p. 3. Aleida Assman is a German professor of literary studies and a leading figure in the field of cultural and communicative memory.

14 Michelle Walmsley, 'Telling disabled people's stories free from the framings of the abled', *The Spinoff*, 27 November 2019; Max Rashbrooke, 'No place like home', *New Zealand Geographic 132*, 2015: www.nzgeo.com/stories/no-place-like-home/; Carole McMinn, 'Lost points of intervention: Pathways to single adult homelessness in Hamilton, New Zealand', PhD thesis, University of Waikato, 2021; Will Hansen, 'A trans history of gay liberation in New Zealand', *The Spinoff*, 27 March 2022.

15 For an early exploration of the role of myth in oral histories see Raphael Samuel and Paul Thompson, *The Myths We Live By* (London: Routledge, 1990); see also the influential chapter by Katherine Borland, '"That's not what I said": Interpretive conflict in oral narrative research', in *Women's Words: The feminist practice of oral history*, eds Sherna Berger Gluck and Daphne Patai (New York: Routledge, 1991), pp. 63–75.

16 See Daniel L. Schacter, *The Seven Sins of Memory: How the mind forgets and remembers* (Boston and New York: Houghton Mifflin Harcourt, 2002) and 'Constructive memory: Remembering the past to imagining the future': www.youtube.com/watch?v=6bWd0ipgI8k; Robin Lindley, 'How memory works: Interview with psychologist Daniel L. Schacter, *History News Network*, 2013: hnn.us/article/152111

17 Charan Ranganath, *Why We Remember: Unlocking memory's power to hold on to what matters* (New York: Random House, 2024), p. 5.

18 Ibid., pp. 282–83.

19. See also Daniel Schacter, 'Constructive memory: Remembering the past to imagining the future': www.youtube.com/watch?v=6bWd0ipgI8k; Robin Lindley, 'How memory works'; and Yifat Gutman, Amy Sodaro and Adam D. Brown, 'Introduction: Memory and the future: Why a change of focus is necessary', in *Memory and the Future: Transnational politics, ethics and society* (Basingstoke: Palgrave Macmillan, 2010), pp. 1–11.
20. The Memory Studies Association was founded in 2016: www.memorystudiesassociation.org
21. Anna Green, 'Individual remembering and "collective memory": Theoretical presuppositions and contemporary debates', *Oral History 32*, 2, 2004, pp. 35–44.
22. Astrid Erll, translated by Sara B. Young, *Memory in Culture* (Basingstoke: Palgrave Macmillan, 2011).
23. For information about oral history planning and conducting an oral history project in New Zealand see Megan Hutching, *Talking History: A short guide to oral history* (Wellington: Bridget Williams Books, 1993); or for a community oral history project see Emily Anderson and Helen Frizzell, 'Hurunui seismic stories', *Oral History in New Zealand 32*, 2020, pp. 5–13. Other good sources include: The National Library https://natlib.govt.nz/researchers/oral-history-advice; NZ History https://nzhistory.govt.nz/hands/a-guide-to-recording-oral-history; and Oral History Society UK www.ohs.org.uk/for-beginners/
24. Linda Tuhiwai Smith, *Decolonizing Methodologies: Research and Indigenous peoples,* 2nd edn (London: Zed Books, 2012); Felicity Ware, Mary Breheny and Margaret Forster, 'Kaupapa kōrero: A Māori cultural approach to narrative inquiry', *AlterNative: An international journal of indigenous peoples 14*, 1, 2017, pp. 45–53.
25. For ethical principles and agreement forms see: www.oralhistory.org.nz/index.php/ethics-and-practice/; Megan Hutching, 'Ethics and oral history', *New Zealand Journal of Public History 4*, 1, 2016, pp. 3–7. For an overview of ethical issues and debates in oral history, see Anna Sheftel and Stacey Zembrzycki, 'Who's afraid of oral history: Fifty years of debates and anxiety about ethics', *The Oral History Review 43*, 2, 2016, pp. 338–66.
26. Eva McMahan, *Elite oral history discourse: A study of cooperation and coherence* (Tuscaloosa: University of Alabama Press, 2015), p. 66.
27. For discussion about remembering and oral history methodology see Anna Green, 'Why family memories and stories matter', *Journal of New Zealand Studies 29,* 2019, pp. 3–19; also Thompson and Bornat, *The Voice of the Past* and Ritchie, *Doing Oral History*.
28. Alessandro Portelli, 'Living voices: The oral history interview as dialogue and experience', *Oral History Review 45*, 2, 2018, pp. 239–48.
29. On the theme of intersubjectivity within the interview see the journal *Oral History 50*, 2022.
30. Mahuika, *Rethinking Oral History and Tradition*; Keenan, 'The past from the paepae', pp. 145–51; and Rawiri Te Maire Tau, *Pikitūroa o Ngāi Tahu: The oral traditions of Ngāi Tahu* (Dunedin: University of Otago Press, 2003).
31. For example, see Te Rina Triponel, 'Auckland iwi head to High Court over Crown approach to land ownership rights', *New Zealand Herald*, 9 February 2021. Concerning the interpretation

of oral history and traditions: Michael Stevens, Atholl Anderson and Te Maire Tau, '"Our ultimate duty": Defending the integrity of Māori tradition', *Te Karaka*, July 2022: https://ngaitahu.iwi.nz/our_stories/our-ultimate-duty-tk90/

32 Anna Green, *British Capital, Antipodean Labour* (Dunedin: Otago University Press, 2001).

33 Luisa Passerini, 'Work ideology under Italian Fascism', *History Workshop Journal* 8, 1979, pp. 82–108 and *Fascism in Popular Memory: The cultural experience of the Turin working class*, trans. Robert Lumley and Jude Bloomfield (Cambridge: Cambridge University Press, 1987).

34 See Richard Candida Smith, 'Review: Popular Memory and Oral Narratives: Luisa Passerini's reading of oral history interviews', *The Oral History Review* 16, 2, 1988, p. 95.

35 See Portelli, 'Living voices', p. 239. See also Alessandro Portelli, 'What makes oral history different', in *The Oral History Reader,* 3rd ed., eds Robert Perks and Alistair Thomson (London and New York: Routledge, 2016), pp. 48–58.

36 Portelli, 'What makes oral history different', p. 49.

37 Ibid., p. 48.

38 Alessandro Portelli, 'Oral history as a genre', in *Narrative and Genre*, eds Mary Chamberlain and Paul Thompson (London: Routledge, 1998), pp. 23–45.

39 See an early article published in 1979 by Ron Grele that demonstrated an alternative structure of historical memory, 'Listen to their voices: Two case studies in the interpretation of oral history interviews', *Oral History* 7, 1, 1979, pp. 33–42.

40 Anna Green, 'Coffee and Bun, Sgt Bonnington, and the Tornado: Myth and place in Frankton Junction', *Oral History* 28, 2, 2000, pp. 26–34.

41 John Kotre, 'Generativity and culture: What meaning can do', in *The Generative Society: Caring for future generations*, eds Ed de St. Aubin, Dan P. McAdams and Tae-Chang Kim (Washington: American Psychological Association, 2004), pp. 35–50; Dan P. McAdams, Ruthellen Josselson and Amia Lieblich, eds, *Identity and Story: Creating self in narrative* (Washington DC: American Psychological Association, 2006).

42 Jerome Bruner, *Making Stories: Law, literature, life* (New York: Farrar, Straus and Giroux, 2002), pp. 15, 20. See also Jerome Bruner, 'Life as narrative', *Social Research: An International Quarterly* 71, 3, 2004, pp. 691–710.

43 McAdams, Josselson and Lieblich, *Identity and Story*, p. 3. Emphasis added. For an alternative view, see: Mark Rowlands, *Memory and the Self: Phenomenology, science and autobiography* (Oxford: Oxford University Press, 2017); Ron Grele's review essay on Lynn Abrams, *Oral History Theory*, in *Oral History Review* 38, 2, 2011, pp. 354–59; Galen Strawson, 'Against narrativity', *Ratio XVII*, 2004, pp. 428–51.

44 Oliver Sachs, *The Man Who Mistook his Wife for a Hat* (London: Pan Macmillan, 2009), pp. 105–06.

45 Sam Wineberg, *Historical Thinking and Other Unnatural Acts: Charting the future of teaching the past* (Philadelphia: Temple University Press, 2001).

46 There is an excellent discussion of these issues in Stéphane Lévesque and Jean-Philippe Croteau, *Beyond History for Historical Consciousness: Students, narrative, and memory* (Toronto: University of Toronto Press, 2020), pp. 152–54.

47 Aleida Assman discussed the difficult relationship between memory and

nationalism in her keynote address at the 2019 Memory Studies Conference in Madrid: www.youtube.com/watch?v=wM04W12CFw4

48 Rowan Light also explores this issue in 'The historians' debate', in *Why Memory Matters: Remembered histories and the politics of the shared past* (Wellington: Bridget Williams Books, 2023).

49 Bain Attwood, *'A Bloody Difficult Subject': Ruth Ross, Te Tiriti o Waitangi and the making of history* (Auckland: Auckland University Press, 2023), pp. 211–12.

CHAPTER 2

1 The Treaty of Waitangi Act 1975, and its Amendment, 1985.
2 W.H. Oliver, *Claims to the Waitangi Tribunal* (Wellington: Department of Justice. Waitangi Tribunal Division, 1991), p. 13.
3 Waitangi Tribunal, *The Kaipara Report* (Wellington: Legislation Direct, 2006).
4 The Ngāti Whatua o Kaipara Claims Settlement Act 2013.
5 See map of the claim area including the location of the five marae and their respective maunga, Woodhill Forest, and the railway line.
6 Waitangi Tribunal, *The Kaipara Report*.
7 Quote from author's notes during an unrecorded interview with Taku at Manawanui, 17 March 2008. The interviewer was the author.
8 Translation and transcription of kaumātua evidence presented in hearing week 8–12 March 1999, WAI 674 Doc 4.1, pp. 5–6.
9 Raupatu Document Bank, Vol. 088, p. 33850.
10 Joan Metge, 'Returning the gift – 'Utu' in intergroup relations: In memory of Sir Raymond Firth', *Journal of the Polynesian Society 111*, 4, 2002, p. 315.
11 *New Zealand Herald*, 6 September 1871, in Bruce Stirling, 'Ngāti Whātua and the Crown 1864–1900', for WAI 312, unpublished, 1998, p. 186.
12 All quotes in this paragraph are from the author's notes during an unrecorded interview with Taku, at Manawanui, 17 March 2008.
13 Richard S. Hill and Brigitte Bönisch-Brednich, 'Politicizing the past: Indigenous scholarship and Crown-Maori reparations processes in New Zealand', *Social & Legal Studies 16*, 2, 2007, p. 171.
14 Waitangi Tribunal, *The Kaipara Report*, p. 314.
15 Ibid.
16 Ibid.
17 Gloria Timoti, 'Brief of Evidence', WAI 312, B9.
18 Judith Binney, 'Stories without end', *Journal of the Polynesian Society 119*, 1, 2010, pp. 5–6.
19 Oral interview with Gloria Timoti at Kakanui, 19 March 2008. Interviewer was author. Transcript with the author.
20 Waitangi Tribunal, *Kaipara Report*, p. 217.
21 Ibid., pp. 218–19, 319.
22 Oral interview with Gloria Timoti, 19 March 2008.
23 Gloria did, finally, receive assistance from Housing New Zealand (formerly called Housing Corporation) and WINZ (Work and Income New Zealand) and moved into a new two-bedroom unit, not at Kakanui but in Helensville in August that year.
24 Personal communication with Barry Rigby, Waitangi Tribunal, 9 December 2022.
25 I rely on Bruce Stirling's report for the WAI 312 claimants, 'Ngāti Whātua and

the Crown 1864–1900', unpublished, December 1998, pp. 178–87, 282–97, for this story of the Kaipara Railway Gift.
26 *Daily Southern Cross*, 24 February 1871, p. 2.
27 Ibid.
28 *New Zealand Herald*, 4 March 1871, in Bruce Stirling, 'Ngāti Whātua and the Crown', p. 181.
29 *New Zealand Herald,* 6 September 1871, in Stirling, 'Ngāti Whātua and the Crown', p. 186.
30 'Auckland-Kaipara Railway Stations', *AJHR,* 1882, p. 683.
31 *New Zealand Gazette 86*, 24 July 1884, p. 1161, 'Land taken for further portion of Kaipara-Waikato Railway (Kumeu-Helensville Section)'.
32 Native Affairs Committee, minutes of evidence on petition 199/1877, Archives New Zealand, LE 1/1877/5, in Stirling, 'Ngāti Whātua and the Crown', p. 292.
33 Personal communication with Bruce Stirling, 23 March 2023.
34 The third reading was on 6 June 2013.
35 Hill and Bönisch-Brednich, 'Politicizing the past', p. 165.
36 Ibid., pp. 166–68.
37 Douglas Graham, *Trick or Treaty?* (Wellington: Institute of Policy Studies, Victoria University of Wellington, 1997), p. 58.
38 Jennifer Cole, 'Painful memories: Ritual and the transformation of community trauma', *Culture, Medicine and Psychiatry* 28, 2004, pp. 87–105.
39 Interview with Sir Tipene O'Regan, 26 September 2019 at Ngāi Tahu offices, Christchurch. Interviewer was author.

CHAPTER 3

1 James Belich is quoted in a *NZ Listener* article as saying 'The inside of people's heads is the most difficult of historian's terrain.' Paul Little, 'An all-inclusive holiday?', *NZ Listener*, 22 April 2023, p. 32.
2 Henry and Marianne Williams arrived in the Bay of Islands in 1823. William and Jane Williams arrived in 1826, moving to a new mission station at Tūranga-nui in 1839.
3 My approach was based on Alistair Thomson's model of remembering, encompassing the relationship between public legends and personal memory, and the idea of composure. Alistair Thomson, *ANZAC Memories. Living with the legend* (Melbourne: Oxford University Press, 1994), p. 8. 'We compose our memories to make sense of our past and present lives … In one sense we compose or construct our memories using the public languages and meanings of our culture. In another sense we compose memories that help us feel relatively comfortable with our lives and identities, that give us a feeling of composure.'
4 Jane Moodie, 'Family myths in oral history: The unsettled narratives of descendants of a missionary-settler family in New Zealand', PhD thesis, University of Waikato, 2004.
5 E.P. Thompson, *The Making of the English Working Class,* rev. edn (Harmondsworth: Middlesex: Penguin, 1968), p. 939.
6 Pierre Bourdieu, 'The forms of capital', in *The Sociology of Economic Life*, eds Mark Granovetter and Richard Swedberg, 3rd edn (New York: Routledge, 2018), pp. 78–92. Bourdieu first proposed these ideas in the 1980s.
7 Charles Crothers, 'Editorial introduction: Special issue on inequality and class in

New Zealand', *New Zealand Sociology 28*, 3, 2013, p. 12.
8. Thompson, *The Making of the English Working Class*, p. 939.
9. Patrick Ongley, 'Class in New Zealand: Past, present and future', *Counterfutures 1*, 2016, pp. 73–77 (italics are mine).
10. Jim McAloon, 'Class in colonial New Zealand. Towards a historiographical rehabilitation', *New Zealand Journal of History 38*, 1, 2004, pp. 3–21.
11. Keith Sinclair, *A History of New Zealand* (Harmondsworth: Penguin, 1959), and *William Pember Reeves: New Zealand Fabian* (Oxford: Oxford University Press, 1965); W.H. Oliver, *The Story of New Zealand* (London: Faber & Faber, 1960) and 'Reeves, Sinclair and the Social Pattern', in *The Feel of Truth: Essays in New Zealand and Pacific history*, ed. Peter Munz (Wellington: A.H. & A.W. Reed, 1969); Erik Olssen, 'Social class in nineteenth-century New Zealand', in *Social Class in New Zealand*, ed. David Pitt (Auckland: Longman Paul, 1977), pp. 22–41; and *Building the New World: Work, politics and society in Caversham 1880s–1920s* (Auckland: Auckland University Press, 1995); John E. Martin, 'Whither the rural working class?' *New Zealand Journal of History 17*, 1, 1983 and *The Forgotten Worker: The rural wage earner in nineteenth-century New Zealand* (Wellington: Allen & Unwin, 1990); Stevan Eldred-Grigg, *A Southern Gentry: New Zealanders who inherited the earth* (Wellington: Heinemann Reed, 1980); Claire Toynbee, 'Class and social structure in nineteenth-century New Zealand', *New Zealand Journal of History 13*, 1, 1979, pp. 65–82; Jim McAloon, *No Idle Rich: The wealthy in Canterbury and Otago 1840–1914* (Dunedin: University of Otago Press, 2002).
12. Tom Brooking, '"Yeotopia" found … but? The Yeoman ideal that underpinned New Zealand agricultural practice into the early twenty-first century, with American and Australian comparisons', *Journal of the Agricultural History Society 93*, 1, 2019, pp. 68–101.
13. Thompson, *The Making of the English Working Class*, p. 11.
14. It was interesting to note that Max Rashbrooke included personal perspectives at the end of each chapter of his recent publication, *Too Much Money* (Wellington: Bridget Williams Books, 2021). It is also noteworthy that Toynbee points to the possibilities of oral history (p. 71), and in his commentary on her paper Brooking agrees, p. 80. An excellent British example of the use of oral history in exploring class is found in the book by Ronald Fraser, *In Search of a Past: The Manor House, Amnersfield, 1933–45* (London: Verso, 1984).
15. Dissenters were those of Protestant religious groups who refused to conform to the Church of England. They were members of a non-established church, often known as Nonconformists.
16. T.C. Williams was the fourth son of Henry and Marianne Williams. He had both farming and business interests. The starting acreage given here is rounded by Tom Williams; according to David Yerex it was 12,000 acres, which by 1890 had grown to 'over 70,000'. David Yerex, *They Came to Wydrop. The Beetham and Williams families, Brancepeth and Te Parae, Wairarapa, 1856–1990* (Wellington: G.P. Print, 1991), pp. 54–61.
17. Tom Williams, interviewed by Jane Moodie, 'Te Parae', Wairarapa, 15 March 2000, Tape 1 side A 6.0–10.0. Interview in author's possession.

18 Tom Williams, Tape 1 side B 2.5, Tape 2 side A 34.0, Tape 1 side B 5.5. These extracts have been considerably condensed in the interests of brevity, and also slightly rearranged in the interests of clarity.
19 Tom Williams, Tape 3 side A 5.5.
20 Tom Williams, Tape 2 side B 8.4.
21 Tom Williams, Tape 2 side B 36.0, Tape 3 side A 11.9.
22 Eric Williams, interviewed by Jane Moodie, Pirongia, Waikato, 2 June 2000, Tape 1 side A 4.0. Interview in author's possession.
23 Eric Williams, Tape 1 side A 6.7.
24 Eric Williams, Tape 1 side B 14.0, 19.6, 28.1, 33.9, 35.7.
25 Elvin Hatch developed a one- and two-table theory of social hierarchy existing among the well-to-do in rural South Canterbury prior to World War II. Two-table families ate apart from their workers, emphasising social distance and hierarchy. Elvin Hatch, *Respectable Lives. Social standing in rural New Zealand* (Berkeley/Los Angeles: University of California Press, 1992), pp. 139–58.
26 Eric Williams, Tape 2 side A 39.4.
27 Eric Williams Tape 1 side A 14.4.
28 Eric Williams, Tape 2 side A 31.9.
29 Eric Williams, Tape 1 side A 22.5, Tape 2 side B 0.8. Heather Scott's mother was Mary Scott, née Clarke; a well-educated woman married to a Pirongia farmer, she was to become a well-known New Zealand author. Mary's grandfather, George Clarke, was a missionary with Henry Williams, and her mother was the daughter of another missionary, Edward Stuart, who later became the second Bishop of Waiapu, a friend of Samuel Williams. *Dictionary of New Zealand Biography, Vol. 4 1921–1940* (Auckland: Auckland University Press, 1998), pp. 462–63.
30 Eric Williams, Tape 2 side A 24.0.
31 Eric Williams, Tape 1 side A 30.0.
32 Eric Williams, Tape 1 side A 35.0.
33 Eric Williams, Tape 2 side A 44.0.
34 Deans: John Deans came to Canterbury in the early 1840s and bought property at Morven Hills and Homebush. Dillon: early settler in Marlborough, also an MP. Teschemaker: described as 'an English gentleman of Dutch descent whose family wealth derived from growing sugar in South America', he had settled in 1860 in Otago, later moving to Marlborough. The Borthwick family owned castles in Scotland, but they had come here as agents for New Zealand Loan and Mercantile, buying up several freezing works.
35 Marianne Williams's father was Wright Coldham, Mayor of Nottingham; her mother, Ann Temple, traced her lineage to the eleventh-century Leofric, Earl of Mercia, who married Lady Godiva. Rex Evans, compiler, *Faith and Farming: Te huarahi ki te ora. The legacy of Henry Williams and William Williams*, rev. edn (Auckland: Evagean, 1998), p. 6.
36 Brooking, 'Commentary' relating to article by Claire Toynbee, 1979, p. 80.
37 Moodie, pp. 322–414.

CHAPTER 4

1 Anna Green, 'Oral history and history', in *Remembering: Writing oral history*, eds Anna Green and Megan Hutching (Auckland: Auckland University Press, 2004), pp. 1–8.
2 See Nēpia Mahuika, 'An outsiders guide to public oral history in New Zealand', *New Zealand Journal of Public History* 5, 1, 2017, pp. 3–18.
3 See Emalani Case, *Everything Ancient Was Once New* (Hawaii: University of Hawaii

Press, 2021), Peter Adds, 'Long-distance prehistoric two-way voyaging: The case for Aotearoa and Hawaiki', *Journal of the Royal Society of New Zealand* 42, 2, 2012, pp. 99–103, and Alice Te Punga Somerville, *Once Were Pacific: Māori connections to Oceania* (Minneapolis: University of Minnesota Press, 2012).

4   See *Tangata o te Moana Nui: The evolving identities of Pacific peoples in Aotearoa New Zealand*, eds Cluny Macpherson, Paul Spoonley, Melani Anae and Sean Mallon (Palmerston North: Dunmore Press, 2001); *Tangata o Le Moana: New Zealand and the people of the Pacific*, eds Kolokesa Mahina-Tuai and Damon Salesa (Wellington: Te Papa Press, 2012).

5   Will 'Ilolahia, interviewed by Helena Cook, Christchurch, October 2022, interview in author's possession.

6   'Ilolahia interview.

7   Ibid.

8   See Teresia Teaiwa and Sean Mallon, 'Ambivalent kinships? Pacific people in New Zealand', *New Zealand Identities: Departures and destinations*, eds James H. Liu, Tim McCreanor, Tracey Mcintosh and Teresia Teaiwa (Wellington: Victoria University Press, 2005) and Karlo Mila-Schaaf, 'Polycultural capital and the Pasifika second generation: negotiating identities in diasporic spaces', PhD thesis, Massey University, 2010.

9   Pākehā is a Māori term traditionally used for settlers of European descent.

10 'Ilolahia interview. Pālagi is the Samoan equivalent of Pākehā.

11 See Cluny Macpherson, 'Empowering Pacific Peoples: Community organisations in New Zealand', in *Tangata o Le Moana: New Zealand and the people of the Pacific*, eds Sean Mallon, Kolokesa Māhina-Tuai and Damon Salesa (Wellington: Te Papa Press, 2012), pp. 179–200.

12 Ibid.

13 'Ilolahia interview.

14 See *Polynesian Panthers: Pacific protest and affirmative action in Aotearoa NZ 1971–1981*, eds Melani Anae, Leilani Tamu, Lautofa Iuli (Wellington: Huia Publishers, 2015) and Melani Anae, *The Platform: The Radical Legacy of the Polynesian Panthers* (Wellington: Bridget Williams Books, 2020).

15 To have sexual relations with more than one man at the party.

16 'Ilolahia interview.

17 Robbie Shilliam, 'The Polynesian Panthers and the Black Power gang: Surviving racism and colonialism in Aotearoa New Zealand', in *Black Power Beyond Borders: The global dimensions of the Black Power movement*, ed. Nico Slate (London: Palgrave Macmillan, 2012), pp. 107–26.

18 Anae, *The Platform*, p. 98.

19 Anae, Tamu, Iuli, eds, *Polynesian Panthers: Pacific protest and affirmative action in Aotearoa NZ 1971–1981*.

20 'Ilolahia interview.

21 Shilliam, 'The Polynesian Panthers and the Black Power gang', p. 116.

22 Anae, *The Platform*, pp. 121–29.

23 'Ilolahia interview.

24 *Dawn Raids*, directed by Damon Fepulea'i, Rachel Jean, and Tarx Morrison (TVNZ, Isola Publications, 2005).

25 Anae, *The Platform*, p. 107.

26 See Sharon Alice Liava'a, 'Dawn Raids: When Pacific Islanders were forced to go "home"', PhD thesis, University of Auckland, 1998.

27 'Ilolahia interview.

28 Anae, *The Platform*, pp. 112–13.

29 'Ilolahia interview.

30 Gershen Kaufman, *Shame: The power of caring* (Vermont: Schenkman Books, 1992), p. 12. For further discussions of shame and memory see, Arnaud

D'Argembeau and Martial Van der Linden, 'Remembering pride and shame: Self-enhancement and the phenomenology of autobiographical memory', *Memory* 16, 5, 2008, pp. 538–47.
31 Tainui Stephens, 'Whakamā: Fighting the taniwha of shame', *The Spinoff*, 13 July 2020.
32 For a discussion of whakamā in a cross-cultural context see Joan Metge, *In and Out of Touch: Whakamaa in cross cultural context* (Wellington: Victoria University Press, 1986).
33 'Ilolahia interview.
34 Philip Fountain and Geoffrey Troughton, 'Christianity and development in the Pacific: An introduction', *Sites: A Journal of Social Anthropology and Cultural Studies* 16, 1, 2019, pp. 1–23.
35 'Ilolahia interview.
36 Ibid.
37 Ibid.
38 Ibid.
39 Ibid.
40 Linda Tuhiwai Smith, *Decolonizing Methodologies: Research and Indigenous peoples* (London: Zed Books, 2012), p. 243.
41 Statement of Tesimoni Fuavao for *Tulou – Our Pacific Voices: Tatala e Pulonga hearing*, 2021: www.abuseincare.org.nz/our-progress/library/v/331/statement-of-tesimoni-fuavao-for-tulou-our-pacific-voices-tatala-e-pulonga-hearing
42 Tuhiwai Smith, *Decolonizing Methodologies*, p. 242.
43 Apulu Reece Autagavaia, 'Dawn Raids ceremony explained: Why Jacinda Ardern sat under a woven mat', *The Spinoff*, 2 August 2021.
44 'Ilolahia interview.
45 Alice Te Punga Somerville, *Once Were Pacific: Māori connections to Oceania*, (Minneapolis: University of Minnesota Press, 2012); Bonnie Etherington, '"I think I believe in civil rights": Re-remembering trans-Indigenous political activism in Pauline Vaeluaga Smith's Dawn Raid', *Studies in the Novel* 54, 3, 2022, pp. 293–311.
46 'Ilolahia interview.

CHAPTER 5

1 Rogers Brubaker and Frederick Cooper, 'Beyond "identity"', *Theory and Society* 29, 1, 2000, pp. 1–47.
2 Peter Finke and Martin Sökefeld, 'Identity in anthropology', in *The International Encyclopedia of Anthropology*, ed. Hilary Callan (New Jersey: John Wiley and Sons, 2018), p. 11.
3 Jo Cribb, 'Focus on families: New Zealand families of yesterday, today, and tomorrow', *Social Policy Journal of New Zealand 35,* June 2009.
4 Robyn Fivush, 'An ecological systems approach to family narratives', *Memory Studies* 9, 3, 2016, pp. 305–14; Robyn Fivush, 'Remembering and reminiscing: How individual lives are constructed in family narratives', *Memory Studies* 1, 1, 2008, pp. 49–58; Elaine Reese, Catherine A. Haden and Robyn Fivush, 'Mother-child conversations about the past: Relationships of style and memory over time', *Cognitive Development* 8, 4, 1993, pp. 403–40.
5 Dan P. McAdams and Kate C. McLean, 'Narrative identity', *Current Directions in Psychological Science 22,* 2013, p. 233.
6 Michael Zuckerman, 'The presence of the present, the end of history', *The Public Historian* 22, 1, Winter 2000, pp. 19–20; Michael Kammen, 'Carl Becker Redivivus: Or, is everyone really a historian?', *History and Theory 39*, May 2000, p. 234.
7 Ian Pool, Arunachalam Dharmalingam and Janet Sceats, *The New Zealand*

Family from 1840 (Auckland: Auckland University Press, 2007), pp. xii–xiv.

8   For example, see A. Bell, 'Reverberating historical privilege of a "middling" sort of settler family', *Genealogy 4*, 2, 2020, pp. 1–17; and Richard Shaw, *The Forgotten Coast* (Auckland: Massey University Press, 2021), pp. 221–22.

9   For two different perspectives on Pākehā identity see: Michael King, *Being Pakeha* (Auckland: Hodder and Stoughton, 1985) and *Being Pakeha Now* (Auckland: Penguin, 1999); Lydia Wevers, 'Being Pakeha: The politics of location', *Journal of New Zealand Studies 4/5*, 2005–6, p. 8.

10 Anna Green, 'Why family memories and stories matter', *Journal of New Zealand Studies 29*, 2, 2019, pp. 3–19. See also the project website: 'The Missing Link' (www.familymemory.nz). The four oral historians were Anna Green, Megan Hutching, Pip Oldham and Helen Frizzell. The research project was funded by the Marsden Fund of the Royal Society Te Apārangi, 2016.

11 Des McSweeney interviewed by Pip Oldham, 9 September 2016, FMP03_1OT2: 3.40. Unless otherwise indicated, subsequent excerpts are taken from this oral history interview, which is currently held by the author.

12 Anna Green, 'Grandparents, communicative memory and narrative identity', *Oral History 47*, 1, 2019, pp. 81–92.

13 Des and Marie McSweeney, 'Arrival in Canterbury', in *McSweeney: Your pioneer story 1850–1962* (Akaroa, n.p., 1995), pp. 3–5.

14 Anna Green and Kayleigh Luscombe, 'Family memory, "things", and counterfactual thinking', *Memory Studies 12*, 6, 2019, pp. 646–59.

15 Catherine Nash, *Of Irish Descent: Origin stories, genealogy, and the politics of belonging* (New York: Syracuse University Press, 2008), p. 72. See also Paul Basu, *Highland Homecomings: Genealogy and heritage tourism in the Scottish diaspora* (London: Routledge, 2007).

16 Interview: FMP_03_2G: 00.43.22. Interviewed by Anna Green, 20 October 2016. Interview in possession of author.

17 Guy Fawkes was an English Catholic who tried unsuccessfully to blow up the British parliament in London in 1605 and is remembered with a bonfire, guy (Guy Fawkes effigy), and fireworks on the night of 5 November.

18 See Angela McCarthy, *Scottishness and Irishness in New Zealand since 1840* (Manchester: Manchester University Press, 2011), pp. 144–45.

19 Patrick O'Farrell, 'Varieties of New Zealand Irishness: A meditation', in *A Distant Shore: Irish migration and New Zealand settlement*, ed. Lyndon Fraser (Dunedin: University of Otago Press, 2000), pp. 135–54.

20 Ed de St Aubin, Dan P. McAdams, and Tae-Chang Kim, eds, *The Generative Society: Caring for future generations* (Washington: American Psychological Association, 2004).

CHAPTER 6

1   My thanks to Terri Elder, whose idea I borrowed for this sentence, and whose feedback on an early draft of this chapter is much appreciated.

2   It is with respect for Marion that I entitle her this way, as she always insisted on being known as Miss Steven in writing.

3   For further reading about Marion's academic career see Roswyn Wiltshire,

'Marion Steven and the Logie Collection', *Journal of New Zealand Studies NS32*, 2021, pp. 96–107.
4   James Logie was Registrar at the (then named) University Canterbury College from 1950 until his death in 1956.
5   Kate Kennedy and Hermione Lee, *Lives of Houses* (New Jersey: Princeton University Press, 2020), p. xiii.
6   Paula Hamilton, 'The Proust effect: Oral history and the senses', in *The Oxford Handbook of Oral History*, ed. Donald A. Ritchie (New York: Oxford University Press, 2011), pp. 219–32.
7   Anna Green, '"Unpacking" the stories', in *Remembering: Writing oral history*, eds Anna Green and Megan Hutching (Auckland: Auckland University Press, 2004), p. 11.
8   Ibid., p. 20.
9   Jane Cox, 'Eulogy for Marion Kerr Steven', James Logie Memorial Collection Archives, University of Canterbury.
10 Emma Jean Kelly, *The Adventures of Jonathan Dennis* (Bloomington: Indiana University Press, 2015), p. 98.
11 Daniel Miller, *Stuff* (Cambridge, UK: Polity Press, 2010), p. 89.
12 Personal communication with Elizabeth Benney, 15 November 2018.

CHAPTER 7

1   The research was funded by a 2015 Asia New Zealand Foundation research grant.
2   The students were boarding at Dr Graham's Homes, a school in the lower Himalayas. Historian Jane McCabe also has connections with Dr Graham's Homes through her family and her research participants. Her work relates to mine in that we both interviewed Anglo-Indians, but her interviews were exclusively associated with the Homes, whereas the participant pool for my research was extended to include any Anglo-Indian who now lived in Aotearoa New Zealand. I interviewed three people who were also involved in Jane's research.
3   L. Caplan, '"Life is only abroad, not here": The culture of emigration among Anglo-Indians in Madras', *Immigrants and Minorities 14*, 1, 1995, pp. 26–46.
4   Robyn Andrews, 'Being Anglo-Indian: Practices and stories from Calcutta', PhD thesis, Massey University, 2005; Alison Blunt, *Domicile and Diaspora: Anglo-Indian women and the spatial politics of home* (Oxford: Blackwell, 2005); L. Caplan, 'Life is only abroad, not here'.
5   Robyn Andrews and Brent H. Otto, 'Religion as capital: Christianity in the lives of Anglo-Indian youth in India', *Journal of Contemporary Religion 32*, 1, 2017, pp. 105–18; Alison Blunt, 'Geographies of diaspora and mixed descent: Anglo-Indians in India and Britain', *International Journal of Population Geography 9*, 2003, pp. 281–94; Blunt, *Domicile and Diaspora*.
6   Patrick Ongley and David Pearson, 'Post-1945 international migration: New Zealand, Australia and Canada compared', *The International Migration Review 29*, 3, 1995, pp. 771–74.
7   Ibid., p. 775.
8   In the New Zealand census people can self-identify as Anglo-Indian, rather than needing to offer any objective 'proof'.
9   Lynne Klap, interview, 6 June 2015. Interview recording held by author.
10 Lynne Klap and Tina Divers, interview, 19 July 2015. Interview recording held by author.
11 Jennifer Moody, interview, 11 July 2015. Interview recording held by author.
12 Lynne Klap, interview, 6 June 2015.

13 Tina in Lynne Klap and Tina Divers, interview, 19 July 2015.
14 Lynne in Lynne Klap and Tina Divers, interview, 19 July 2015.
15 Lynne Klap, personal email correspondence, 30 September 2015.
16 'Partition' is the term used for the splitting of India into two nations, India and Pakistan, on the dissolution of the British Raj. This was immediately followed by mass migration mostly of Hindus to India and Muslims to Pakistan, accompanied by terrible communal violence.
17 Christine, personal email correspondence, 24 May 2023.
18 Christine, interview, 10 November 2015. Interview recording held by author. All further quotes of Christine's in this chapter are from this interview.
19 Parvati Erikson, interview, 19 November 2015. Interview recording held by author.
20 Tasman Empire Airways Limited, now known as Air New Zealand Limited.
21 Patricia Springer, interview, 24 August 2015. Interview recording held by author.
22 Chris McGowan, interview, 10 May 2016. Interview recording held by author.
23 Richard Pollock, interview, 16 August 2016. Interview recording held by author.
24 The headline from a newspaper story, 7 May 1888: 'New Zealand in the 19th century strived to be a "Britain of the South Seas" and Pākehā saw non-white migrants as undesirable', Ministry for Culture and Heritage, 'Anti-Chinese hysteria in Dunedin', see: https://nzhistory.govt.nz/anti-chinese-hysteria-dunedin
25 Simon Daisley, interview, 3 December 2015. Interview recording held by author.
26 Jane McCabe, 'Kalimpong Kids: The lives and labours of Anglo-Indian adolescents resettled in New Zealand between 1908 and 1938', PhD thesis, University of Otago, 2014.
27 This phenomenon of holidaying in places one feels genealogically connected to is referred to by Wessendorf as 'roots tourism'. Susanna Wessendorf, '"Roots migrants": Transnationalism and "return" among second-generation Italians in Switzerland', *Journal of Ethnic and Migration Studies 33*, 7, 2007, pp. 1083–1102. Paul Basu also writes about the phenomenon and questions the terminology: 'Roots tourism as return movement: Semantics and the Scottish diaspora', in *Emigrant Homecomings: The return movement of emigrants, 1600–2000*, ed. Marjory Harper (Manchester: Manchester University Press, 2005).
28 Preface of this book.

CHAPTER 8

1 Roberto Rabel in *A Fair Sort of Battering: New Zealanders remember the Italian campaign,* ed. Megan Hutching (Auckland: HarperCollins NZ, 2004), p. 21.
2 Ibid., p. 22.
3 Maurice Shadbolt, *Voices of Gallipoli* (Auckland: Hodder & Stoughton, 1988).
4 Paula Hamilton and Linda Shopes, eds, 'Building partnerships between oral history and memory studies', in *Oral History and Public Memories* (Philadelphia, USA: Temple University Press, 2008), p. vii, quoted in Graham Smith, 'Toward a public oral history', *The Oxford Handbook of Oral History*, ed. Donald A. Ritchie (New York: Oxford University Press, 2010), p. 439.
5 William Flint, interviewed by Megan Hutching, 5 February 2002, side 3.

Interview archived at Alexander Turnbull Library, Wellington, OHInt-0802-05. Used with permission of the Chief Historian, Te Manatū Taonga Ministry for Culture and Heritage. Extracts from the interview were published in *Inside Stories: New Zealand prisoners of war remember*, ed. Megan Hutching (Auckland: HarperCollins NZ, 2002).
6. See: https://literariness.org/2019/03/22/picaresque-novels-and-novelists/
7. Flint, 5 February 2002, side 7.
8. Flint, 5 February 2002, side 6.
9. Flint, 5 February 2002, side 6.
10. Flint, 5 February 2002, side 7.
11. Flint, 5 February 2002, side 3.
12. Eric Williams, *The Wooden Horse* (London: Collins, 1949); Paul Brickhill, *The Great Escape* (London: Faber, 1951). There are films of both books – *The Wooden Horse* (1950) and *The Great Escape* (1963).
13. Paul J. Springer, 'Prisoners of war on film and in memory', *Orbis 54*, 2010, p. 669, quoted in Matthew Johnson, 'Resisting captivity: An analysis of the New Zealand POW experience during World War Two', PhD thesis, University of Waikato, 2018, p. 11.
14. Many former prisoners of war wrote memoirs about their experiences. For a useful list, see Matthew Johnson, 'Resisting captivity', pp. 272–74. Johnson also discusses the strengths and weaknesses of using memoirs in his introduction, pp. 29–34, but has surprisingly little to say about the use of oral history interviews (despite using published versions of them in his thesis).
15. Graham Smith, 'Toward a public oral history', p. 439.
16. Few members of New Zealand military personnel have been involved in active combat since the war in Vietnam. In countries such as the United States, where their military has been almost continually involved in active conflict, this argument is more tenuous.
17. Graham Dawson and Bob West, 'Our finest hour? The popular memory of World War II and the struggle over national identity', in *National Fictions: World War Two in British Film and Television*, ed. Geoffrey Hurd (London: BFI Publishing, 1984), p. 11.
18. Smith, 'Toward a public oral history', p. 440.
19. Matthew Johnson, 'Resisting captivity', p. 260.

CHAPTER 9

1. For example, Judith Fyfe and Hugo Manson, 'Oral history and how to approach it', Oral History Centre, Alexander Turnbull Library, 1995 and subsequent revisions.
2. Sean Nugent, 'Aspiring Station matriarch served rural community for decades', *Otago Daily Times*, 7 July 2018.
3. Phyllis Aspinall, interviewed by Helen Frizzell, 22–23 March 2010. Interview archived at Alexander Turnbull Library, Wellington, OHInt-0984-02, GEM_PASPIT03, 30:20.
4. A. Maud Moreland, *Through South Westland: Journey to the Haast and Mount Aspiring* (London: Witherby & Co., 1911).
5. J.C. Aspinall, 'High country sheep station', in *A Bulletin for Schools*, GP Serial No. 51, 197.
6. George Evans, 'The woman of the west', 1901.
7. GEM_PASPIT03, 53:49.
8. GEM_PASPIT03, 32:08-44:10.
9. Photograph by Helen Buttfield, supplied by interviewee and archived with the

oral history file name *aspinall_william_MtAspiringHomestead_ed*.

10 Short section removed where interviewee and interviewer are talking at cross purposes, T03 43:21 to 43:48.

11 J.C. Aspinall, 'High country sheep station', p. 197.

12 Alex Hedley, *High Country Legacy: Four generations of Aspinalls at Mt Aspiring Station* (Auckland: HarperCollins NZ, 2012).

13 For example, Laurel Teirney, 'Phyllis Aspinall of Mount Aspiring – a tribute for an inspiring woman' (Wanaka: Wanaka Arts Society, January 2018).

14 Studs Terkel with Tony Parker, 'Interviewing and interviewer', in *The Oral History Reader*, 2nd edn, eds Robert Perks and Alastair Thomson (Oxford: Routledge, 2006), pp. 124–25.

15 Anna Bryson and Sean McConville, *The Routledge Guide to Interviewing* (Oxford: Routledge, 2014), p. 137.

16 Jane Moodie, 'The moral world of the Waikite Valley', in *Remembering, Writing Oral History*, eds Anna Green and Megan Hutching (Auckland: Auckland University Press, 2004), pp. 39–59.

17 GEM_PASPIT03, 12:48.

18 GEM_PASPIT02, 28:00.

19 GEM_PASPIT02, 1:06:03.

20 GEM_PASPIT03, 07:41 and 08:08.

21 GEM_PASPIT06, 02:21.

22 Helen Leach, *Kitchens: The New Zealand kitchen in the 20th century* (Dunedin: University of Otago Press, 2014), pp. 10–11.

23 Ibid., p. 101.

24 GEM_PASPIT07, 32:57.

25 Jerry Aspinall, *Farming Under Aspiring* (Alexandra: Macpherson Publishing, 1993), p. 86.

26 GEM_PASPIT04, 05:45.

27 GEM_PASPIT06, 05:31.

28 GEM_PASPIT03, 40:46.

29 GEM_PASPIT03, 54:56.

30 GEM_PASPIT03, 24:09.

31 GEM_PASPIT07, 15:31.

32 GEM_PASPIT07, 14:15.

CHAPTER 10

1 The voices of trans individuals, whakawāhine or Māori trans women and men, who worked in parlours, from the streets, and privately indoors during this period are also critical to the wider Royal Society of New Zealand Marsden Fund Fast-Start project on which this chapter is based: 'Untold Intimacies: Histories of sex work in Aotearoa'.

2 Robert Atkinson, 'The life story interview as a bridge in narrative inquiry', in *Handbook of Narrative Inquiry: Mapping a Methodology*, ed. D. Jean Clandinin (California: SAGE Publications Inc, 2007), p. 224.

3 Barbara Brooks, *A History of New Zealand Women* (Wellington: Bridget Williams Books, 2016), p. 408; Jacqueline O'Neill, '"She asked for it": A textual analysis of the re-negotiation of the meaning of rape in the 1970s–1980s', MA thesis, Massey University, 2006.

4 Christine Dann, *Up from Under: Women's Liberation in New Zealand 1970–1985* (Wellington: Allen & Unwin, Port Nicholson Press, 1985), pp. 133–34.

5 Barbara Sullivan, 'Prostitution and consent: Beyond the liberal dichotomy of "free or forced"', in *Making Sense of Sexual Consent*, eds Mark Cowling and Paul Reynolds (Aldershot, England: Ashgate, 2004), p. 128.

6 Grace Millar, 'Women's lives, feminism and the New Zealand Journal of History', *New Zealand Journal of History* 52, 2, 2018, p. 145.

7. Leonie Pihama et al., 'Māori cultural definitions of sexual violence', *Sexual Abuse in Australia and New Zealand 7*, 1, 2016, p. 43.
8. Ibid., p. 48.
9. Ibid.
10. Erin Ford Cozens, '"Our particular abhorrence of these particular crimes": Sexual violence and colonial legal discourse in Aotearoa/New Zealand, 1840–1855', *Journal of the History of Sexuality 24*, 3, 2015, pp. 378–401; Ani Mikaere, 'Māori women caught in the contradictions of a colonised reality', *Waikato Law Review 6*, 2, 1994, pp. 125–149; Angela Wanhalla, 'Interracial sexual violence in 1860s New Zealand', *New Zealand Journal of History 45*, 1, 2011, pp. 71–84.
11. Penny Summerfield, 'Culture and composure: Creating narratives of the gendered self in oral history interviews', *Cultural and Social History 1*, 2004, pp. 69–70; Penny Summerfield, 'Dis/composing the subject: intersubjectivities in oral history', in *Feminism & Autobiography: Texts, theories, methods*, eds Tess Coslett, Celia Lury and Penny Summerfield (London: Routledge, 2000), p. 93.
12. Wendy Rickard, 'Oral history – "More dangerous than therapy?" Interviewees' reflections on recording traumatic or taboo issues', *Oral History 26*, 2, 1998, p. 42; Alistair Thomson, 'Anzac memories: Putting popular theory into practice in Australia', in *The Houses of History: A critical reader in twentieth-century history and theory*, eds Anna Green and Kathleen Troup (Manchester: Manchester University Press, 1999), p. 243.
13. Melissa Matutina Williams, *Panguru and the City: Kāinga Tahi, Kāinga Rua. An urban migration history* (Wellington: Bridget Williams Books Ltd., 2015), p. 25.
14. Oral historian Wendy Rickard has highlighted the legal risks she and the women she interviewed faced when speaking about sex work in Britain. See 'Collaborating with sex workers in oral history', *Oral History Review 30*, 1, 2003, p. 51.
15. Sex work was decriminalised in Belgium in June 2022.
16. Kate, interviewed by Cheryl Ware, Wellington, 11 June 2021. Interview in author's possession. Italics indicate emphasis in narrator's voice.
17. Anna Bracewell-Worrall, 'Calls mount for "stealthing" – covert condom removal during sex – to be explicitly recognised as rape', *Newshub*, 2 October 2021.
18. Cheryl Ware, 'Sex workers' responses to the HIV and AIDS epidemic in Aotearoa New Zealand', *Women's History Review 29*, 2, 2020, pp. 289–307.
19. Thank you to Kate for this observation.
20. 'Designer rapist', *Siren: Sex Industry Rights and Education Network*, July 1990, p. 10.
21. Sophie Day, 'What counts as rape? Physical assault and broken contracts: Contrasting views of rape among London sex workers', in *Sex and Violence: Issues in representation and experience*, eds Penelope Harvey and Peter Gow (London: Routledge, 1994), pp. 172–73.
22. Kate, interview 11 June 2021.
23. Frankie, interviewed by Cheryl Ware, Auckland, 19 May 2021. Interview in author's possession.
24. Anna Green, '"Unpacking" the stories', in *Remembering: Writing oral history*, eds Anna Green and Megan Hutching (Auckland: Auckland University Press, 2004), p. 19.
25. Lynzi Armstrong, 'Managing risks of violence in decriminalised street-based sex work: A feminist (sex worker rights) perspective', PhD thesis, Victoria University of Wellington, 2011, p. 46.

CHAPTER 11

1. Susan T. interviewed by Dean Broughton, 15 January 2023, 0:03. Interview in author's possession.
2. Anna Green and Megan Hutching, 'Preface', in *Remembering: Writing oral history*, eds Anna Green and Megan Hutching (Auckland: Auckland University Press, 2004), p. vii.
3. Marine Department, 'Memorandum on the Shipping and Seamen Act 1952: Penalties for desertion', 1957 Series 16612, Box 22, Record 15/3/856, Archives New Zealand, R19978141 Seamen – Engagement and Discharge – Desertion from Overseas Ships.
4. Miscellaneous files, R19978141 'Seamen – Engagement and Discharge – Desertion from Overseas Ships', Series 16612, Box 22, Record 15/3/856, Archives New Zealand.
5. *A Record of Achievement: The work of the National Government 1949–1957* (Wellington: The National Party, 1957), p. 111; E.R. Martin, Memorandum to Mr O'Halloran and Mr Hobbs re: Ship Deserters, 16 December 1955, Series 16612, Box 22, Record 15/3/856, Archives New Zealand, R19978141 Seamen – Engagement and Discharge – Desertion from Overseas Ships.
6. Annabel Ahuriri Driscoll, Denise Blake, Helen Potter, Kim McBreen and Ani Mikaere, 'A "forgotten" whakapapa: Historical narratives of Māori and closed adoption', *Kotuitui; New Zealand Journal of Social Sciences Online 18*, 2, 2022, p. 136.
7. Ruth Greenaway and Megan Hutching, *Threads of Caring: A history of the Anglican Trust for Women and Children* (Auckland: Anglican Trust for Women and Children, 2021), pp. 124–25.
8. Anne Else, *A Question of Adoption* (Wellington: Bridget Williams Books, 1991), p. 197.
9. Susan T. interview, 47:17.
10. Susan T. interview, 01:33.
11. Susan T. interview, 02:43.
12. Susan T. interview, 03:36.
13. Susan T. interview, 04:56.
14. Susan T. interview, 06:17.
15. *New Zealand Police Gazette*, 12 April 1961, R15423795 Archives New Zealand, Wellington, p.260; *New Zealand Police Gazette*, 14 June 1961, 'Prisoners Released', R15423795, Archives New Zealand, Wellington, p. 609.
16. Charles Edward Martin, Employment Record C.R.S 10, Fifth Register of British Merchant Seamen, Records of the Registrar General of Shipping and Seamen and Successor. Copy in author's possession.
17. Bevan Martin, *Maritime Law in New Zealand* (Wellington: Thomson Reuters New Zealand Ltd, 2016), pp. 10–11; Shipping and Seamen Act 1952, Sections 157 and 158.
18. Susan T. interview, 05:03.
19. Susan T. interview, 05:42.
20. *New Zealand Police Gazette*, 12 April 1961; *New Zealand Police Gazette*, 14 June 1961.
21. 'Details about your child', copy of a social welfare report on the adoption of a newborn baby to Mr and Mrs R**, 1961. Copy held by the author.
22. Susan T. interview, 05:54.
23. Susan T. interview, 06:17.
24. Susan T. interview, 10:04.
25. Susan T. interview, 10:56.
26. Susan T. interview, 16:17.
27. Susan T. interview, 19:32.
28. Susan T. interview, 21:30.
29. Susan T. interview, 22:48.
30. Susan T. interview, 24:32.

31. Susan T. interview, 32:22.
32. Susan T. interview, 30:12.
33. Susan T. interview, 51:20.
34. Alessandro Portelli, 'What makes oral history different', in *The Oral History Reader,* 3rd edn, eds Robert Perks and Alistair Thomson (London and New York: Routledge, 2016), p. 52.
35. Ibid., p. 51.

CHAPTER 12

1. Alessandro Portelli, 'What makes oral history different', in *The Oral History Reader,* 3rd edn, eds Robert Perks and Alistair Thomson (London and New York: Routledge, 2016), pp. 48–58.
2. Ruth Greenaway and Megan Hutching, *Threads of Caring: A history of the Anglican Trust for Women and Children* (Auckland: Anglican Trust for Women and Children, 2021) and Kay Morris Matthews, *Who Cared: Childhoods within Hawke's Bay children's homes and orphanages* (Napier: East Institution of Technology, 2013) are examples of histories of children's care institutions which used oral histories.
3. *Appendix to the Journal of the House of Representatives,* Session 1, 1925, E-4, p. 20.
4. Lydia Murdoch, *Imagined Orphans: Poor families, child welfare, and contested citizenship in London* (New Jersey: Rutgers University Press, 2006), p. 2.
5. I found some evidence of the local Child Welfare department advising parents to place their children in the Home. See Elizabeth Ward, 'Such a work as this: A case study of the All Saints' Children's Home, Palmerston North', MA thesis, Massey University, 2015, pp. 125–27.
6. Lynn Abrams, *Oral History Theory,* 2nd edn (London: Routledge, 2016), p. 80.
7. These interviews are archived at the Ian Matheson City Archives, Palmerston North.
8. These can be found in Ward, 'Such a work as this', p. 169.
9. Matron's Daybook, Series 4, Box 1, May 1960–August 1964, All Saints' Children's Home Archive, Ian Matheson City Archives, Palmerston North.
10. For more detail on the last years of the Home see Ward, 'Such a work as this', pp. 137–42.
11. Correspondence and Subject Files. Series 7, Folder 5, Annual Report, All Saints' Children's Home Archive, Ian Matheson City Archives, Palmerston North.
12. For more detail on the All Saints' Children's Home Trust see Ward, 'Such a work as this', pp. 153–54.
13. Peggy Crawford, *Only an Orphan: First-hand accounts of life in children's institutions* (Lower Hutt: MJC Publishing, 1995) and Morris Matthews, *Who Cared,* both contain excerpts from oral histories conducted by the authors.
14. Abrams, *Oral History Theory,* p. 16.
15. Christine R., interviewed by Elizabeth Ward, Palmerston North, 6 November 2014, Ian Matheson City Archives, Palmerston North.
16. Christine R. interview.
17. Howard E., interviewed by Elizabeth Ward, Wellington, 26 June 2014, Ian Matheson City Archives, Palmerston North.
18. Paula Hamilton, 'The Proust effect: Oral history and the senses', in *The Oxford Handbook of Oral History,* ed. Donald A. Ritchie (New York: Oxford University Press, 2010), p. 219.
19. Christine R. interview.
20. Penny Summerfield, *Reconstructing Women's Wartime Lives* (Manchester: Manchester University Press, 1998),

pp. 216–19; Abrams, *Oral History Theory*, p. 44.
21 Christine R. interview.
22 Howard E. interview.
23 Christine R. interview.
24 Howard E. interview. This incident is mentioned in Matron's Daybook July 1963. Matron's Daybook, Series 4, Box 1, May 1960–August 1964, All Saints' Children's Home Archive, Ian Matheson City Archives, Palmerston North.
25 Howard E. interview.
26 Abrams, *Oral History Theory*, p. 117.
27 Christine R. interview.
28 Howard E. interview.
29 https://manawatuheritage.pncc.govt.nz/item/40f7181e-520d-46e7-829a-514f91ae2f4d
30 The difference in the distance between the two churches and the Home is small, but St Oswald's was closer to the school the children attended, so may have been seen as more part of the natural community of the Home.
31 Matron's Daybook, Series 4, Box 1, May 1960–August 1964, All Saints' Children's Home Archive, Ian Matheson City Archives, Palmerston North.
32 Christine R. interview.
33 Howard E. interview.
34 Christine R. interview.
35 Howard E. interview.
36 Matron's Daybook, Series 4, Box 1, May 1960–August 1964, All Saints' Children's Home Archive, Ian Matheson City Archives, Palmerston North.
37 Crawford, *Only an Orphan*, pp. 39–51. These are also a theme in Morris Matthews but, as she dealt with each home separately, they are scattered throughout the book.
38 Howard E. interview.
39 Ibid.
40 Ibid.
41 This was confirmed by the principal, Ken Gregory, in an interview with author 12 August 2014. See Ward, 'Such a work as this', p. 110.
42 During the period covered, physical punishment of the children is not mentioned. It is mentioned earlier in the life of the Home. See Ward, 'Such a work as this', pp. 109–10.
43 Many of the other oral histories mention corporal punishment, Howard's experience within the Home was not unique. For example, see Mavis H. interviewed by Elizabeth Ward, Palmerston North, 25 June 2014, Ian Matheson City Archives, Palmerston North, and Owen W. interviewed by Elizabeth Ward, Palmerston North, 17 June 2014, Ian Matheson City Archives, Palmerston North.
44 Bronwyn Dalley, *Family Matters: Child welfare in twentieth century New Zealand* (Auckland: Auckland University Press, 1998), pp. 249–51.
45 Ken Gregory, in an interview with author, 12 August 2014, discussed how concerned he was about the treatment of the children and the avenues open to him.

CHAPTER 13

1 Deborah Dunsford, *Doing It Themselves: The story of Kumeū, Huapai and Taupaki* (Auckland: Kumeū District History Project, 2002).
2 See for example David Yerex, *Empire of the Dairy Farmers* (Petone: N.Z. Dairy Exporter Books, 1989); Rex Monigatti, *Fruitful Fields: The development of New Zealand's fruit industry from 1916 to 1966* (Wellington: New Zealand Fruitgrowers' Federation, 1991); Michael Cooper, *The Wine and Vineyards of New Zealand* (Auckland: Hodder & Stoughton, 1984); Patricia O'Shea, *The*

Golden Harvest: A history of tobacco growing in New Zealand (Christchurch: Hazard Press, 1997).

3   Recent examples of memoirs of rural life include: Doug Avery, *The Resilient Farmer* (Auckland: Random House New Zealand, 2017); Colin Crump, *In Endless Fear: A true story* (Auckland: Penguin Books, 2002); Frans Jansen, *Of Horses and Men: Tales from a rural New Zealand farrier* (New Zealand: Wild Side Publishing, 2020); Catherine Stewart, *A Wife on Gorge River* (Auckland: Random House, 2017).

4   See for example, Dunsford, *Doing It Themselves*; H.R. Locker, *Jade River: A history of the Mahurangi* (Auckland: Friends of the Mahurangi, 2001); Alice M. Rea, *They Came For Kauri But ... The history of Waimauku and Muriwai, 1863–1963* (Auckland: n.p., 1963); Ruth E. Low, *On the Hoof: The untold story of drovers in New Zealand* (Auckland: Penguin, 2014); Ruth E. Low, *The Shearers: New Zealand legends* (Auckland: Penguin, 2019).

5   *Auckland Star*, 28 March 1914, p. 4.

6   *New Zealand Herald*, 20 March 1915, p. 11.

7   Ibid.

8   Dunsford, *Doing It Themselves*, pp. 187–88.

ABOUT THE CONTRIBUTORS

ROBYN ANDREWS is an Associate Professor in Social Anthropology and a Research Fellow at Massey University. Her 2005 PhD thesis was based on ethnographic research with the Anglo-Indian Community in Kolkata, India. It was the first of several Anglo-Indian Studies projects she is engaged with in India and the diaspora.

DEAN BROUGHTON is a PhD candidate at Te Herenga Waka Victoria University of Wellington and is completing a comprehensive study of ship-jumping seafarers in New Zealand between 1945 and 1980. His general research focuses on New Zealand and British seafarers in the nineteenth and twentieth centuries. He comes from a merchant navy background and is passionate about the seafaring narrative being more prominent in New Zealand history. Dean has worked as a researcher and tutor in a range of historical and political subjects at Te Herenga Waka.

HELENA COOK is a Samoan/Irish lecturer in the School of Educational Studies and Leadership at Te Whare Wānanga o Waitaha University of Canterbury. Her research has two broad areas of interest: historically 'othered' bodies within institutions and Pacific and indigenous ways of knowing and being in higher education. These interests draw on her background in tertiary education and political science and her passion for telling stories about the world we inhabit.

DEBORAH DUNSFORD is an independent historian. She records interviews for archival purposes, and her books *Doing It Themselves: The story of Kumeu, Huapai, and Taupaki* (2002) and *Mt Albert Then and Now: A history of Mt Albert, Morningside, Kingsland, St Lukes, Sandringham, and Owairaka* (2016) draw extensively on her oral history interviews. She is currently working on a history of the Auckland suburb of Milford and its early days as a popular seaside holiday and entertainment resort.

HELEN FRIZZELL is a freelance oral historian based in Ōtepoti Dunedin. She has over 35 years of experience in recording, presenting and teaching oral history and is a Winston Churchill Fellow. Helen's interviews have been used in publications, play scripts and exhibitions such as *Shirakee: Children in Walker Street 1900–1920*.

ANNA GREEN is an adjunct professor at Te Herenga Waka Victoria University of Wellington's Stout Research Centre for NZ Studies. She specialises in memory and oral history using an interdisciplinary approach drawn from psychology, anthropology, sociology and literature. Anna serves as president of The National Oral History Association of New Zealand and contributes to various international scholarly associations and journals.

MEGAN HUTCHING has worked as an oral historian for over 30 years, including at Auckland Libraries and Te Manatū Taonga. She has published on a wide range of topics, including immigration and New Zealand's involvement in World War II and has an abiding interest in the history of women's political activism.

MARGARET KAWHARU (Te Taoū, Ngāti Whātua) has been dedicated to pursuing and implementing the Ngāti Whātua o Kaipara Treaty claim for 35 years. She managed the claim through the Waitangi Tribunal and negotiations processes to a settlement with the Crown. She served as a trustee of the post-settlement governance entity and is currently a director of the commercial subsidiary, chairing the two forestry companies. Margaret has a PhD from the Stout Research Centre for New Zealand Studies at Te Herenga Waka Victoria University of Wellington.

NATALIE LOOYER worked as a curatorial assistant at the Teece Museum of Classical Antiquities while completing her Master of Arts in Classics at Te Whare Wānanga o Waitaha University of Canterbury in 2019. She diverted her attention to modern history and is now a PhD candidate at Te Herenga Waka Victoria University of Wellington, researching the history of rock climbing as a sport in Aotearoa New Zealand.

JANE MOODIE became interested in oral history while involved in the Frankton Oral History Project at the University of Waikato in the 1990s. Later projects have included a study of the lives of soldier-settlers and their families in the Waikite Valley after World War II, and a study of the lives of Hungarian refugees in New Zealand 50 years after the 1956 Hungarian Revolution. More recently, Jane's focus has been on the significance of family memory, particularly in relation to Pākehā New Zealand families.

PIP OLDHAM has been a freelance oral historian since 2003 and co-edits the journal *Oral History in New Zealand* with Megan Hutching. She is particularly interested in applying the methodology developed by Judith Fyfe and Hugo Manson to short interviews recorded at intervals over months or years to create a longitudinal picture of an interviewee's life. Examples are a multi-year project, begun in March 2020, exploring the impacts of the Covid-19 pandemic, and recordings with artists and art dealers.

MEGAN PŌTIKI (Kāi Tahu, Te Āti Awa) hails from Ōtākou. Her PhD is on the factors contributing to the death of the Māori language at Ōtākou. Her research interests are focused on the loss of te reo Māori at Ōtākou, traditional mōteatea and new waiata composition, takiaue (death and Māori customs pertaining to the dead), and the written Māori archives of the past that have a particular geographical focus on her tribal region of Kāi Tahu.

ELIZABETH WARD is the manager of Heritage Marlborough. She has previously worked as a contract researcher and lectured at Massey University in the History and Politics programmes. Her PhD thesis was on the origins and development of the Reform Party, and she has recorded a number of oral history projects, including those for her master's thesis on The All Saints Children Home in Palmerston North.

CHERYL WARE is a historian of sex, gender and health in late twentieth-century Aotearoa New Zealand and Australia. She has held multiple competitive research awards, including a Marsden Fund Fast-Start grant, a Judith Binney Writing Award, and a Kate Edger Postdoctoral Research Fellowship. Cheryl is the author of *Untold Intimacies: Histories of sex workers in Aotearoa New Zealand* (Auckland University Press, forthcoming 2025) and *HIV Survivors in Sydney: Memories of the epidemic* (Palgrave Macmillan, 2019).

SELECT BIBLIOGRAPHY

Abrams, Lynn, *Oral History Theory,* 2nd edn (London: Routledge, 2016)

Adds, Peter, 'Long-distance prehistoric two-way voyaging: The case for Aotearoa and Hawaiki', *Journal of the Royal Society of New Zealand* 42, 2, 2012, pp. 99–103

Anae, Melani, Leilani Tamu, Lautofa Iuli, eds, *Polynesian Panthers: Pacific protest and affirmative action in Aotearoa NZ 1971–1981* (Wellington: Huia Publishers, 2015)

Anae, Melani, *The Platform: The radical legacy of the Polynesian Panthers* (Wellington: Bridget Williams Books, 2020)

Anderson, Emily and Helen Frizzell, 'Hurunui seismic stories', *Oral History in New Zealand* 32, 2020, pp. 5–13

Andrews, Robyn and Brent H. Otto, 'Religion as capital: Christianity in the lives of Anglo–Indian youth in India', *Journal of Contemporary Religion* 32, 1, 2017, pp. 105–18

Aspinall, Jerry, *Farming Under Aspiring* (Alexandra: Macpherson Publishing, 1993)

Atkinson, Robert, 'The life story interview as a bridge in narrative inquiry', in *Handbook of Narrative Inquiry: Mapping a methodology,* ed. D. Jean Clandinin (Thousand Oaks, CA: SAGE Publications Inc, 2007), pp. 224–45

Attwood, Bain, *'A Bloody Difficult Subject': Ruth Ross, Te Tiriti o Waitangi and the making of history* (Auckland: Auckland University Press, 2023)

Autagavaia, Apulu Reece, 'Dawn Raids ceremony explained: Why Jacinda Ardern sat under a woven mat', *The Spinoff,* 2 August 2021

Avery, Doug, *The Resilient Farmer* (Auckland: Random House New Zealand, 2017)

Basu, Paul, *Highland Homecomings: Genealogy and heritage tourism in the Scottish diaspora* (London: Routledge, 2007)

Basu, Paul, 'Roots-tourism as return movement: Semantics and the Scottish diaspora', in *Emigrant Homecomings: The return movement of emigrants, 1600–2000,* ed. Marjory Harper (Manchester: Manchester University Press, 2005), pp. 131–50

Beaglehole, Ann, *A Small Price to Pay: Refugees from Hitler in New Zealand, 1936–1946* (Wellington: Bridget Williams Books, 1998)

Belich, James, *Paradise Reforged: A history of the New Zealanders: From the 1880s to the year 2000* (Auckland: Penguin Random House, 2001)

Bell, Avril, 'Reverberating historical privilege of a "middling" sort of settler family', *Genealogy* 4, 2, 2020, pp. 1–17

Blunt, Alison, *Domicile and Diaspora: Anglo–Indian women and the spatial politics of home* (Oxford: Blackwell, 2005)

Blunt, Alison, 'Geographies of diaspora and mixed descent: Anglo–Indians in India and Britain', *International Journal of Population Geography* 9, 2003, pp. 281–94

Borland, Katherine, '"That's not what I said": Interpretive conflict in oral narrative research', in *Women's Words: The feminist practice of oral history,* eds Sherna Berger

Gluck and Daphne Patai (New York: Routledge, 1991), pp. 63–75

Bourdieu, Pierre, 'The forms of capital', in *The Sociology of Economic Life,* 3rd edn, eds Mark Granovetter and Richard Swedberg (New York: Routledge, 2018), pp. 78–92

Brickell, Chris, *Mates and Lovers: A history of gay New Zealand* (Auckland: Penguin Random House, 2008)

Brickhill, Paul, *The Great Escape* (London: Faber & Faber, 1951)

Brooking, Tom, '"Yeotopia" found … but? The yeoman ideal that underpinned New Zealand agricultural practice into the early twenty-first century, with American and Australian comparisons', *Journal of the Agricultural History Society* 93, 1, 2019, pp. 68–101

Brooks, Barbara, *A History of New Zealand Women* (Wellington: Bridget Williams Books, 2016)

Brubaker, Rogers and Frederick Cooper, 'Beyond "identity"', *Theory and Society* 21, 1, 2000, pp. 1–47

Bruner, Jerome, 'Life as narrative', *Social Research: An International Quarterly* 71, 3, 2004, pp. 691–710

Bruner, Jerome, *Making Stories: Law, literature, life* (New York: Farrar, Straus and Giroux, 2002)

Bryson, Anna and Sean McConville, *The Routledge Guide to Interviewing* (Oxford: Routledge, 2014)

Caplan, Lionel, *Children of Colonialism: Anglo-Indians in a post-colonial world* (Oxford: Berg, 2001)

Caplan, Lionel, 'Dimensions of urban poverty: Anglo-Indian poor and their guardians in Madras', *Urban Anthropology* 25, 4, 1996, pp. 311–346

Caplan, Lionel, '"Life is only abroad, not here": The culture of emigration among Anglo-Indians in Madras', *Immigrants and Minorities* 14, 1, 1995, pp. 26–46

Case, Emalani, *Everything Ancient Was Once New* (Hawaii: University of Hawaii Press, 2021)

Chan, Elizabeth, 'Women trailblazers in the law: The New Zealand women judges oral histories project', *Victoria University of Wellington Law Review* 45, 2014, pp. 407–27

Charlton, Thomas L., Lois E. Myers and Rebecca Sharpless, *Thinking About Oral History: Theories and applications* (Lanham: AltaMira Press, 2008)

Cole, Jennifer, 'Painful memories: Ritual and the transformation of community trauma', *Culture, Medicine and Psychiatry* 28, 2004, pp. 87–105

Cooper, Michael, *The Wine and Vineyards of New Zealand* (Auckland: Hodder & Stoughton, 1984)

Coslett, Tess, Celia Lury and Penny Summerfield, eds, *Feminism & Autobiography: Texts, theories, methods* (London: Routledge, 2000)

Crawford, Peggy, *Only an Orphan: First-hand accounts of life in children's institutions* (Lower Hutt: MJC Publishing, 1995)

Cribb, Jo, 'Focus on Families: New Zealand families of yesterday, today, and tomorrow', *Social Policy Journal of New Zealand* 35, June 2009, pp. 4–16

Crothers, Charles, 'Editorial introduction: Special issue on inequality and class in New Zealand', *New Zealand Sociology* 28 3, 2013, p. 12

Crump, Colin, *In Endless Fear: A true story* (Auckland: Penguin Books, 2002)

D'Argembeau, Arnaud and Martial Van der Linden, 'Remembering pride and shame: Self-enhancement and the phenomenology of autobiographical memory', *Memory* 16, 5, 2008, pp. 538–47

Dalley, Bronwyn, *Family Matters: Child welfare in twentieth century New Zealand* (Auckland: Auckland University Press, 1998)

Dann, Christine, *Up from Under: Women's liberation in New Zealand 1970–1985* (Wellington: Allen & Unwin, Port Nicholson Press, 1985)

Dawson, Graham and Bob West, 'Our finest hour? The popular memory of World War

II and the struggle over national identity', in *National Fictions: World War Two in British film and television*, ed. Geoffrey Hurd (London: BFI Publishing, 1984)

Day, Sophie, 'What counts as rape? Physical assault and broken contracts: Contrasting views of rape among London sex workers', in *Sex and Violence: Issues in representation and experience*, eds Penelope Harvey and Peter Gow (London: Routledge, 1994), pp. 172–89

Driscoll, Annabel Ahuriri, Denise Blake, Helen Potter, Kim McBreen and Ani Mikaere, 'A "forgotten" whakapapa: Historical narratives of Māori and closed adoption', *Kotuitui: New Zealand Journal of Social Sciences Online* 18, 2, 2022, pp. 135–52

Dunsford, Deborah, *Doing It Themselves: The story of Kumeū, Huapai and Taupaki* (Auckland: Kumeū District History Project, 2002)

Eldred-Grigg, Stevan, *A Southern Gentry: New Zealanders who inherited the earth* (Wellington: Heinemann Reed, 1980)

Else, Anne, *A Question of Adoption* (Wellington: Bridget Williams Books, 1991)

Erll, Astrid, *Memory in Culture*, trans. Sara B. Young (Basingstoke: Palgrave Macmillan, 2011)

Etherington, Bonnie, '"I think I believe in civil rights": Re-remembering trans-Indigenous political activism in Pauline Vaeluaga Smith's Dawn Raid', *Studies in the Novel* 54, 3, 2022, pp. 293–311

Evans, Rex, *Faith and Farming: Te huarahi ki te ora. The legacy of Henry Williams and William Williams*, rev. edn (Auckland: Evagean, 1998)

Finke, Peter and Martin Sökefeld, 'Identity in anthropology', in *The International Encyclopedia of Anthropology*, ed. Hilary Callan (Hoboken, NJ: John Wiley and Sons, 2018), pp. 1–13

Fivush, Robyn, 'An ecological systems approach to family narratives', *Memory Studies* 9, 3, 2016, pp. 305–14

Fivush, Robyn, 'Remembering and reminiscing: How individual lives are constructed in family narratives', *Memory Studies* 1, 1, 2008, pp. 49–58

Ford Cozens, Erin, '"Our particular abhorrence of these particular crimes": Sexual violence and colonial legal discourse in Aotearoa/New Zealand, 1840–1855', *Journal of the History of Sexuality* 24, 3, 2015, pp. 378–401

Fountain, Philip and Geoffrey Troughton, 'Christianity and development in the Pacific: An introduction', *Sites: A Journal of Social Anthropology and Cultural Studies* 16, 1, 2019, pp. 1–23

Fraser, Ronald, *In Search of a Past: The Manor House, Amnersfield, 1933–45* (London: Verso, 1984)

Graham, Douglas, *Trick or Treaty?* (Wellington: Institute of Policy Studies, Victoria University of Wellington, 1997)

Green, Anna, *British Capital, Antipodean Labour* (Dunedin: Otago University Press, 2001)

Green, Anna, 'Coffee and Bun, Sgt Bonnington and the Tornado: Myth and place in Frankton Junction', *Oral History* 28, 2, 2000, pp. 26–34

Green, Anna, 'Grandparents, communicative memory and narrative identity', *Oral History* 47, 1, 2019, pp. 81–92

Green, Anna, 'Individual remembering and "collective memory": Theoretical presuppositions and contemporary debates', *Oral History* 32, 2, 2004, pp. 35–44

Green, Anna, 'Oral history and history', in *Remembering: Writing oral history*, eds Anna Green and Megan Hutching (Auckland: Auckland University Press, 2004), pp. 1–8

Green, Anna, '"Unpacking" the stories', in *Remembering: Writing oral history*, eds Anna Green and Megan Hutching (Auckland: Auckland University Press, 2004), pp. 9–24

Green, Anna, 'Why family memories and stories matter', *Journal of New Zealand Studies* 29, 2, 2019, pp. 3–19

Green, Anna and Kayleigh Luscombe, 'Family memory, "things", and counterfactual thinking', *Memory Studies 12*, 6, 2019, pp. 646–59

Greenaway, Ruth and Megan Hutching, *Threads of Caring: A history of the Anglican Trust for Women and Children* (Auckland: Anglican Trust for Women and Children, 2021)

Grele, Ron, 'Listen to their voices: Two case studies in the interpretation of oral history interviews', *Oral History 7*, 1, 1979, pp. 33–42

Gubrium, Jaber F. and James A. Holstein, eds, *Handbook of Interview Research* (Thousand Oaks, CA: Sage, 2011)

Gutman, Yifat, Adam D. Brown and Amy Sodaro, eds, *Memory and the Future: Transnational politics, ethics and society* (Basingstoke: Palgrave Macmillan, 2010)

Gutman, Yifat, Amy Sodaro and Adam D. Brown, eds, 'Introduction: Memory and the future: Why a change of focus is necessary', in *Memory and the Future: Transnational politics, ethics and society* (Basingstoke: Palgrave Macmillan, 2010), pp. 1–11

Gutman, Yifat and Jenny Wüstenberg, eds, *The Routledge Handbook of Memory Activism* (London: Routledge, 2023)

Hamilton, Paula and Linda Shopes, eds, *Oral History and Public Memories* (Philadelphia: Temple University Press, 2008)

Hamilton, Paula, 'The Proust effect: Oral history and the senses', in *The Oxford Handbook of Oral History*, ed. Donald A. Ritchie (New York: Oxford University Press, 2010), pp. 218–32

Hansen, Will, 'A trans history of gay liberation in New Zealand', *The Spinoff*, 27 March 2022

Hatch, Elvin, *Respectable Lives: Social standing in rural New Zealand* (Berkeley/Los Angeles: University of California Press, 1992)

Hedley, Alex, *High Country Legacy: Four generations of Aspinalls at Mt Aspiring Station* (Auckland: HarperCollins NZ, 2012)

Hill, Richard S. and Brigitte Bönisch-Brednich, 'Politicizing the past: Indigenous scholarship and Crown–Māori reparations processes in New Zealand', *Social & Legal Studies 16*, 2, 2007, p. 163–81

Hutching, Megan, ed., *A Fair Sort of Battering: New Zealanders remember the Italian campaign* (Auckland: HarperCollins NZ, 2004)

Hutching, Megan, ed., *Against the Rising Sun: New Zealanders remember the Pacific War* (Auckland: HarperCollins NZ, 2006)

Hutching, Megan, ed., *A Unique Sort of Battle: New Zealanders remember Crete* (Auckland: HarperCollins NZ, 2001)

Hutching, Megan, 'Ethics and oral history', *New Zealand Journal of Public History 4*, 1, 2016

Hutching, Megan, ed. *Inside Stories: New Zealand prisoners of war remember* (Auckland: HarperCollins NZ, 2002)

Hutching, Megan, ed., *Last Line of Defence: New Zealanders remember the war at home* (Auckland: HarperCollins NZ, 2007)

Hutching, Megan, *Talking History: A short guide to oral history* (Wellington: Bridget Williams Books, 1993)

Hutching, Megan, ed., *The Desert Road: New Zealanders remember the North African campaign* (Auckland: HarperCollins NZ, 2005)

Jansen, Frans, *Of Horses and Men: Tales from a rural New Zealand farrier* (Maungaturoto: Wild Side Publishing, 2020)

Kammen, Michael, 'Carl Becker Redivivus: Or, is everyone really a historian?', *History and Theory 39*, May 2000, pp. 230–42

Kaufman, Gershen, *Shame: The power of caring* (Vermont: Schenkman Books, 1992)

Keenan, Danny, 'The past from the paepae: Uses of the past in Māori oral history', in *Remembering: Writing oral history*, eds Anna Green and Megan (Auckland: Auckland University Press, 2004), pp. 145–51

Kelly, Emma Jean, *The Adventures of Jonathan Dennis* (Bloomington: Indiana University Press, 2015)

Kennedy, Kate and Hermione Lee, *Lives of Houses* (New Jersey: Princeton University Press, 2020)

King, Michael, *Being Pakeha* (Auckland: Hodder and Stoughton, 1985)

King, Michael, *Being Pakeha Now* (Auckland: Penguin, 1999)

Kotre, John, 'Generativity and culture: What meaning can do', in *The Generative Society: Caring for future generations*, eds Ed de St. Aubin, Dan P. McAdams and Tae-Chang Kim (Washington: American Psychological Association, 2004), pp. 35–50

Kukutai, Tahu, Nepia Mahuika, Heeni Kani, Denise Ewe and Karu Hura Kukutai, 'Survivance as narrative identity: Voices from a Ngā Tiipa oral history project', *MAI Journal 9*, 3, 2020, pp. 309–20

Leach, Helen, *Kitchens: The New Zealand kitchen in the 20th century* (Dunedin: Otago University Press, 2014)

Lévesque, Stéphane and Jean-Philippe Croteau, *Beyond History for Historical Consciousness: Students, narrative, and memory* (Toronto: University of Toronto Press, 2020)

Light, Rowan, *Why Memory Matters: Remembered histories and the politics of the shared past* (Wellington: Bridget Williams Books, 2023)

Lindley, Robin, 'How memory works: Interview with psychologist Daniel L. Schacter', History News Network 2013: http://hnn.us/article/152111

Little, Paul, 'An all-inclusive holiday?', *NZ Listener*, 22 April 2023, p. 32

Locker, H.R., *Jade River: A history of the Mahurangi* (Auckland: Friends of the Mahurangi, 2001)

Low, Ruth E., *On the Hoof: The untold story of drovers in New Zealand* (Auckland: Penguin, 2014)

Low, Ruth E., *The Shearers: New Zealand legends* (Auckland: Penguin, 2019)

MacDonald, Liana, 'Shifting perspectives of the Wairau Affray', *Oral History in New Zealand 33*, 2021, pp. 1–14.

Macpherson, Cluny, Paul Spoonley, Melani Anae and Sean Mallon, eds, *Tangata o te Moana Nui: The evolving identities of Pacific peoples in Aotearoa New Zealand* (Palmerston North: Dunmore Press, 2001)

Mahina-Tui, Kolokesa and Damon Salesa, eds, *Tangata o Le Moana: New Zealand and the people of the Pacific* (Wellington: Te Papa Press, 2012)

Mahuika, Nēpia, 'An outsiders guide to public oral history in New Zealand', *New Zealand Journal of Public History 5*, 1, 2017, pp. 3–18

Mahuika, Nēpia, *Rethinking Oral History and Tradition: An Indigenous perspective* (Oxford: Oxford University Press, 2019)

Martin, Bevan, *Maritime Law in New Zealand* (Wellington: Thomson Reuters New Zealand, 2016)

Martin, John E., *The Forgotten Worker: The rural wage earner in nineteenth-century New Zealand* (Wellington: Allen & Unwin, 1990)

Martin, John E., 'Whither the rural working class?', *New Zealand Journal of History 17*, 1, 1983, pp. 21–42

Matthews, Kay Morris, *Who Cared: Childhoods within Hawke's Bay children's homes and orphanages* (Napier: Eastern Institution of Technology, 2013)

Matutina Williams, Melissa, *Panguru and the City: Kāinga Tahi, Kāinga Rua. An urban migration history* (Wellington: Bridget Williams Books, 2015)

McAdams, Dan P. and Kate C. McLean, 'Narrative identity', *Current Directions in Psychological Science 22*, 2013, pp. 233–38

McAdams, Dan P., Ruthellen Josselson and Amia Lieblich, eds, *Identity and Story: Creating self in narrative* (Washington DC: American Psychological Association, 2006)

McAloon, Jim, 'Class in colonial New Zealand: Towards a historiographical rehabilitation', *New Zealand Journal of History 38*, 1, 2004, pp. 3–21

McAloon, Jim, *No Idle Rich: The wealthy in Canterbury and Otago 1840–1914* (Dunedin: Otago University Press, 2002)

McCabe, Jane, *Kalimpong Kids: The New Zealand story, in pictures* (Dunedin: Otago University Press, 2020)

McCarthy, Angela, *Scottishness and Irishness in New Zealand since 1840* (Manchester: Manchester University Press, 2011)

McMahan, Eva, *Elite Oral History Discourse: A study of cooperation and coherence* (Tuscaloosa: University of Alabama Press: 2015)

McSweeney, Des and Marie, *McSweeney: Your pioneer story 1850–1962* (Akaroa, n.p., 1995)

Metge, Joan, *In and Out of Touch: Whakamaa in cross cultural context* (Wellington: Victoria University Press, 1986)

Metge, Joan, 'Returning the gift – 'utu' in intergroup relations: In memory of Sir Raymond Firth', *Journal of the Polynesian Society 111*, 4, 2002, pp. 311–38

Midgley, Mary, *The Myths We Live By* (London: Routledge, 2004)

Mikaere, Ani, 'Māori women caught in the contradictions of a colonised reality', *Waikato Law Review 6*, 2, 1994, pp. 125–149

Millar, Grace, 'Women's lives, feminism and the New Zealand Journal of History', *New Zealand Journal of History 52,* 2, 2018, pp. 134–52

Miller, Daniel, *Stuff* (Cambridge, UK: Polity Press, 2010)

Monigatti, Rex, *Fruitful Fields: The development of New Zealand's fruit industry from 1916 to 1966* (Wellington: New Zealand Fruitgrowers' Federation, 1991)

Moodie, Jane, 'The moral world of the Waikite Valley', in *Remembering, Writing Oral History*, eds Anna Green and Megan Hutching (Auckland: Auckland University Press, 2004), pp. 39–59

Moreland, A. Maud, *Through South Westland, Journey to the Haast and Mount Aspiring* (London: Witherby & Co., 1911)

Munz, Peter, 'Reeves, Sinclair and the social pattern', in *The Feel of Truth: Essays in New Zealand and Pacific history*, ed. Peter Munz (Wellington: A.H. & A.W. Reed, 1969)

Murdoch, Lydia, *Imagined Orphans: Poor families, child welfare, and contested citizenship in London* (New Brunswick, NJ: Rutgers University Press, 2006)

Nash, Catherine, *Of Irish Descent: Origin stories, genealogy, and the politics of belonging* (New York: Syracuse University Press, 2008)

New Zealand National Party, *A Record of Achievement: The work of the National Government 1949–1957* (Wellington: The National Party, 1957)

NZ History: https://nzhistory.govt.nz/hands/a-guide-to-recording-oral-history

O'Farrell, Patrick, 'Varieties of New Zealand Irishness: A meditation', in *A Distant Shore: Irish migration and New Zealand settlement*, ed. Lyndon Fraser (Dunedin: Otago University Press, 2000), pp. 135–54

O'Shea, Patricia, *The Golden Harvest: A history of tobacco growing in New Zealand* (Christchurch: Hazard Press, 1997)

Oliver, W.H., *Claims to the Waitangi Tribunal* (Wellington: Department of Justice. Waitangi Tribunal Division, 1991)

Oliver, W.H., *The Story of New Zealand* (London: Faber & Faber, 1960)

Olssen, Erik, *Building the New World: Work, politics and society in Caversham 1880s–1920s* (Auckland: Auckland University Press, 1995)

Olssen, Erik, 'Social class in nineteenth-century New Zealand', in *Social Class in New Zealand*, ed. David Pitt (Auckland: Longman Paul, 1977), pp. 22–41

Ongley, Patrick, 'Class in New Zealand: Past, present and future', *Counterfutures 1*, 2016, pp. 73–77

Ongley, Patrick and David Pearson, 'Post-1945 international migration: New Zealand, Australia and Canada compared', *The International Migration Review 29*, 3, 1995, pp. 771–74

Parekowhai, Cushla, 'Korero taku whaea: Talk my aunt: Learning to listen to Māori women', *Oral History in New Zealand 4*, 1992, pp. 1–4

Passerini, Luisa, *Fascism in Popular Memory: The cultural experience of the Turin working class,* trans. Robert Lumley and Jude Bloomfield (Cambridge: Cambridge University Press, 1987)

Passerini, Luisa, 'Work ideology under Italian Fascism', *History Workshop Journal 8,* 1979, pp. 82–108

Perks, Robert and Alistair Thomson, eds, *The Oral History Reader* (London: Routledge, 1998, 2006, 2016)

Pihama, Leonie et al., 'Māori cultural definitions of sexual violence', *Sexual Abuse in Australia and New Zealand 7,* 1, 2016, pp. 43–51

Pool, Ian, Arunachalam Dharmalingam and Janet Sceats, *The New Zealand Family from 1840* (Auckland: Auckland University Press, 2007)

Portelli, Alessandro, 'Living voices: The oral history interview as dialogue and experience', *Oral History Review 45,* 2, 2018, pp. 239–48

Portelli, Alessandro, 'Oral history as a genre', in *Narrative and Genre,* eds Mary Chamberlain and Paul Thompson (London: Routledge, 1998), pp. 23–45

Portelli, Alessandro, 'What makes oral history different', in *The Oral History Reader,* 3rd edn, eds Robert Perks and Alistair Thomson (London and New York: Routledge, 2016), pp. 48–58

Rabel, Roberto, 'Up the Strada', in *A Fair Sort of Battering: New Zealanders remember the Italian campaign,* ed. Megan Hutching (Auckland: HarperCollins NZ, 2004), pp. 19–44

Raganath, Charan, *Why We Remember: Unlocking memory's power to hold on to what matters* (New York: Random House, 2024)

Rashbrooke, Max, 'No place like home', *New Zealand Geographic 132,* 2015: www.nzgeo.com/stories/no-place-like-home/

Rashbrooke, Max, *Too Much Money: How wealth disparities are unbalancing Aotearoa New Zealand* (Wellington: Bridget Williams Books, 2021)

Rea, Alice M., *They came for kauri but …: The history of Waimauku and Muriwai, 1863–1963* (Auckland: n.p., 1963)

Reese, Elaine, Catherine A. Haden and Robyn Fivush, 'Mother-child conversations about the past: Relationships of style and memory over time', *Cognitive Development 8,* 4, 1993, pp. 403–40

Reeves, William Pember, *Long White Cloud (Ao Tea Roa),* rev. 3rd edn (London: Allen & Unwin, 1924)

Rickard, Wendy, 'Collaborating with sex workers in oral history', *Oral History Review 30,* 1, 2003, pp. 47–59

Rickard, Wendy, 'Oral history: "More dangerous than therapy?" Interviewees' reflections on recording traumatic or taboo issues', *Oral History 26,* 2, 1998, pp. 34–48

Ritchie, Donald A., *Doing Oral History: A practical guide,* 3rd edn (New York: Oxford University Press, 2014)

Rogers, Brubaker and Frederick Cooper, 'Beyond "identity"', *Theory and Society 29,* 1, 2000, pp. 1–47

Rowlands, Mark, *Memory and the Self: Phenomenology, science and autobiography* (Oxford: Oxford University Press, 2017)

Royal, Charles, 'Oral history and hapū development', *Oral History in New Zealand 5,* 1993, pp. 4–6

Royal, Te Ahukaramu Charles, 'Politics and knowledge: Kaupapa Māori and matauranga Māori', *New Zealand Journal of Educational Studies 47,* 2, 2012, pp. 30–37

Sachs, Oliver, *The Man Who Mistook His Wife for a Hat* (London: Pan Macmillan, 2009)

Samuel, Raphael and Paul Thompson, *The Myths We Live By* (London: Routledge, 1990)

Schacter, Daniel L., *The Seven Sins of Memory: How the mind forgets and remembers* (Boston and New York: Houghton Mifflin Harcourt, 2002)

Shadbolt, Maurice, *Voices of Gallipoli* (Auckland: Hodder & Stoughton, 1988)

Shaw, Richard, *The Forgotten Coast* (Auckland: Massey University Press, 2021)

Sheftel, Anna and Stacey Zembrzycki, '"Who's afraid of oral history": Fifty years of debates and anxiety about ethics', *The Oral History Review 43*, 2, 2016, pp. 338–66

Shilliam, Robbie, 'The Polynesian Panthers and the Black Power Gang: Surviving racism and colonialism in Aotearoa New Zealand', in *Black Power Beyond Borders: The global dimensions of the Black Power Movement*, ed. Nico Slate (London: Palgrave Macmillan, 2012), pp. 107–26

Sinclair, Keith, *A History of New Zealand* (Harmondsworth: Penguin, 1959)

Sinclair, Keith, *William Pember Reeves, New Zealand Fabian* (Oxford: Clarendon Press, 1965)

Smith, Graham, 'Toward a public oral history', in *The Oxford Handbook of Oral History,* ed. Donald A. Ritchie (New York: Oxford University Press, 2010), pp. 430–47

Smith, Linda Tuhiwai, *Decolonizing Methodologies: Research and Indigenous peoples,* 2nd edn (London: Zed Books, 2012)

St Aubin, Ed de, Dan P. McAdams and Tae-Chang Kim, eds, *The Generative Society: Caring for future generations* (Washington: American Psychological Association, 2004)

Stephens, Tainui, 'Whakamā: Fighting the taniwha of shame', *The Spinoff*, 13 July 2020

Stevens, Michael, Atholl Anderson and Te Maire Tau, '"Our Ultimate Duty": Defending the integrity of Māori tradition', *Te Karaka*, July 2022: https://ngaitahu.iwi.nz/our_stories/our-ultimate-duty-tk90/

Stewart, Catherine, *A Wife on Gorge River* (Auckland: Random House, 2017)

Strawson, Galen, 'Against narrativity', *Ratio XVII*, 2004, pp. 428–51

Sullivan, Barbara, 'Prostitution and consent: Beyond the liberal dichotomy of "free or forced"', in *Making Sense of Sexual Consent*, eds Mark Cowling and Paul Reynolds (Aldershot: Ashgate, 2004), pp. 127–39

Summerfield, Penny, 'Culture and composure: Creating narratives of the gendered self in oral history interviews', *Cultural and Social History 1*, 2004, pp. 65–93

Summerfield, Penny, 'Dis/composing the subject: Intersubjectivities in oral history', in *Feminism & Autobiography: Texts, Theories, Methods*, eds Tess Coslett, Celia Lury and Penny Summerfield (London: Routledge, 2000), pp. 91–106

Summerfield, Penny, *Reconstructing Women's Wartime Lives* (Manchester: Manchester University Press, 1998)

Tau, Te Maire Rawiri, *Pikitūroa o Ngāi Tahu: The oral traditions of Ngāi Tahu* (Dunedin: Otago University Press, 2003)

Te Punga Somerville, Alice, *Once Were Pacific: Māori connections to Oceania*, (Minneapolis: University of Minnesota Press, 2012)

Teaiwa, Teresia and Sean Mallon, 'Ambivalent kinships? Pacific people in New Zealand', in *New Zealand Identities: Departures and destinations*, eds James H. Liu, Tim McCreanor, Tracey Mcintosh and Teresia Teaiwa (Wellington: Victoria University Press, 2005), pp. 207–29

Terkel, Studs with Tony Parker, 'Interviewing and interviewer' in *The Oral History Reader,* 2nd edn, eds Robert Perks and Alastair Thomson (Oxford: Routledge, 2006), pp. 147–52

The National Library: https://natlib.govt.nz/researchers/oral-history-advice

Thompson, E.P., *The Making of the English Working Class*, rev. edn (Harmondsworth: Penguin, 1968)

Thompson, Paul and Joanna Bornat, *The Voice of the Past: Oral history*, 4th edn (Oxford: Oxford University Press, 2017)

Thomson, Alistair, *ANZAC Memories. Living with the legend* (Melbourne: Oxford University Press, 1994)

Thomson, Alistair, 'Anzac Memories: Putting popular theory into practice in Australia', in *The Houses of History: A critical reader in twentieth-century history and theory*, eds Anna Green and Kathleen Troup (Manchester: Manchester University Press, 1999), p. 243

Toynbee, Claire, 'Class and social structure in nineteenth-century New Zealand', *New Zealand Journal of History* 13, 1, 1979, pp. 65–82

Walmsley, Michelle, 'Telling disabled people's stories free from the framings of the abled', *The Spinoff*, 27 November 2019

Wanhalla, Angela, 'Interracial sexual violence in 1860s New Zealand', *New Zealand Journal of History* 45, 1, 2011, pp. 71–84

Ware, Cheryl, 'Sex workers' responses to the HIV and AIDS epidemic in Aotearoa New Zealand', *Women's History Review* 29, 2, 2020, pp. 289–307

Ware, Cheryl and Linda Bryder, '"We'd just get together … and talk about cancer", Commissioned oral histories and the professional historian', *Health and History* 21, 2019, pp. 47–68

Ware, Felicity, Mary Breheny and Margaret Forster, 'Kaupapa kōrero: A Māori cultural approach to narrative inquiry', *AlterNative: An International Journal of Indigenous Peoples* 14, 1, 2017, pp. 45–53

Wessendorf, Susanna, '"Roots migrants": Transnationalism and "return" among second-generation Italians in Switzerland', *Journal of Ethnic and Migration Studies* 33, 7, 2007, pp. 1083–1102

Wevers, Lydia, 'Being Pakeha: The politics of location', *Journal of New Zealand Studies* 4/5, 2005–6, pp. 1–10

Williams, Eric, *The Wooden Horse* (London: Collins, 1949)

Wiltshire, Roswyn, 'Marion Steven and the Logie Collection', *Journal of New Zealand Studies* NS32, 2021, pp. 96–107

Wineberg, Sam, *Historical Thinking and Other Unnatural Acts: Charting the future of teaching the past* (Philadelphia: Temple University Press, 2001)

Yerex, David, *Empire of the Dairy Farmers* (Petone: N.Z. Dairy Exporter Books, 1989)

Yerex, David, *They Came to Wydrop: The Beetham and Williams families, Brancepeth and Te Parae, Wairarapa, 1856–1990* (Wellington: G.P. Print, 1991)

Zuckerman, Michael, 'The presence of the present, the end of history', *The Public Historian* 22, 1, Winter 2000, pp. 19–20

INDEX

Bold denotes illustrations

activism/activists 62, 140–41, 142, 144
    see also Polynesian Panthers
adoption
    Adoption Act 1955 152
    Adult Adoption Information Act 1985 152–53
    birth parents, search for/finding 153–55, 157–58
    closed stranger adoption 151, 152–53
    Margaret (adopted Sue's birth mother) 153–60
    oral history and 159
    ship jumping and 151
    Sue (interviewee) 151, 153–60
Akaroa 72, 73, **79**
Alexander Turnbull Library 15, 124
All Saints' Children's Home 161, 162, 163–70
'All things bright and beautiful' (Alexander) 50
ancestry
    ancestor histories 96–97, 110
    Anglo-Indians 96–97, 100–101, 110
    genealogy 54, 71, 100, 101
    identity and 96–97
    Māori/whakapapa 10, 13, 18, 28, 30, 34, 141
    McSweeney, Des 72–81
    pride/respect 47, 81
    'roots tourism' 111
    Williams, Tom 53
Andrews, Robyn 96
Anglican Church 46, 51, 55, 163, 168, 170
    see also All Saints' Children's Home
Anglo-Indians
    ancestry/ancestor histories 96–97, 100–101, 110
    Atkinson, Christine (née Palman) 98, 102–05, 108, 109, 111
    Auckland/Tāmaki Makaurau 98, 102, 103, 104, 105
    census information 98
    definition 97
    Erikson, Parvati 98, 105–07, 108, 109, 111
    ethnicity 100, 108, 111
    Hay, Frederica (née Coventry) 95, 96, 98, 99–102, 109–10, 111
    identity/self-identification 100–101, 104–05, 107, 108–09, 110, 111
    interviews 96, 98–107, 108–10
    misidentification 108–09
    New Zealand, living in 97–98, 100, 102–04, 105–06
    New Zealand, migration to 95, 96, 97–98, 102–03, 105, 107, 108
    pride in being Anglo-Indian 110
    racism/discrimination towards 100, 104, 109–10
    self-identification 100–101, 104–05
    see also India
approaches, oral history *see* methodologies, oral history
Araparera marae **26**, 31
archival history *see* written/archival histories versus oral history
Ardern, Jacinda 69
Ask the Fellows Who Cut the Hay (Evans) 14
Aspinall, Amy 124, 127, 131, 132, 135–36, 137
Aspinall, Jerry 124–26, 127, 132, 133, 134, 136–38
Aspinall, John (Jack) 124, 130, 135
Aspinall, Phyllis
    background/early life 134–35
    domestic responsibilities 127–33, 135–36, 138
    marriage *see* Aspinall, Jerry

Mount Aspiring Station and homestead
124–33, 135–36, **125**, **129**
obituary 124
perception from oral history 124, 133–34, 138
perception, public/traditional 124, 133
recipe books 138
Aspinall, William **129**
Assman, Aleida 15–16
Atkinson, Christine (née Palman) 98, 102–05, 108, 109, 111
Attwood, Bain 22
Auckland/Tāmaki Makaurau
Anglo-Indians 98, 102, 103, 104, 105
Bastion Point protest 63–64
Mount Albert 59
Ōtara 60
Ponsonby 60
Remuera 105
sex work industry 146, 148
see also Polynesian Panthers
Auckland Weekly News (newspaper) **177**
Aunty Gloria *see* Timoti, Gloria (Aunty Gloria)
Australia 15, 97, 109
authenticity 12–13, 20
see also reliability/cross-referencing of information; subjectivity

Banks Peninsula 23, 72–73, 75, 76–77, **77**, **78**, **79**, 80, 81
Bastion Point protest 63–64
Beetham family 44, 46
benefits/advantages of oral histories 9, 123, 139
class, understanding of 41, 43, 44, 52–53, 54
Dawn Raids 57–58, 69–70
institutional care 161, 162, 167, 170–71
military history, adding nuance to 113–14, 120
non-verbal clues 134
past and present, connecting 9, 20, 23, 47, 68–70, 71–72, 74, 80, 111, 149, 178
subjectivity/inconsistency of remembered experience 22–23, 112, 162, 171
understanding those with little power 161, 170

war/conflict 113–14, 120
written/archival histories, versus 9, 22–23, 35, 57–58, 95–96, 114, 120, 124, 161, 162, 170–71, 181
bisexuality 145, 146
Black Panthers (USA) 57, 61
see also Polynesian Panthers
Bourdieu, Pierre 41, 42, 54
Brooking, Tom 43, 54
Bruner, Jerome 21
Bryson, Anna 134

capital, cultural 42, 54, 55
capital, economic 42
capital, social 42, 53
care, institutional
All Saints' Children's Home 161, 162, 163–70
Child Welfare Office 162, 170
Christine (children's home resident) 163–70
corporal punishment 169–70
extracurricular activities 168–69
Howard (children's home resident) 163–70
interviews 162–70
living conditions/routine 164–66
New Zealand homes 161–62
official documentation 161, 162, 163, 167, 168, 169, 170–71
oral history and 161, 162, 167, 170, 171–72
relationships/interactions between children 166–68
censuses 43, 98, 104
Christchurch
Canterbury Museum 90
Marion Steven's home 83, 84–88, 89, 90, 91–93
St Bede's College 73
University of Canterbury 83–84, 90
Christianity 30, 66, 97, 108
Anglicanism 46, 51, 55, 163, 168, 170
Christine (children's home resident) 163–70
Clark, Helen 114
class
capital, cultural 42, 54, 55
capital, social 42, 53

colonial society 42–43
consciousness/conditioning, class 44, 47–53
definition, conceptual 41–43
egalitarianism 23, 41, 42, 49, 52, 55–56
ethnicity/race and class 42, 47, 49, 54, 55–56
gender 56
identity and 42, 47
middle class 43–44
oral history and 41, 43, 44, 52–53, 54
upper class 53, 54
wealth relating to class 42, 43, 51, 53, 54, 56
working class 42, 60
yeoman ideal 43, 51, 52
see also inequality/inequity
Coldham, Alister 45
Coldham, Guy 45
collective history/memory 17, 18, 22, 34, 35, 38, 68, 113, 119, 120, 123
see also social memory
colonisation 9–10, 36, 42–43, 49, 72–76, 141
community focus 14, 22, 15, 60, 62
Crown, the (Ngāti Whātua Treaty Claim) 25–38, 49
see also government, New Zealand
cultural capital 42, 54, 55

Daily Southern Cross (newspaper) 36
Dapp, Paul 62, **63**
Dawn Raids
 counter-raids by Polynesian Panthers 64–65
 government, New Zealand 60, 62, 63, 64, 69
 memory 68–69
 oral histories, benefits from 57–58, 69–70
 police actions 57, 62, 64, 65
 Polynesian Panthers 57, 61–65, **63**, 66, 70
 premise for 57
 whakamā/shame 65
Dawson, Graham 120
Day, Sophie 144
demographics 43, 71–72, 98, 104
Dennis, Jonathan 92
deportation, compulsory 151–52, 155, 156
Depression years *see* Great Depression

diaspora, Pacific 58–60
discrimination *see* racism/discrimination
domestic life, New Zealand
 Aspinall, Phyllis **125**, 127–33, 135–36, 138
 Mrs Schumacher's Gems (interviews project) 123
Dr Graham's Homes 105, 106

economic capital 42
egalitarianism 23, 41, 42, 49, 52, 55–56
England 51, 58, 59, 80, 144, 155, 156, 157, 158–59
Entertaining with Graham Kerr (Kerr) 138
Erikson, Parvati 98, 105–07, 108, 109, 111
Etherington, Bonnie 70
ethics 17–18, 141–42, 162–63
ethnicity 96
 Anglo-Indians in New Zealand 100, 108, 111
 class and 42, 47, 49, 54, 55–56
 see also Māori
Evans, George Ewart 14

Falconer, Earl **67**
Falloon, John 46
family
 family memory/stories 41, 52, 54, 55–56, 69, 71–81
 identity and 71, 81
farming/farmers
 labourers/workers 14, 43, 49–50
 Lincoln Agricultural College 73
 Māori farm workers 55
 McSweeney, Des 73, 76–79
 peasant farming 73
 Pirongia 51
 Te Miro 52
 Te Parae/Te Aute 45, 48–50, 55
 Wild Cattle Hill 76–79, **77**, **78**
 Wye Valley/Anna Green 13–14
 yeoman (family) farmers 43, 51, 52
 see also rural New Zealand and oral history; Williams, Eric; Williams, Tom
Farming under Aspiring (Aspinall) 136–37
Felix, Nari 61
feminism/women's liberation 139, 140, 141, 144–45

Fickling, Bill 174–76, **175**, 178, 179–80, 181–82, 183
Fickling, Emma 174, 178, 179, 181, 182, 183
Fickling, Phyllis 173, 174–83
Flint, William (Bill) 114–21
Frankie (sex worker) 146–50
Frizzell, Helen 123, 127, 134, 138
funding of oral history 15, 81, 139
Fyfe, Judith 123

Gair, George 64, 65
gender 20, 56, 123–24, 134, 138, 145, 149
genealogy 54, 71, 100, 101
  see also ancestry; whakapapa
Germany/Germans 75, 77, 114–15, 117, 118
Glen Finnan (homestead) 124–26, 127
glossary of terms 185–86
government, New Zealand
  Dawn Raids 60, 62, 63, 64, 69
  House of Representatives 36, 37
  immigration policy 97–98
  Labour governments 60, 62, 69, 73, 81
  Manatū Taonga/Ministry for Culture and Heritage 15
  National governments 64, 152
  Pacific peoples, relations with/treatment of 57, 60, 62, 69, 70
  see also individual politicians
Great Britain *see* England
Great Depression 11, 44, 52, 134–35, 182
Greece 115–17
Green, Anna 13–17, 91, 149, 151

Hamilton, Paula 91, 115
Haranui marae 25, **26**, 35
Harawira, Hone 62
Hassan, Norman **67**
Hay, Frederica (née Coventry) 95, 96, 98, 99–102, 109–10, 111
history education 22, 69
home and identity/memory 83, 84–88, 89–91
horseracing/racing industry 46
Housing New Zealand 33
Howard (children's home resident) 163–70
Huapai/Huapai Estate **175, 177**
  advertising versus reality 176–78
  creation/development 173, 174–77

Fickling, Bill 174–76, **175**, 178, 179–80, 181–82, 183
Fickling, Bob 182
Fickling, Emma 174, 178, 179, 181, 182, 183
Fickling, Phyllis 173, 174–83
Northern Fruitlands Ltd 173, **175**, 176, 178, 179, 182
self-sufficiency/daily work 178–80, 183
Hutching, Megan 15, 113–14, 123, 151

identity
  ancestor histories 96–97
  Anglo-Indians 100–101, 104–05, 107, 108–09, 110, 111
  class and 42, 47
  definition 70
  family and 71, 81
  generational change/attitudes 110
  home and 83, 84–88, 89–91
  'Ilolahia, Will 58
  loss of identity 32
  Marion Steven's Christchurch home 83, 84–88, 89, 90, 91–93
  McSweeney, Des 81
  misidentification 108–09
  Pacific peoples 58, 63
  self-identification 100–101, 104–05, 107, 108
  shame and 58
  stories creating identity 21, 22, 23, 71
'Ilolahia, Will **67**
  identity 58
  inspirations 61–62
  interview with Helena Cook 58–70
  migration to Aotearoa New Zealand 58–59
  Polynesian Panthers 57, 61–65, 66, 70
  racism 59
  shame 66–68
immigration 62–63, 97–98, 152
  see also Anglo-Indians; Pacific peoples
India 95, 97, 99–101, 102–03, 104, 105, 106–07
  Kolkata 96, 100, 101
  see also Anglo-Indians
Indigenous peoples *see* Māori
inequality/inequity 15–16, 33, 41
  see also class
institutional care *see* care, institutional

interviews/interviewing
   academic oral history 16
   activist oral history 16
   commissioned oral history 15
   ethics 17–18
   interviewer/interviewee relationship 43
   'life story' approach 21, 80, 140, 162
   methodologies/techniques 17–18, 72, 140, 162–63
   narrative form 21, 41, 43, 44–45
   non-verbal clues, significance of 134
   orality 20
   preservation of 15
interviews, list of
   Anglo-Indians 96, 98–107, 108–10
   Aspinall, Phyllis 123–38, **125**
   Atkinson, Christine (née Palman) 102–05
   Christine (children's home resident) 164–70
   Erikson, Parvati 98, 105–07
   Fickling, Phyllis 173, 174–83
   Flint, William (Bill) 114–21
   Frankie (sex worker) 146–50
   Howard (children's home resident) 164–70
   Jane (Marion Steven's niece) 84–87, 90, 91–92
   Jennifer (Frederica Hay's great-grandchild) 99–100
   Kate (sex worker) 142–45, 149–50
   Lynne (Frederica Hay's great-grandchild) 99, 100–101
   'Ilolahia, Will 58–70
   Marion Steven's students 83, 88
   McSweeney, Des 72–81
   O'Regan, Tipene 39
   Richard and Alison (Marion Steven's colleagues) 86–88
   settler descendants 72–81
   Simon (Anglo-Indian) 110
   Sue (ship jumping interviewee) 151, 153–60
   Timoti, Gloria (Aunty Gloria) 32–33
   Tina (Frederica Hay's great-grandchild) 99, 100, 101
   Wikiriwhi, Takutaimoana (Uncle Doc) 28–30, 31
   Williams, Eric 47–53, 54, 55
   Williams, Tom 44–47, 53–54, 55, 56

Ireland/Irish 49, 54, 73–75, 80, 81
Iuli, Ta **63**
iwi/hapū
   Ngāi Tahu/Kāi Tahu 13, 23
   Ngā Tamatoa 62, 70
   Ngāti Whātua 25–39, **26**, **29**, **33**
   see also Māori; Treaty of Waitangi (Te Tiriti o Waitangi); *individual people*

James Logie Memorial Collection 83–84, 88, 90–91
Jane (Marion Steven's niece) 84–87, 90, 91–92

Kā Huru Manu (Ngāi Tahu mapping project) 13
Kaipara/Kaipara Harbour 25–28, **26**, **29**, 30, 31–32, 34, 36
Kāi Tahu/Ngāi Tahu 13, 23
Kakanui marae **26**, 31
Kate (sex worker) 142–45, 149–50
Kaufman, Gershen 65
Kawharu, Margaret 27, 28
Kelly, Emma-Jean 92
Kerr, Graham 138
Kirk, Norman 60, 62
Koroheke, Maata Tira 36

Labour Party, New Zealand 60, 73, 81
Lands for Settlement Act 44
Lange, David 61
Leach, Helen 135
Lee, Hermione 83, 89
legislation
   Adoption Act 1955 152
   Adult Adoption Information Act 1985 152–53
   Lands for Settlement Act 44
   Public Works Act 37
   Treaty of Waitangi Act 1975 25
Lincoln Agricultural College 73
Lives of Houses (Lee) 83, 89
Logie, James 84, 86
Looyer, Natalie 83–84
Low, Ruth E. 174

Manatū Taonga/Ministry for Culture and Heritage 15
Manson, Hugo 123

Māori
　colonisation, effects of 9–10, 141
　disempowerment 38, 142
　farm workers 55
　grievance(s) 25, 27, 28, 30, 34, 35–37
　inequity 33, 34
　kaumātua/kuia 12, 27, 34, 39; *see also individual people*
　land acquisition/confiscation by Crown 26, 27, 30, 32, 35–37, 49
　Māori scholars on sexual violence 141
　marae 9, 12, 25, **26**, 27–28, 31, 35, 38
　mātauranga 11, 12, 13, 17
　Pacific peoples, relationship with 62–64
　Pākehā and Māori (relating to class) 47, 49, 54, 55–56
　Pākehā, relationship with/attitudes from 36, 47, 55, 62
　tangihanga 10, 12, 185
　te reo 10, 12–13, 35
　tikanga 9–10, 11–12, 17, 30
　tino rangatiratanga 31, 62
　Treaty claims, Ngāti Whātua 25–39, **26, 29, 33**
　transmission of knowledge through oral history 11–12, 18–19, 57
　utu 30
　whakamā 23, 65, 68, 69, 70
　whakapapa 10, 13, 18, 28, 34, 141
　see also iwi/hapū; Treaty of Waitangi (Te Tiriti o Waitangi); *individual people*
marae 12, 25
　Araparera **26**, 31
　Haranui 25, **26**, 35
　Kakanui **26**, 31
　Ōtākou 9, 12
　Puatahi **26**
　Reweti **26**, 27–28, 31
Margaret (adopted Sue's birth mother) 153–60
Martin, Charles Edward (Ted) 154–55, 156, 157–59
mātauranga/mātauranga Māori 11, 12, 13, 17
Matukituki valley 124, 126
McCabe, Jane 110
McConville, Séan 134
McSweeney, Des **79**
　early life 72–73
　education 73, 75
　family/ancestry 72–81
　family museum 78–79, **79**
　farming 73, 76–79
　history, interest in 79–80
　identity 81
media, New Zealand
　Auckland Weekly News (newspaper) **177**
　Daily Southern Cross (newspaper) 36
　Huapai Estate 176
　Pacific peoples, portrayal of 60, 61
　sex work industry 141, 143–44
　Siren: Sex Industry Rights and Education Network (magazine) 144
　war commemoration 119
memory
　collective memory 17, 18, 22, 34, 35, 38, 68, 113, 119, 120, 123
　Dawn Raids 68–69
　family memory 41, 52, 54, 55–56, 69, 71–81
　home and 83, 84–88, 89–91
　memory activism 15–16
　memory studies 16–17
　multiple memories 32
　myth and 22, 41
　neurology/physiology 16–17
　place and 93
　public memory 119, 120
　shame and 65–68
　smell 164
　social/family memory 16, 17, 22–23, 41, 52, 54, 55, 69
　trauma/traumatic memory 141
　see also methodologies, oral history; remembering
methodologies, oral history
　academic oral history 16
　activist oral history 15–16
　analytic 14, 16
　commissioned oral history 15, 18
　community focus 14, 15
　framework 123
　interpretive 14, 16, 18–19, 20, 120, 139, 140, 160, 161
　settler descendants interviews 72
　see also interviews/interviewing
migration/migrants *see* Anglo-Indians; immigration; Pacific peoples

military history 113–14, 118
  see also war/conflict
Millar, Grace 141
Miller, Daniel 92
Moodie, Jane 41, 47–50, 134
Moreland, Maud 126
Mount Aspiring Station 124–26, **125**
Muldoon, Robert 64
myth and memory 22, 41

narrative form/interviews 21, 41
National Oral History Association Te Kete Kōrero-a-Waha o Te Motu (NOHANZ) 14–15, 17–18
National Party, New Zealand 64
Nee Nee, Henry 64–65
neuroscience 16–17
New Zealand Families Commission 70
New Zealand Police Gazette 155
Ngāi Tahu/Kāi Tahu 13, 23
Ngā Tamatoa 62, 70
Ngāti Whātua Treaty claims 25–39, **26**, **29**, **33**
Northern Fruitlands Ltd 173, **175**, 176, 178, 179, 182

official history *see* written/archival histories versus oral history
Oldham, Pip 72, 75, 77–78
Ongley, Patrick 42
oral history/histories
  adoption and 159
  class and 41, 43, 44, 52–53, 54
  definition, Anna Green's 13–17
  definition, Megan Pōtiki's 9–13
  disempowerment caused by oral histories 142
  ethics 17–18, 141–42, 162–63
  funding 15, 81, 139
  institutional care and 161, 162, 167, 170, 171–72
  National Oral History Association Te Kete Kōrero-a-Waha o Te Motu (NOHANZ) 14–15, 17–18
  rural New Zealand and 23, 173, 174, 178; *see also* Aspinall, Phyllis; farming/farmers; Huapai/Huapai Estate
  sex work industry and 139–40, 141, 146, 147, 149–50
  transmission of knowledge through oral history 11–12, 14, 18–19, 57
  Waitangi Tribunal, importance to 34–35
  war/conflict and 113–14, 120
  written sources, versus 9, 22–23, 57–58, 95–96, 124, 162, 170–71, 181
  see also benefits/advantages of oral histories; methodologies, oral history
orality 20
O'Regan, Tipene 39
orthodox history *see* written/archival histories versus oral history
Ōtākou 9–10, 209
Ōtākou marae 9, 12
overstayers 57, 58, 60, 62, 64, 66–68, 69

Pacific peoples
  attitudes of New Zealanders towards 59–62
  identity 58, 63
  Māori, relationship with 62–64
  media, portrayal by 60
  migration 58–60
  New Zealand government, relations with/treatment by 57, 60, 62, 69, 70
  overstayers 57, 58, 60, 62, 64, 66–68, 69
  Pākehā, relationship with 60–61, 62–63, 69
  police, treatment by 60–61, 62
  Polynesian Panthers 57, 61–65, **63**, 66, 70
  racism/discrimination towards 57, 62, 64
  religion 65–66
  Samoa/Samoans 60
  Tonga/Tongans 58, 60, 62
  transmission of knowledge through oral history 57
  see also Dawn Raids
Pākehā
  colonisation 36, 49
  laws/policies 31
  Māori, relationship with/attitudes towards 36, 47, 55, 62
  Pacific peoples, relationship with/attitudes to 60–61, 62–63, 69
  settlers, colonial 53, 58, 72–78, **77**, 100
Palmerston North 168–69
  see also All Saints' Children's Home
Passerini, Luisa 19–20, 21

past and present, connecting 9, 20, 23, 47, 68–70, 71–72, 74, 80, 111, 149, 178
Pihama, Leonie 141
Pirongia 48, 51
place and oral history 83, 84–88, 89–91, 93
  see also whakapapa
police (New Zealand) 57, 60–61, 62, 64, 65, 140, 141, 155
Polynesian Panthers 57, 61–65, **63**, 66, 70
Polynesians see Pacific peoples
Pomare, Māui 46–47
Ponsonby Black Panthers 61
popular history 21, 22, 118, 120–21
Portelli, Alessandro 18, 20, 21, 117, 159–60, 161, 170
Pōtiki, Megan 9–13
psychology 16–17, 21, 71, 80
Puatahi marae **26**
Public Works Act 37
Pukehou 48, 50

Rabel, Roberto 113
race see ethnicity
racism/discrimination 57, 59, 60, 64, 100, 104, 109–10
  see also Māori
Ranganath, Charan 16–17
rape see sexual violence/rape *under* sex work industry
reframing of existing historical perspectives 7, 58, 145, 161, 162, 170, 181–82
reliability/cross-referencing of information 13, 18–19
  see also authenticity; subjectivity
religion
  Anglicanism 46, 51, 55, 163, 168, 170
  Catholicism 75, 103
  Christianity 30, 66, 97, 108
  Ireland 75
  Pacific peoples 65–66
remembering 16–17
  connecting past, present and future 68–70, 74, 178
  dynamic/subjective nature of 115, 118–19
  memory studies 17
  see also memory; methodologies, oral history

Remembering: Writing oral history (Green and Hutching) 91, 151
Reweti marae **26**, 27–28, 31
Richard and Alison (Marion Steven's colleagues) 86–88
Royal Society Te Apārangi 81
rural New Zealand and oral history 23, 173, 174, 178
  see also Aspinall, Phyllis; farming/farmers; Huapai/Huapai Estate

Sachs, Oliver 21
Samoa/Samoans 60
Schmidt, Fred 62, **63**
Scott, Heather 51, 52
Seale, Bobby 61
Seize the Time: The story of the Black Panther Movement and Huey P. Newton (Seale) 61
settlers, colonial 53, 58, 72–78, **77**, 100
sex work industry
  abolitionism 143, 144–45
  Auckland/Tāmaki Makaurau 146, 148
  consent 139–41, 142–44, 145–48, 150
  decriminalisation 139–40, 142, 148
  discrimination 140
  Frankie (sex worker) 146–50
  interviews 139, 140, 142–50
  Kate (sex worker) 142–45, 149–50
  legal cases/law reform 140–41, 143–44
  London 144
  Māori on sexual violence 141
  media coverage 141, 143–44
  New Zealand Prostitutes' Collective 144, 147, 150
  oral history, significance of 139–40, 141, 146, 147, 149–50
  parlour work 142, 143, 145, 146, 147–48
  public perception 139–40, 148
  sexual violence/rape 139, 140–41, 142–43, 143–44, 148
  Siren: Sex Industry Rights and Education Network (magazine) 144
  stereotyping 142, 148–49
  strip club work 146
  Wellington 142, 143, 145
  women's liberation/feminism 139, 140, 141, 144–45
sexuality 139, 145, 146

Shadbolt, Maurice 114
shame
    Dawn Raids 65
    identity and 58
    'Ilolahia, Will 66–68
    memory and 65–68
    whakamā 23, 65, 68, 69, 70
    see also trauma/traumatic memory
Sheehan, John 36
ship jumping
    deportation of ship jumpers 151–52, 155, 156
    Martin, Charles Edward (Ted) 155, 159
    New Zealand, in 152
    Sue (interviewee) 151, 153–60
Shopes, Linda 115
Siren: Sex Industry Rights and Education Network (magazine) 144
smell and memory 164
social capital 42, 53
social memory 16, 17, 22–23, 41, 52, 54, 55, 69
    see also collective history/memory
sovereignty, indigenous 31, 62, 63
St Bede's College 73
Stephens, Tainui 65
Steven, Marion
    background/career 83–84
    book collection 84, 87, 90
    Christchurch home 83, 84–88, 89, 90, 91–93
    Elizabeth (Marion's friend) 93
    James Logie Memorial Collection 83–84, 88, 90–91
    Jane (Marion Steven's niece) 84–87, 90, 91–92
    personality/appearance 84, 85, 86, 88, 89, 91–92, 93
    Richard and Alison (Marion Steven's colleagues) 86–88
    students of Marion 83, 88, 89
    Sue (Marion's twin sister) 88
Stuff (Miller) 92
subjectivity 19–20, 22–23, 76, 81, 112, 115, 117–19, 159–60, 162, 171
    see also authenticity; reliability/cross-referencing of information
Sue (ship jumping interviewee) 151, 153–60
Sullivan, Barbara 140–41

Tāmaki Makaurau *see* Auckland/Tāmaki Makaurau
tangihanga 10, 12, 185
Tawhai, Hone Mohi 37
Te Aute College/village 48–49, 50–51, 52, 54, 55
Te Awahou (Foxton) 90
Te Kawau, Apihai 36
Te Miro (farm) 51
Te Papa Tongarewa Museum of New Zealand 90
Te Parae homestead 44–45, 46, 55, 56
Te Punga Somerville, Alice 69–70
te reo Māori 10, 12–13, 35
Te Reweti, Wiremu 36
Te Tinana, Ihikiera 36
Te Tiriti o Waitangi *see* Treaty of Waitangi (Te Tiriti o Waitangi)
teaching history 22, 69
Teavae, Nooroa **63**
Terkel, Studs 134
Teschemaker, Nancy 45
Thompson, E.P. 41–42, 43
tikanga 9–10, 11–12, 17, 30
Timoti, Gloria (Aunty Gloria) 27, 31–33, **33**, 37, 39
tino rangatiratanga 31, 62
Tipene, Wiremu 30
Tonga/Tongans 58, 60, 62
    see also 'Ilolahia, Will
transmission of knowledge through oral history 11–12, 14, 18–19, 57
transphobia 145
trauma/traumatic memory 141
    see also shame
Treaty of Waitangi (Te Tiriti o Waitangi)
    Ngāti Whātua claim 25–39, **26, 29, 33**
    Treaty of Waitangi Act 1975 25
    Waitangi Tribunal 25–27, 28, 30–31, 32, 34–35, 37–38
Trendall, Dale 90
Tuhaere, Paora 37
Tuhiwai Smith, Linda 68, 69

UB40 (band) **67**
Uncle Doc *see* Wikiriwhi, Takutaimoana (Uncle Doc)
University of Canterbury 83–84, 90
utu (reciprocity) 30

Vete, Semi (Sam) **63**
Voices of Gallipoli (Shadbolt) 114

wāhi *see* place and oral history
Wairarapa *see* Te Aute College/village; Te Parae Homestead
Waitangi Tribunal 25–27, 28, 30–31, 32, 34–35, 37–38
Wales 13–14
Wanganui Collegiate 46, 47
war/conflict
    commemorations/remembrance 23, 113, 118–20
    Flint, William (Bill) 114–21
    individuals' experiences 113
    oral history, benefit of 113–14, 120
    prisoners of war 113, 115–18, 120–21
    Returned Services Association 118, 120
    Voices of Gallipoli (Shadbolt) 114
    World War I 10, 14, 119
    World War II 10, 15, 50, 113–18, 119, 120–21
Washington, George 59
wealth relating to class 42, 43, 51, 53, 54, 56
Wellington 90, 142, 143, 145, 155
Wells, Peter 92
West, Bob 120
whakapapa 10, 13, 18, 28, 34, 141
    see also genealogy; place and oral history
Wikiriwhi, Takutaimoana (Uncle Doc) 27–31, **29**, 37, 39
Wild Cattle Hill farm 76–79, **77, 78**
Williams, Eric
    background/early life 44, 50–51, 52, 53
    class 47–48, 50, 52, 54, 55–56
    family 49, 53
    interview 47–53, 54, 55
    Māori/Pākehā relationship 55
    Te Aute 48–50, 51, 54
Williams family 41, 42, 43–47, 50–55
Williams, Guy 44, 45
Williams, Heather (née Scott) 51, 52
Williams, Henry 43–44, 53
Williams, Marianne (née Coldham) 43–44, 45, 53
Williams, Melissa Matutina 142
Williams, Thomas Coldham 44, 45
Williams, Tom
    background/early life 44, 45–46, 52
    class 53
    cultural capital 55
    interview 44–47, 53–54, 55, 56
    Māori/Pākehā relationship 47
    Te Parae homestead 44–45, 46–47, 56
    Williams family 45, 47, 53–54, 55, 56
women's liberation/feminism 139, 140, 141, 144–45
'Work Ideology and Consensus under Italian Fascism' (Passerini) 19–20
World War I 10, 14, 119
World War II 10, 15, 50, 113–18, 119, 120–21
    see also war/conflict
written/archival histories versus oral history 9, 22–23, 35, 57–58, 95–96, 114, 120, 124, 161, 162, 170–71, 181
Wye Valley (Wales) 13–14

Yerex, David 46